T0360505

ROUTLEDGE LIBRARY EDITIONS:
EMPLOYMENT AND
UNEMPLOYMENT

Volume 6

UNEMPLOYMENT, SCHOOLING AND TRAINING IN DEVELOPING COUNTRIES

UNEMPLOYMENT, SCHOOLING AND TRAINING IN DEVELOPING COUNTRIES

Tanzania, Egypt, the Philippines and Indonesia

Edited by
M. D. LEONOR

Routledge
Taylor & Francis Group
LONDON AND NEW YORK

First published in 1985 by Croom Helm Ltd

This edition first published in 2019
by Routledge
2 Park Square, Milton Park, Abingdon, Oxon OX14 4RN

and by Routledge
52 Vanderbilt Avenue, New York, NY 10017

Routledge is an imprint of the Taylor & Francis Group, an informa business

British Library Cataloguing in Publication Data
A catalogue record for this book is available from the British Library

ISBN: 978-1-138-38855-0 (Set)
ISBN: 978-0-429-02498-6 (Set) (ebk)
ISBN: 978-0-367-08654-1 (Volume 6) (hbk)
ISBN: 978-0-429-02380-4 (Volume 6) (ebk)

Publisher's Note
The publisher has gone to great lengths to ensure the quality of this reprint but points out that some imperfections in the original copies may be apparent.

Disclaimer
The publisher has made every effort to trace copyright holders and would welcome correspondence from those they have been unable to trace.

Unemployment, Schooling and Training in Developing Countries

TANZANIA, EGYPT, THE PHILIPPINES AND INDONESIA

Edited by
M.D.Leonor

A study prepared for the International Labour Office within the framework of the World Employment Programme

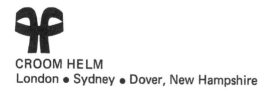

CROOM HELM
London ● Sydney ● Dover, New Hampshire

© 1985 International Labour Organisation
Croom Helm Ltd, Provident House, Burrell Row,
Beckenham, Kent BR3 1AT
Croom Helm Australia Pty Ltd, Suite 4, 6th Floor,
64-76 Kippax Street, Surry Hills, NSW 2010, Australia

British Library Cataloguing in Publication Data

Unemployment, schooling and training in developing countries
    (Tanzania, Egypt, the Philippines and Indonesia): a study prepared
    for the International Labour Office within the framework of the
    World Employment Programme.
    1. Unemployment—Developing countries
    I. Leonor, M.   II. International Labour Office
    331.13'7804   HD5852
    ISBN 0-7099-1329-X

Croom Helm, 51 Washington Street, Dover,
New Hampshire 03820, USA

Library of Congress Card Number: 85-5949
Library of Congress Cataloging in Publication Data applied for.

Printed and bound in Great Britain
by Billing & Sons Limited, Worcester.

CONTENTS

FOREWORD
PREFACE

CHAPTER 1. INTRODUCTION 1
           Mauricio Leonor

CHAPTER 2. TANZANIA 11
           Mauricio Leonor

           Introduction 11
           The employment situation 12
           Unemployment and underemployment 12
           Economic growth and growth in
             employment 17
           Expansion of schooling 21
           Migration of workers 23
           Employment of school-leavers 27
           The origins of unemployment 28
           The political economy of change
             and slow growth 28
           Educational policy and unemployment ... 33
           Towards education for self-reliance   33
           The primary school-leaver crisis 34
           The students' revolt 35
           Education for self-reliance 37
           The strikes of vocational school
             students 40
           Lessons from Tanzanian experience 44
           Bibliography 50

CHAPTER 3. EGYPT 55
           Karima Korayem, Abdel Aziz El-Koussy,
           Mohy. Khairy Harby and Mauricio Leonor

           Overview 55
           Mauricio Leonor

           Unemployment and labour market policies 60
           Karima Korayem

           Unemployment 60
           Rural/urban unemployment 61
           Age and sex of the unemployed 61

Educational attainment of
    unemployed workers 66
Labour market policies 68
Direct policies 68
    Free-tuition policy 68
    Short work-week in public
        enterprises 70
    Guaranteed jobs 70
    Lengthening the period of
        military conscription 72
    Untrammelled emigration 73
Indirect policies 73
    Central planning policy 74
    Open-door policy 75
Impact on wage scale 76
Impact on employment structure 77

Mis-education and its supposed remedies   80
Abdel Aziz El-Koussy
and Mohy. Khairy Harby

Historical background 80
Aspects of mis-education 89
Quantitative imbalances 90
Educational remedies 91
    Attempts to relate general
        education to employment 92
    Attempts in vocational training ... 94
    Attempts in non-formal education .. 96
New trends 96

Conclusion 97
Mauricio Leonor

Bibliography 101

CHAPTER 4. THE PHILIPPINES 109
Edita A. Tan and Mauricio Leonor

Overview 109
Mauricio Leonor

Background 109
  Trends in the economy 109
  Trends in unemployment 112
  Pattern of labour absorption 114
Lessons from policy responses 118
  Reducing the supply of graduates .. 118
  Curricular reforms 119
  Non-formal education 121
  Training for employment overseas .. 122

A market model 124
Edita A. Tan

Introduction 124
Theoretical considerations 126
  The nature and choice of
    education capital 126
  Ability and cost of education 127
  Supply of skills in labour markets 128
  The responsibility of the schools
    in unemployment 131
  The quality problem 131
  The role of the Government in
    education 131
Empirical evidence 133
  The school system 134
  Unemployment trends 135
  Returns on college education 147
  College enrolment and graduates ... 149
Concluding remarks 157
Chapter Appendix 160
Bibliography 165

CHAPTER 5. INDONESIA 169
Ruth Daroesman

Introduction 169
The dimensions of unemployment 171
  The labour force of Indonesia in 1980 171
  Labour force participation rates .. 172
  Unemployment rates 174
  Underemployment 174
  Unemployment and education 178
  The 1976-78 tracer study 181

Entry into the labour force and
 duration of unemployment 181
The job search 182
Aspirations 184
The schools and unemployment 186
Movement into employment 186
Trends in educated unemployment 188
The education system and unemployment 191
The education system 191
 Introduction 191
 The pattern of growth 192
 Growth of expenditure 195
Educational issues affecting
 employment 195
Compulsory primary education
 and the drop-out problem 195
The general/vocational balance
 of secondary schools 197
Non-formal education and other
 forms of delivery 198
Curriculum 198
Other quality factors: time,
 teachers and equipment 199
University reform 199
Stock and flow of educated
 manpower 200
Self-employment status of the
 educated 202
Occupational structure of the
 educated labour force 202
The civil service 210
Looking ahead 210
Socio-economic policies influencing
 education and employment 211
The impact of policies on wage
 structure and demand for
 educated labour 214
Public service wages 216
Allocation of skilled manpower 217
Minimum wages 219
Regional wage variations 219
Wages and occupations 220
Male/female wage differentials 222

Current and future issues - and some
 approaches 224
 General economic issues 224
 The mismatch issue 227
 Primary school drop-out 229
 Secondary school expansion 229
 Educational quality 230
 The role of vocational schools 230
  Training for what? 231
  Where? 231
  Form and cost? 232
 Labour absorption and wages 232
 Some approaches 233
Summary 236
Bibliography 244

CHAPTER 6. SUMMARY, LESSONS AND ISSUES 249
   Mauricio Leonor

Summary 249
 Introduction 249
 On the unemployment of educated
  labour 250
  Tanzania 251
  Egypt 252
  The Philippines 252
  Indonesia 254
 Lessons 258
 Direct intervention in the labour
  market 259
 Guaranteed jobs in the public
  sector 259
 Reducing the labour force 259
  Expansion of the school system .. 259
  Military service 260
  National service 260
 Control of the size of the
  educated labour force 261
 Control of wages 261
 Permissive emigration 262
 Indirect intervention through
  schools as training systems 263
 Increased vocational instruction
  in schools 263

Redirection of attitudes towards
  work and village life 265
Diversification of specific skills
  and their labels 266
Upgrading quality 269
Issues 269
Wage differentials 270
Appropriate designs of school and
  training systems 271
Convention No. 142: Human
  resources development 273
Bibliography 277

INDEX 279

FIGURES

1. Changes in the educational profile of
   Tanzania 22
2. Labour market for graduates and skilled
   workers, I 129
3. Labour market for graduates and skilled
   workers, II 162
4. Growth of Indonesian education, 1900–1980 .. 193
5. Dynamics of vocational school curricula
   and employment opportunity sets 274

TABLES

CHAPTER 2

1. The Tanzanian labour force, 1965 13
2. Unemployment in Tanzania cross-classified
   by education, sex and age, 1965 14
3. Unemployment and underemployment in
   Tanzania, 1965 15
4. Invisible underemployment in Tanzania, 1965 16
5. Annual growth rates of gross domestic
   product by industrial origin, 1966 prices 18
6. Annual growth rates of wage employment
   by industry, 1965-76 20
7. Rates of rural-urban migration for four
   education groups in three time periods:
   Tanzanian males 25
8. Educational attainments of rural population of Tanzania in 1965 and 1980 26

CHAPTER 3

9.   Unemployment by sectors in Egypt,
     1960 and 1976 62
10a. Distribution of the unemployed
     labour force by age and sex in
     1960 and 1976 64
10b. Distribution of unemployed labour
     by age, sex and type of workers,
     1960 and 1976 65
11. Unemployment by educational level,
     1960 and 1976 67
12. Distribution of the unemployed labour
     force by educational level in 1960
     and 1976 69
13. Educational expansion in Egypt 71
14. Distribution of the employed by economic
     activities in 1960 and 1976 78
15. Distribution of the employed by educational
     level in the different economic
     activities in 1960 82
16. Distribution of the employed by educational
     level in the different economic
     activities in 1976 84

17. Distribution of the employed by educational
    level and by public and private
    institutions in 1976 86

CHAPTER 4

18. Utilisation rates of human resources 113
19. Unweighted average absorption rates and
    monthly incomes of college graduates,
    1969 116
20. Overseas contract workers by major
    occupational group, 1975-80 123
21. Average annual tuition fees in universities
    and colleges by field of study and type
    of school 136
22. Growth and distribution of enrolment in
    private colleges by field of study,
    1967-72 138
23. Educational attainment of faculty of the
    University of the Philippines and
    private schools, 1968-69 140
24. Number and per cent distribution of
    unemployed labour by nature of
    unemployment, 1956-75 142
25. Open unemployment rate of experienced
    labour force, by sector and occupation,
    1956-71 144
26. Reported unemployment by educational
    attainment, 1961, 1965, 1977 146
27. Percentage distribution of college
    graduates, by waiting time from
    graduation to first job in 1970, 1978 ... 148
28. Number and per cent distribution of
    employed graduate respondents, by
    reasons for delay in job and by
    waiting period, 1978 150
29. Absorption rate by school type 152
30. Growth of enrolment in higher education
    by sector, 1945-46 to 1975-76, selected
    years 153
31. Growth and distribution of college
    graduates by area of specialisation 154
32. Increments in supply of college graduates
    and in employment, 1951-55 to 1975-77 ... 156

CHAPTER 5

33. Labour force participation rates, 1980 173
34. Labour force participation rates by
    educational level, 1980 175
35. Unemployment rates by sex, age and
    urban/rural location, 1980 176
36. Unemployed workers, by period of time
    seeking work 177
37. Unemployment rates by educational level,
    1980 179
38. Unemployment by age and level of
    education, 1978 180
39. Duration of unemployment of the employed
    and unemployed 183
40. Employment, unemployment and schooling
    rates, one and two years after upper
    secondary school 187
41. Unemployment rates by age and sex, urban and
    rural residence, various sources, 1970-80   189
42. Unemployment rates by educational attain-
    ment and sex, various sources, 1971-80 ..   190
43. Share of education in the development
    budget 196
44. Population by educational attainment,
    1971-80 201
45. Educational distribution of the population
    and of the labour force, 1971-80 203
46. Enrolment in tertiary education,
    around 1978 204
47. Enrolments in tertiary non-degree
    programmes (state institutions only)   206
48. Estimate of Sarjana (5-year) graduates
    1950-80 by field of study (state
    universities and teacher-training
    institutes only) 207
49. Educational and occupational distribution
    of employed workers, 1980 208
50. Index of monthly wages per employed person
    by educational level (urban areas of
    Indonesia) 215
51. Index of average wages by occupation, 1978   221
52. Daily wages of skilled and unskilled
    workers in construction 1971/72
    and 1981/82 223

FOREWORD

Increasing doubt is being shed on the simple proposition that higher levels of education in developing countries are an unmitigated good. In 1973 the International Labour Office published a study by Mark Blaug in which he foresaw that the problem of unemployed school-leavers could only be solved by the "slow and patient reform" of primary education. As this study of four developing countries makes clear this is not the way that education authorities have responded. Rather they have increased the amount of vocational instruction given in school in the hope of making school-leavers "employable" and they have intervened as best they could, but fruitlessly, to change attitudes towards different types of work. Training programmes within schools have become more specialised. But as Mauricio Leonor shows, this has made school curricula more rigid as well as increasing the cost of schooling. As a further result the necessary improvements in primary education, which all agree are essential, have been pushed further into the background.

The subject of educated unemployment and the waste and frustration which it involves is one of natural interest to the International Labour Office. This study was prepared within the programme of research of the ILO's World Employment Programme.

ILO, Geneva

P.J. Richards
Head
International Policies Unit
Employment and Development Department

The path of social policy for alleviating
unemployment may be paved with good intentions, but the
latter are not sufficient to prevent the effects of
policy errors from making the problem even worse. A
major source of these errors is a dated knowledge base
itself, because it obstructs new information and
innovations, including a wide range of measures that are
incompatible or inconsistent with the corpus of knowledge
that is held as "truth" but most of which -- in Hunter's
terms -- now belongs to mythology. Besides, a dated
knowledge base may spin off irrelevant policy measures
which, in many cases, are very expensive in terms of
missed opportunities for development.

The present volume examines the ways by which four
poor countries tried to alleviate a particular sort of
problem, namely, the widespread joblessness of university
graduates and school-leavers, more popularly known as
"educated unemployment". The approach is not that of an
exhaustive inventory of causes nor an assessment of the
effects of a constellation of these causes. Rather, it
is a focus on the role of schooling and training, whether
well or badly applied (i.e. mis-education), as a supposed
cause of so-called educated unemployment and on certain
labour market policies that were used to help solve the
problem. Mis-education, however, has many variants, and
so has what might be called "proper" education, each
being dependent on a particular, perhaps dated, knowledge
base.

Indeed even the authors of the country studies in
this volume seem to exhibit differences in opinions and
views. They write from their individual perspectives,
although they started from one general outline. The
author on Tanzania writes, for example, as an "outsider
looking in", spinning most of his observations from
secondary sources (that is, through published materials
and numerous interviews with many friends who spent some
time in that country), and checking these observations by
fieldwork in Dar es Salaam and its environs. The style is

that of an outsider who is unconstrained by power relations within the country's politics and misses some of the subtle and fine details of what has actually taken place there.

The main contributors to the chapter on Egypt are "insiders" who have been participant observers of what has been happening in that country. Prof. Karima Korayem is a distinguished economist who is connected with Al-Azhar University and the IBM Trade Centre in Cairo. Profs. Abdel Aziz El-Koussy and Mohy. Khairy Harby are not only well-known academics but also seasoned officials (now retired) of the Ministry of Education and, later (Prof. El-Koussy) of ALECSO, a regional organisation under the aegis of the UNESCO. These contributors, writing in their personal capacity, are familiar with details of the local situation that are often beyond the grasp of outsiders.

Prof. Edita A. Tan is also a distinguished economist and currently professor of economics in the University of the Philippines. She is therefore thoroughly familiar with the local scene as her perceptive essay on a market model reveals.

Ms. Ruth Daroesman, the author of the chapter on Indonesia, is both an "insider" and an "outsider". She worked for some time in Indonesia, particularly with the US-AID and the Ministry of Education and has kept in touch with the local situation there, through her work as Assistant Editor of the Bulletin of Indonesian Economic Studies and later as Fellowship Programme Officer, Office of the Chancellor of the Australian National University in Canberra.

From their own individual perspectives and knowledge bases the authors may have put particular countries under a magnifying glass and have exposed themselves to the hazards of this exercise. For instance, after the chapter on Tanzania was written, a Tanzanian ex-cabinet minister, who was then visiting professor in the United States, put forward a diagnosis of his country's under-development in an article in a London daily. That diagnosis might be right in principle, but it could be judged wrong because it was different from the official position. This hazard brings us to the domain of politics which is beyond the scope of this volume.

However, good knowledge base is a starting point, albeit a very important one, for social policy. From there, many unknown factors mediate or intervene. The next steps are to get the correct information and advice to policy makers, not by making them theorists but by exposing them to the information so they may become Machiavelli's enlightened philosopher princes or princesses.

Further, it may be said that in the course of its evolution this volume owes so much to so many. My colleague Peter Richards provided guidance, encouragement and administrative support from the inception of the study to its completion. Lothar Richter, Juan Mesa, John H. Richards, Robert S. Ray, Bernardo Bergerie-Pagadoy and Robert Caldwell read either a part or the entire manuscript and shared their comments and suggestions for improving its presentation. C. Hennis assisted in transforming unorthodox format and prose to good house style, while Irene Pearson, Ann Meade, Heather Kelland, Mary Dominguez and Marlene Rivo helped type the manuscript at various stages. Many friends also helped in some ways but, in their self-effacing style, they prefer to remain anonymous.

M.D. Leonor

ILO, Geneva

INTRODUCTION

This study is about unemployment, and about how schools as training institutions react or fail to react to unemployment in Tanzania, Egypt, the Philippines and Indonesia. It is also about the use of policies in education, training and the labour market as means to alleviate the problem in these countries. Lastly, it is about the lessons to be learned from the experience of these countries in trying to cope with unemployment in their educated labour force.

The study investigates mis-education as the major supposed cause of widespread unemployment among school-leavers and university graduates in poor countries. Its focus is on schooling and training rather than on macro-economic variables.

Macro-economic diagnoses suppose that unemployment is a result of inappropriate economic structures and low overall demand that inhibits a full utilisation of available labour. Low demand and unemployment manifestly co-exist and co-vary, thus leaving little doubt as to a direct, and perhaps reciprocal, relation between the two. But the inappropriateness of an economic structure and its complex effect on unemployment are not readily obvious, as shown in detailed analysis by many ILO Employment Strategy Missions. And when this effect varies directly with the educational level of prospective workers, there is good reason to believe in the presence of other, doubtless more profound and specific, causes.

The general situation in the countries chosen for the study was that unemployment tended to be always greater among new workers with more schooling than among those with little or no schooling at all. Rough and ready explanations for this observation do not seem to explain fully certain differences in unemployment rates. One such explanation is that educated workers have higher labour force participation rates and are therefore more liable to be counted as unemployed. Another is that those who never went to school have more time for job-search.[1] The latter explanation might

well be partly true but it does not seem to square up to
the widely held tenet that education and skills are
scarce "commodities" in poor countries and should be
employed more than the purely manual contributions of
uneducated workers. So it is likely that a good part of
the mysteries of unemployment of educated workers lies
beyond the reach of economic causes and explanations.

Thus the focus of enquiry was shifted to
mis-education, principally to two of its variants, both
suggesting that unemployment can be blamed on certain
characteristics of school systems. The first of these
is that schools fail to develop among school-leavers the
flexibility to adjust to changing labour markets, and
the second is that schools fail to equip the
school-leavers with employable skills for which there is
a foreseeable demand.

These variants, however, are not mutually
exclusive. But it is useful to keep their identities
separate because they stem from different perspectives
and they require different remedial approaches. The
corrective for the first emphasises mental agility and
preparedness to acquire new skills required by new work
opportunities; it does not, however, define the location
and manner of skill acquisition. The cure for the
second is silent on mental preparedness; instead it lays
stress on the immediate and direct acquisition of
practical skills. Further, it specifies the location of
training, i.e. as part of formal curricula in schools.

The four countries studied were predisposed to
diagnose the second variant rather than the first,
perhaps by reason of history. These countries long had
their systems of educating their aristocracy or the
ruling upper class. This education was mainly in the
"3Rs" and had no skill specific to any occupation. But
popular expansion of schools did not strictly follow
this model of education. Instead the content of
schooling veered towards what was often supposed to be
the educational need of the people. In colonies or
non-self-governing territories this need was deemed by
colonial administrators to be for practical subjects,
indeed as it still is today in many technical assistance
programmes. This need appeared even more compelling to
the four countries when unemployment of educated labour
changed from bad to worse. The driving force behind
this need was so strong that other solutions to the
problem seemed out of the question.

Because none of the countries diagnosed the first
variant, it is not possible to illustrate the effects of
action taken to solve the alleged failure of schools to
develop mental flexibility. But inferences can be drawn
from within country differences, i.e. from certain

effects of parallel systems of general academic and vocational schools on earnings and unemployment. It is found, for example, that vocational school graduates tend to have lower average earnings and higher unemployment rates than graduates of general academic schools, suggesting certain differences in ability to adjust to labour markets. But many factors influence or intervene in this seemingly straightforward relation, so that categorical statements are difficult to defend. So our arguments were extended from the empirical to the speculative.

The choice of the countries was arbitrary. It was based on what lessons could be learned from the country's experience that might contribute to a usable body of knowledge.

Tanzania

Tanzania is one of the 25 poorest countries on earth. But it is also a young and innovative one whose strong leadership and dynamic experiments in socialism have been shining examples of how to break away from Africa's colonial past. When it acceded to Independence, the country was in the limelight of world attention and was receiving aid, not in trickles but in massive quantities, almost to the point of dependency. When aid was reduced substantially, almost every development programme collapsed. However, our interest in the lessons from Tanzania is not in the politics of aid but in what the country did after deciding to ignore the unemployment problem.

Tanzania has effectively prevented the emergence of educated unemployment at the level of university graduates. By socialistic planning she has restricted the expansion of higher education and thus of the supply of graduates. But this has nudged the problem to secondary and primary school-leavers, who are unloaded in their quasi-totality onto a sluggish labour market. In other words, tight control at the university level has pushed unemployment to those with lower qualifications.

This unemployment was considered in certain quarters as being of the voluntary sort because, according to official circles, there was much work to do on the abundantly available land. What was needed was to orient idle school-leavers back to ujamaa villages and to the land. A series of measures such as Education for Self-Reliance (ESR) and National Service was meant to provide this orientation. All this, however, appears to be a futile exercise in an unimproving economy, and school-leavers continued to leave their villages as in

the past. Besides, unprecedented innovations in ESR
were feared to have deleterious effects on the mental
preparedness of pupils and students either for further
studies and new work opportunities or for vocational
training.

Egypt

Egypt is rich not only in cultural history but also
in a newly found resource - oil. In 1981 Egypt was
already a middle-income country, with a per capita GNP
of about $540, as against a figure of only $260 in
1973. Its 43 million people are predominantly Muslim
and Arabic in cultural origin, and seem to have been
intricately entwined in Middle East politics since the
remote past.
Political change was the context, the origin of
policies whose ultimate aim was something much greater
than merely alleviating unemployment. Unemployment
could have been worse, were it not for Egypt's proximity
to and cultural affinities with other Arab States whose
demand for Egyptian skilled labour was large.
Several lessons from Egypt reveal the
self-defeating effects of certain policies. Rapid
expansion of schools as a gambit for keeping labour
force participation rates and unemployment temporarily
low had a large and adverse cumulative effect. This was
compounded by a guaranteed jobs policy with the
prevailing grade system and wage scales which led to
overstaffing in government offices and public
enterprises. But all these negative effects were a
small price to pay for achieving broad social objectives
and promoting stability when the country was in the
throes of political change.
Measures taken in the school system were likewise
self-defeating, because they were in conflict with
actual wage scales and opportunities. Social demand was
for the traditionally well-rewarded academic schooling
rather than for low-paid practical trade training. Yet
the authorities established more and more vocational
schools and even increased the vocational content of
school curricula. Many practical schools were diverted
from their original purpose but were "saved" by being
transformed into institutions for higher studies; they
were thus a roundabout way of preparing for the
university. The consequence was a stream of
school-leavers who were neither well prepared for
university studies nor trained for immediate employment.
The result is regrettably not peculiar to Egypt,
being common among ex-colonies whose prevailing concepts

about schooling and training can be traced back to
colonial times.

The Philippines

The Philippines is an ASEAN[2] country of about 49
million people with a per capita gross domestic product
(GDP) of $822 in 1981. Its economy has been heavily
affected by rising fuel prices and a fall in the demand
for its products.

The country's major peculiarity in this study is
the presence of a large private sector in high school
and higher education which, in conventional theory,
should be more flexible and responsive to manpower
demand than state-controlled systems. But the leads and
lags of supply and demand for specific manpower are
rather long, and made longer by a school system whose
characteristics are more relevant to a large rich
country than to a poor one. Hence, waiting periods for
available jobs became unnecessarily long, and
unemployment of newly educated labour rather severe;
they would have been even worse if it had not been for
the fact that opportunities for overseas employment were
available.

But the lessons from Philippine experience are not
of the speed and ease of response by the state schools
to alleged scarcity of skills but rather of the
clumsiness and negative effects of such response; not
the flexibility of private schools but rather of the
need for quality control; not of curricular reforms to
make schools more vocationally oriented but rather of
the efficient delivery of specific skills through ad hoc
training systems.

Indonesia

Indonesia is a big country of 153 million people
who are mostly Muslim (about 90 per cent) but who are
non-Arabic in ethnic origins. Indonesia is rich in
natural resources, chiefly in forestry, agriculture and
oil. It is an OPEC country whose income from oil has
increased its per capita GNP from $109 in 1972 to $475
in 1980.

Oil has financed Indonesia's employment-creating
development programmes. But the fast expansion of these
programmes - perhaps too soon - to the far-flung corners
of the archipelago was a heavy liability when there was
a glut of oil and oil prices fell in the world market.
When the country's development programmes slowed down,
unemployment became worse. School-leavers and graduates
outnumbered the supply of modern sector jobs, while

university campuses became politically restive with
dissatisfaction about the national economy when the
fortunes from oil began to slip away.

The Indonesian study reports that unemployment of
school-leavers and graduates is a distorted Western view
of one of the problems of poor countries. It qualifies
this unemployment as a leisurely transition from school
to further schooling or to work and later back to
school. It appears to be a rational form of behaviour
of students who come from the upper strata of Indonesian
society and who can afford to hold out for whatever time
is necessary to get a relatively decent job. In a
country whose culture does not encourage youngsters to
cut loose from their families at an early age, the need
to find jobs in a great hurry after graduation is
perhaps not as compelling as in the West.

This transition was seen as nothing serious in a
country where underemployment, unproductivity and
poverty loom large. Accordingly, effort in the field of
schooling and training has been largely in augmenting
the productive capacity of the population, rather than
in reducing unemployment as such.

Moreover, the description of this transition, based
on results of a tracer study, leads to an understanding
of flow problems in which new crops of school-leavers
and graduates overload the absorptive capacity of
existing employers. Overloading was not a question of
over-supply because overall manpower requirements for
modernising Indonesia were thought to be very large.
Hence, control of flows or of supply even to match
actual absorptive capacity of employers was out of the
question, provided quality could be sustained. Quality
was related to many issues, among which are the design
features of the school system, improvement of which
could remove certain aspects that prolong waiting time
for jobs and entrench occupational immobility.

Some terms

At this point it is perhaps worthwhile to introduce
some terms whose meanings varied from one country to
another. The term graduates, for example, is specific
to university graduates in Tanzania and Egypt, but not
so in Indonesia and the Philippines. In the last two
countries the term is used rather generally. It,
therefore, requires a qualifier for specifying which
level is referred to. Thus the terms primary school
graduates, high school graduates and college graduates
are used in Indonesia and the Philippines, which in
Tanzania and Egypt mean primary school-leavers,

secondary school-leavers and graduates, respectively. It becomes obvious that the term school-leavers is not synonymous with drop-outs. Strictly speaking, the expression "school-leavers" refers to students who have completed secondary school instruction and passed the so-called secondary school-leaving examination. Unless the level is specified, the term school-leaver applies to those who have completed their studies and passed the corresponding examination for leaving either the lower secondary or the upper secondary school in Egypt or in Tanzania. In some instances, the term is extended to cover the primary school level by using the appropriate limiter as in primary school-leavers already mentioned above.

In this babel of tongues there are also other terms, namely, training, non-formal education and educated unemployment, which readers might also wish to have defined.

The term training has gathered new meanings and has become a source of confusion when undefined for a given context. In this study we distinguish two nuances of the generic term training, namely, the technical and the political. In its technical sense, training is defined by the International Dictionary of Education as "Systematic practice in the performance of a skill".[3] Another authoritative source defines training as "the special kind of teaching and instruction in which goals are clearly determined, are usually readily demonstrated and call for a degree of mastery ...".[4] These definitions are general in that they apply "regardless whether [training] takes place within the system of formal education or outside it" (Recommendation No. 150, Paragraph 5(1), and ILO Convention No. 142, Article 2), wherever and whatever is its administrative support.

However, training according to the political nuance is less broad because it is only a part of training in the general technical sense, i.e. it is called training only if it takes place outside schools. Thus, to use a rather striking example, language courses are training when conducted and administered by the ILO's clientele of labour ministries of member States, but not when undertaken under the jurisdiction of the Ministry of Education, Culture and Sports. In this example, use of the word "training" is simply a political device for distinguishing which ones are within or outside official power and control.

In this study we prefer the broad technical definition of training to the political one, for good reason. A broad definition avoids the use of "blinkers" and transcends artificial boundaries. It permits a good perspective to be had of a wide range of training activities, as indeed is needed in analysis. Further, much instruction for well-defined goals such as direct preparation for specific occupations or even for specific jobs takes place in schools. Not recognising this instruction as training is merely nearsighted, especially because under changing conditions or in dynamic labour markets such instruction, as argued later in this study, ought to be provided outside of schools.

The adjective non-formal is used to differentiate a particular sort of teaching and learning from the formal and informal forms of education. Formal education refers to schooling or to any portion of it, from primary and secondary grades up to the university. Non-formal education consists of deliberate teaching and learning activities which are not part of school curricula. The word "deliberate" distinguishes the non-formal from the informal sort of education. The latter experience takes place as day-to-day learning events like those in work experience and even in leisure. In this nomenclature, training in the technical sense may occur as part of formal or of non-formal education but hardly of informal education. In the political sense, however, the term training has taken on a new meaning, and is specific only to non-formal education.

"Educated unemployment" is an ugly formation, especially to English purists. It found currency when university graduates in many poor countries could hardly find suitable jobs. At first it was synonymous with graduate unemployment and was peculiar to unemployed university graduates. But when joblessness spread, the term "educated unemployment" was also extended to those with lower levels of schooling. In this study the usage varies from one country to another, principally because the determination of who is educated enough is problematic. Casting absolutes aside and adopting a heuristic approach, we extended the coverage of the term "educated unemployment" to primary school-leavers in Tanzania but only down to the secondary school-leavers in Egypt or to high school graduates in Indonesia as well as in the Philippines, where perhaps the term should only be applied to unemployed college graduates.

Notes

1 M. Blaug: "Educated unemployment in Asia with special reference to Bangladesh, India and Sri Lanka", in Economic Bulletin for Asia and the Pacific, Vol. XXVIII, No. 1/2, June-Dec. 1977, ST/ESCAP/47, pp. 120-137.

2 ASEAN is an acronym for Association of Southeast Asian Nations.

3 G. Terry Page and J.B. Thomas: International Dictionary of Education (London, Kogan Page, 1977), p. 346.

4 C.V. Good: Dictionary of Education (New York, McGraw-Hill Book Co., 3rd ed., 1973), p. 613.

I. INTRODUCTION

Tanzania is noticeably different from the other countries in this study because she does not have the so-called "educated unemployment", the widespread joblessness of high school-leavers[1] and university graduates, in the form and on the scale known in many poor countries.

By socialistic planning and control, the country has prevented the emergence of the problem or, at least, minimised it. By expanding the university-preparatory high schools and the university slowly, she has assured herself a supply of an élite cadre of graduates, well within her economy's absorptive capacity. And by institutionalising school reforms towards self-reliance, she has been preparing the minds of the country's youth for communal employment, principally in the rural areas. At the same time, however, the vast expansion of primary schooling, the limited opportunities for secondary education and a languishing economy have created a phenomenon of unemployment at the level of the primary and lower secondary school-leavers.

These observations are discussed in the subsequent sections. Section II describes the employment situation in Tanzania. The discussion starts with the country's 1965 Labour Force Survey, follows this up with information on economic development since then, and draws attention to the general picture, that is, that the situation in recent years is not much better than in 1965. Section III tells how the situation developed or persisted within the socialistic framework of government, while Section IV traces how the Tanzanian education system was used to cope with the persisting problem and why the success in this effort was rather limited. Finally, Section V draws lessons from Tanzanian experience.

II.   THE EMPLOYMENT SITUATION

1.   Unemployment and underemployment

Statistics show that unemployment in Tanzania in 1965 was rather low.[2]   The labour force survey of that year showed that the unemployment rates were only 7.0 and 3.9 per cent in the urban and rural sectors, respectively (Table 1).   These figures were based on the simple notion of unemployment, that is, when a person is completely out of work.

To a casual observer the population might have seemed to be quite busy.   But on closer scrutiny the situation was already serious at that time.   First, conventional unemployment as defined above hit on the young and educated workers particularly hard, especially those with only primary schooling (Table 2).   Second, underemployment rates were very high.[3]   The labour force survey mentioned above revealed that about 36 per cent of the rural labour force suffered from critical underemployment, in the sense of a condition characterised by very low earnings or by long hours of work with very low income or productivity.

Perhaps the gravity of the situation might be understood better if the underemployment were converted to its arithmetic equivalent in unemployment.   Based on a 45-hour work-week, visible underemployment (Table 3) would have added about 4.2 and 14.8 percentage points to the unemployment rates in the urban and rural sectors, respectively.   Thus the unemployment rates for these same sectors would have been 11.2 and 18.7 or 18.4 for the country as a whole.   And based on an income standard of Tsh.150/ per month, invisible underemployment (Table 4) would have added 5.1 and 55.1 percentage points to the basic unemployment figures above, placing the country's theoretical unemployment at 12.1 and 59.0 per cent in the urban and rural sectors, respectively.

Without a doubt these rates are exceedingly alarming.   They are so because the reference point of Tsh.150/ per month, the urban minimum wage (roughly US$18.00) at that time, is perhaps unrealistically high.

But replacing this reference point by Tsh.100, the rural minimum wage also at that time, would only have reduced the unemployment rate of the rural sector from 59.0 to 55.2 per cent.   Of course, lowering the point of reference - down to a level at which it would be meaningless in terms of the goods and services it could buy - would decrease the estimated unemployment rates.   But anything lower than the rural minimum wage would not accord with the Government's series of upward

Table 1:   The Tanzanian labour force, 1965
            (in thousands)

	Total	Rural	Urban
Population	10 248	9 783	465
Labour force	3 806	3 663	143
Employed	3 654	3 ىلا	133
Unemployed	152	142	10
Unemployment rate (%)	4.0	3.9	7.0

Sources: R.S. Ray, 1966, Tables 2.2 and 2.18.

Table 2: Unemployment in Tanzania cross-classified by education, sex and age, 1965
(in thousands)

Sex and age group	Total	Highest year of formal education completed			
		No formal education	Standard I to IV	Standard V to VIII	Form I or higher
Total unemployed	152	45	56	42	9
14-44 years of age	139	38	52	41	8
45-64 years of age	12	7	4	2	*
65 years and over	1	*	*	-	-
Male unemployed	132	37	52	37	7
14-44 years of age	121	31	48	36	7
45-64 years of age	10	5	3	2	*
65 years and over	1	1	*	-	-
Female unemployed	20	8	4	5	2
14-44 years of age	18	6	4	5	1
45-64 years of age	1	1	*	-	-
65 years and over	*	*	-	-	-

* Less than 500.
Details may not add to totals because of rounding (sic).

Source: Ray, op. cit., p. 76.

Table 3:   Unemployment and underemployment in
            Tanzania, 1965 (in thousands)[1]

	Total	Rural	Urban
Labour force	3 806	3 663	143
Unemployed	152	142	10
Unemployment rates (%)	4.0	3.9	7.0
Unemployment equivalent of visible underemployment	549	543	6
Equivalent unemployment rates (%)	14.4	14.8	4.2
Unemployment and underemployment combined	701	685	16
Combined unemployment rates (%)	18.4	18.7	11.2

[1] Except if indicated otherwise.

Source: Ray, op. cit., p. 83.

Table 4: Invisible underemployment in Tanzania, 1965 (in thousands)

Severity of degree of underemployment	Under-employment		Equivalent in unemployment	
	Rural	Urban	Rural	Urban
NONE or persons fully employed	(883)	(101)	0	0
Persons employed or earning:				
75% to 90% of standard (MILD)	109	7	19 075	1 225
50% to 75% of standard (MODERATE)	254	10	69 850	2 750
25% to 50% of standard (HEAVY)	413	4	258 125	2 500
10% to 25% of standard (SEVERE)	608	1	501 600	0 825
less than 10% of standard (CRITICAL)	1 254	*	1 169 982	*
TOTAL	3 521	123	2 018 632	7 300
% of the labour force			55.1	5.1

* less than 500

Source: Ray, op. cit., pp. 65-68.

adjustments of the urban minimum wage from Tsh.150/ in 1965 to Tsh.480/ in 1980.

All these figures seem to tell us that the unemployment situation in Tanzania in 1965 was very serious indeed. No direct evidence exists as to whether this situation has improved or deteriorated in the intervening period, but recourse may be had to the following indirect evidence. First, an examination of the sectoral growth of the economy and trends in wage employment may tell something about the country's capacity to absorb more labour in gainful employment. Second, an accounting of the supply of educated labour, that is, the expansion of the school system and its output, can show the supply condition of the labour market. And third, an analysis of the migration of Tanzanian workers should give information on where the workers go and the sort of labour market condition created by their mobility.

2. Economic growth and growth in employment

At first sight the Tanzanian economy has been doing fairly well. From 1966 to 1979 it grew by between 4 and 5 per cent yearly, rates that were much better than those of most other African countries. This first impression, however, changes to something less favourable if the country's fast population growth of about 3.28 per cent a year is considered. The suggestion of economic deterioration is supported by the slowing down of growth in the monetary sector, from 5.4 per cent in 1966-70 to 4.0 per cent in 1973-76, the latter rising again to 4.3 per cent in 1976-79, primarily due to a buoyant services sector consisting mainly of public administration and other services.

The faltering rate of growth of the monetary sector, however, was counterbalanced by growth in the subsistence sector, mainly in food production and construction of village dwellings. Hence, the overall growth rate of the economy seems to have kept fairly steady, as shown in Table 5.

But in terms of wage employment, the picture has been less rosy. Employment in estate agriculture, mining and quarrying was falling rapidly, while growth spurts in public utilities and construction in 1965-67 could not be maintained. In fact, the figures for 1965-72 and 1972-76 in Table 6 seem to indicate that employment in these two subsectors was also falling sharply. The only sectors showing some growth were manufacturing, commerce and transport. These three sectors propped up the employment growth of the whole monetary sector from a modest 1.93 per cent in 1965-67

Table 5: Annual growth rates of gross domestic product by industrial origin, 1966 prices

Sectors	1966–70	1970–73	1973–76	1976–79
Monetary sector				
Agriculture	3.1	0.7	1.2	4.5
Mining and quarrying	-15.0	-2.1	-8.4	-5.5
Manufacturing and handicrafts	8.1	7.4	2.5	0.9
Electricity and water	10.4	7.4	7.3	5.6
Construction	11.8	9.8	-6.5	0.5
Transport, storage and communication	10.9	7.5	4.3	3.4
Trade, restaurants and hotels	4.5	1.8	1.2	8.1
Finance, insurance, real estate and business services	11.7	7.1	4.7	2.5
Public Administration and other services	5.9	10.1	13.1	5.5
Monetary GDP at factor cost	5.4	4.9	4.0	4.3

Subsistence production

Agriculture	1.1	4.3	7.3	9.9
Construction	2.8	2.3	-0.5	5.8
Owner-occupied dwellings	2.8	2.9	2.5	2.5
Total subsistence production	1.5	3.9	6.1	8.4
Total GDP at factor cost	4.2	4.6	4.6	5.5

Note: The data are for Tanzania mainland only.

Source: Calculations are based on figures from Table 2.2 of the World Bank Report No. 3086-TA, Jan. 1981

Table 6:   Annual growth rates of wage employment by
industry, Tanzania, 1965-76

	1965-67	1965-72	1972-76	1965-76
Industry				
Estate				
agriculture	-5.6	-2.8	3.8	-0.5
Mining	-6.4	-4.0	-1-5	-3.1
Manufacturing	10.1	11.6	8.2	10.3
Public utilities	22.2	14.6	5.1	11.0
Construction	15.5	7.4	-4.5	2.9
Commerce	6.1	4.8	11.3	7.1
Transport and				
communications	6.1	4.9	9.0	6.4
Services	3.2	2.9	3.0	3.9
Finance	na*	na*	9.3	na*
Total wage sector	1.93	2.83	4.33	3.37

* na means "not available".

Source: Calculations are based on Appendix Table 3,
Valentine, p. 268, citing Tanzania: Employment
and earnings for years 1962-1976.

to a high 4.33 per cent in 1972-76, or an overall annual growth figure of 3.37 per cent for the period 1965-76.

From 1976 onwards, data on wage employment are not available. But it can be reckoned from Table 5 that the country's annual growth of gross domestic product (GDP) in 1976-79 was greater by only about 0.3 per cent than in 1973-76. If the same improvement is assumed for wage employment, then the employment situation in 1976-79 was only infinitesimally better than in the preceding years. This inference, of course, is based on figures that may have wide variances as do most statistics from less developed countries. In fact, there are observers who suspect that the figures are over-estimates (Jamal, 1981). Hence, the employment situation in Tanzania may not have changed markedly since 1965. It could be supposed, however, that there had been qualitative changes, especially after the Arusha Declaration in 1967.[4] But increasing population pressure, rapid expansion of primary schooling, and rural migration seem to destroy such a supposition.

3. Expansion of schooling

The change in the educational profile of Tanzania can be described briefly. In the beginning the profile was like a pole stuck to a pedestal. The pole has remained tall and slender, while the pedestal has been broadening rapidly since the country's Independence in 1961.

The university enrolment is only a tiny proportion of the population between ages 20-24. Even if enrolment in other post-high school institutions is taken into account, the enrolment-to-population ratio is still small.

This is the tall, slender pole shown in Figure 1, in spite of striking increases in admissions. When the University of Dar es Salaam started as a law school in 1963, it had only 34 students. In 1965 this number increased to 261, rising to 1,309 in 1970 and to 3,268 in 1975. There were also other post-secondary schools offering diploma courses in technical subjects whose enrolment was also expanding rapidly. But all this was only a very small fraction of the population for this level, producing an élite few university graduates. The graduates enjoyed good positions in government and in para-statal agencies. Their salaries were many times greater than the wages of unskilled workers, and not unnaturally this difference in remuneration created a keen demand for schooling among the public at large.

Growth in secondary school attendance was very fast. Enrolment was 22,980 in 1965, almost doubling

Figure 1:   Changes in the educational profile of Tanzania,
            public schools only

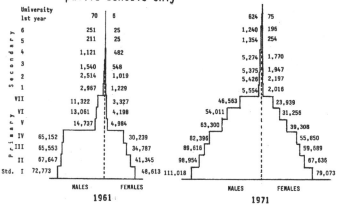

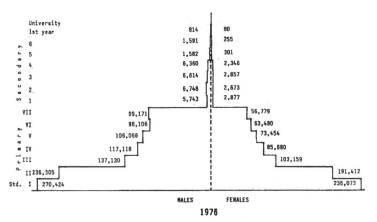

Source of data: Sectoral Planning Unit of the Ministry of
National Education, Tanzania.

to 41,178 in 1970. In the next five years it rose to 53,623 and to 66,273 in 1979.

The increase in enrolment was much greater in secondary schools than in the University. Hence, the number of secondary school-leavers who were entering the labour market was large. Many of them delayed this step by taking diploma or certificate courses in technical subjects or in teacher training. But this delay only served to swell the contingent that would soon be unloaded on the labour market. Each year there was an increasing supply of school-leavers, with or without further training, who were needing or demanding jobs, almost exclusively in the modern sector.

At the primary school level the expansion in absolute figures was greater. The enrolment of 710,000 pupils in 1965 rose to 1,573,000 in 1975, a doubling achieved in only a decade. The enrolment rose to 3,275,000 in 1979, a doubling in only four years. This has brought Tanzania closer to achieving universal primary education than any poor country in Africa, Asia or Latin America. As early as 1979 the country's uptake of Standard 1 pupils was already 94 per cent of 7-year-old children, only a few points below the 98 per cent target recommended by the World Employment Conference in 1976. In addition, the adult literacy rate had improved apace from about 9.5 per cent in 1960 to 28.1 per cent in 1970; a recent estimate (ca. 1978) has put it at 66 per cent, a figure that is substantially higher than the 40 per cent that England attained during the Industrial Revolution.

4. Migration of workers

The increasingly better educated Tanzanians have not been sedentary. They have been mobile, just like their ancestors, when the country - then Tanganyika and Zanzibar - was under the rule of the Germans and later the British.

In those days the Tanganyikans responded to climatic changes. When drought set in they walked long distances in search of water. When food crops failed, they went looking for paid work in the mines, on estate plantations in coastal areas, or in developing towns. Many Tanzanians still do so today.

After the country's Independence, the "Tanzanisation" of public offices accelerated migration, especially of the literate Tanzanians, towards the growing towns and cities. The attendant employment opportunities and expatriate wage rates ensured a steady flow of people with some schooling towards the cities, a

flow that was speeded up by the widening differentials
between wages or incomes in villages and in towns. This
combination of circumstances had the effect of creaming
off the better-educated Tanzanians from the rural areas.

The above observation is borne out by the changing
educational level of the migrants.   In 1961 about 33
per cent of the rural-urban migrants never had any
formal schooling, but in 1970 this figure was down to
only 7 per cent. And in recent years (ca. 1978) the
migrants had two-and-a-half times the average schooling
of those who remained in the rural areas (Mascarenhas,
p. 20).

This   is   supported   by   the   changing   rates   of
rural-urban migration, not only across levels of
schooling but also over time.   In Table 7 the rates per
100 rural dwellers increased from 0.011 (!) for those
with no schooling to 0.035 for those with (secondary)
Form 1 or better schooling.   The rates also increased
from 0.022 in the 1955-61 arrival period to 0.085 in
1967-70.   The figures for the latter period rose even
more sharply with the level of schooling. The migration
rate of those with at least Form 1 was almost 23 times
as great as that of those with no schooling.

This is not saying that more schooling is the cause
of migration, but simply that schooling seems to
predispose Tanzanians to it.   If this is so, the
increased   supply   of   school-leavers   could   have
accelerated rural to urban migration from 1970 to the
present.   There is no direct statistical evidence to
this effect, and the well-established migratory flow of
educated Tanzanians might have undergone other
influences, for instance if prospects in the rural areas
had been improving dramatically.   But this improvement
has not occurred, even if significant increases in
subsistence production of food and construction of
village dwellings have been reported.

This leads to a conclusion that the towns and
cities of Tanzania are teeming with school-leavers, from
primary if not from secondary schools. This conclusion
is, in fact, supported by the evidence in Table 8. The
educational profile of the rural part of Tanzania in
1980 hardly differs from that of 1965. The proportions
of the rural population with primary schooling seem not
to have changed at all, despite the rapid expansion of
primary schools since 1965. An exception, however, may
be mentioned for females who had Standards 5 to 8
schooling and who stayed on in the villages.   But at
the secondary or higher levels, the sharply falling
percentage as between 1965 and 1980 can only reflect an
unmistakable drift of both females and males away from
the villages towards towns and cities.

Table 7: Rates of rural-urban migration for four education groups in three time periods: Tanzanian males (per 100 rural dwellers)

Current age	Arrival period[a]	None	Standard 1-4	Standard 5-8	Form 1 and up	Aggregated over education
20-24	1967-1970	.014	.047	.277	.318	.085
25-34	1962-1966	.013	.038	.144	.399	.047
35 and up	1955-1961	.012	.030	.106	.180	.022
Aggregated over age groups (time periods): 1955-1970		.011	.032	.123	.249	.035

[a] Period which the majority of migrants in the age sub-group arrived in town.

Source: H.N. Barnum and R.H. Sabot: Migration, education and urban surplus labour: The case of Tanzania. Paris, OECD, 1976, p. 57.

Table 8: Educational attainments of rural
population of Tanzania in 1965 and 1980

	Labour force Survey, 1965 Per cent	Rural Household Survey, 1980 Per cent
Total 5 years old and over		
No schooling completed	51.3	49.2 (9.6)[1]
Standards 1 to 4	30.6	31.1
Standards 5 to 8	14.7	19.1
Secondary or higher	3.4	0.6
Total	100.0	100.0
Male		
No schooling completed	39.6	42.5 (7.8)[1]
Standards 1 to 4	35.0	35.9
Standards 5 to 8	20.1	20.8
Secondary or higher	5.3	0.8
Total	100.0	100.0
Female		
No schooling completed	62.9	55.7 (11.4)[1]
Standards 1 to 4	26.3	26.4
Standards 5 to 8	9.3	17.5
Secondary or higher	1.5	0.4
Total	100.0	100.0

[1] Figures in parentheses are for adult literates.

Sources: (a) R.S. Ray: Labour force survey. Ministry of
Economic Affairs and Development Planning, The
United Republic of Tanzania, Jan. 1966, p. 88,
Table 6.2; (b) Paul Collier, et al.: Ujamaa
and rural development: Labour and poverty in
rural Tanzania (Geneva, ILO, forthcoming),
typescript, p. 31, Table 3.3.

5. Employment of school-leavers

Employment seems not to be a problem for school-leavers who have completed their secondary education, i.e. with Form 6 or better schooling. Estimates by the World Bank show shortfalls which are expected to increase when direct entry to the university will be made to rise twofold. These shortfalls may be expected even without augmenting the number of school-leavers needed in other economic and social activities. The latter are mainly public sector posts and in National Service, a para-military-cum-civic volunteer service.

But the situation for those with less than Form 6 education has not been as good. A tracer survey of Form 4 school-leavers conducted in November 1981 showed that of the 39 per cent who were not allocated to further studies, only "7 per cent were referred to job(s), while the remaining 32 per cent were unplaced, ... (or) were left to find their own employment" (Munch-Petersen, p. 17). Previous estimates by the ILO Employment Strategy Mission to Tanzania in 1976 showed that Form 4 school-leavers had problems of employment. From one-fourth to almost one-third of these school-leavers were not placed in employment, pre-service training, nor in further schooling.

Perhaps the unplaced school-leavers were those who could not be accounted for by the government office which looked after their allocation and employment. It is also possible, as the ILO mission hinted, that the unplaced school-leavers could be those who did not register as unemployed for fear of being "rounded up ... and sent to rural areas" (Mission Report, p.23). Whether the school-leavers were indeed unemployed the mission did not definitely say, but other observers revealed that a surplus of school-leavers definitely existed. "Many educated (workers were) doing jobs for which they were over-qualified ... and some secondary school-leavers (had) in fact 'filtered down' to jobs which could be done by primary school-leavers" (Mascarenhas, p. 20). It was also reported that the unimproving employment situation in the urban areas might have pushed some of the school-leavers back to smaller towns and to the villages, places where unemployment was already severe.

III. THE ORIGINS OF UNEMPLOYMENT

The political economy of
change and slow growth

The political economy of Tanzania is too vast a
subject to describe in detail in this chapter. So the
discussion below focuses only on certain aspects which
heavily influence unemployment, starting at the time of
British rule under mandate from the League of Nations.[5]

Tanganyika's links with international markets were
well established when the country was governed by
Britain. During the Second World War Tanganyika's
primary products - mostly plant fibres and other
tropical crops - were of great importance to the Allies
because alternative supplies from the Far East and Latin
America risked being cut off. And when the War was
over, Tanganyika's links to the market in the allied
countries were maintained.

There was always a ready export market for
Tanganyikan products. All that was needed was to
produce more, and doing this was not too complicated
because the technology and skills needed were simple
farm routines. Tanganyika had the land and abundant
labour, while Britain had the administrators who could
instil discipline into and secure compliance from the
Tanganyikans. The enterprising organisation of these
factors produced a steady stream of commodities - mostly
sisal, tea, cotton, coffee and some minerals - to
international markets via the British connection.

The education needed for production was simple.
Training was an on-the-job affair, while schooling was
necessary only to prepare some workers for following
easy written instructions, for keeping production
records, or for the low-level tasks of servicing port
towns and depots. These forms of education were never
expanded beyond the needs of the economy, and hence the
problem of "educated unemployment" was unheard of.

But when Tanganyika gained independence and later
joined with Zanzibar to form the Republic of Tanzania,
things started to change. Government had to change
hands, from European expatriates to Tanzanians. More
and more Tanzanians had to be trained for their new
responsibilities. Many had to be sent overseas for
advanced education and training. And soon many
Tanzanians took up high positions in government and, in
some instances, in large business firms. But the
overall control of the latter was still in the hands of
the expatriates.

Expatriate control was dominant not only in estate agriculture but also in mining, manufacturing, and finance. The scale of activities in these sectors increased as did the participation of Tanzanians, but the controlling relationship remained almost the same, even after expatriates lost much of their role in government. This control was sustained by links between business interests and governmental functions. A number of Tanzanian officials in key government offices also held named posts in large business firms, an unholy link which was later broken by the leadership code of the Arusha Declaration.[6]

This controlling relationship, according to Tanzanian scholars (Rweyemamu, 1971), was not in the best interest of the country. Expatriate control of production, so the argument ran, exacted an unconscionable share of what the Tanzanians produced. Capital and expatriate services were overvalued, while Tanzanian labour was paid cheaply. In addition, products were sold overseas at book values that were much lower than what was considered by Tanzanians to be a fair price. Hence, even if business records showed only break-even transactions, a huge invisible profit had already been extracted.

Whether this claim is true or not can always be debated, especially in the light of subsequent experience but it was something real in the minds of Tanzanians who wanted to wrest control of big business firms from expatriate hands. And so the private firms were nationalised.

With nationalisation came the severance of market links. Business organisation was impaired, production fell, while output could not be sold at even the previous prices. Meagre foreign earnings dropped further and did not suffice to cover importation of the capital goods needed by industry let alone the consumer items which Tanzanians in towns and cities were used to. The economy was in dire straits.

Attempts were made to re-establish and restructure the broken market links. The East African Economic Community composed of Kenya, Tanzania and Uganda, was formed. The Community tried to pool its resources, agreed on what to produce in which country, and attempted to continue to trade freely among the three member countries. This regional group was intended to be like the European Economic Community, a parallel that did not last long (Guruli, 1972, pp. 88-95; Smith, pp. 156f).

Tanzania could export virtually nothing to the other members of the East African Community. Her agricultural cash crops competed with those of her

neighbours without much success; her nationalised
industries frightened away capital; and her
manufactured products did not have any comparative
advantage within the Community. Further, foreign goods
which entered the Community - whether legally or
illegally - could move freely to Tanzania, penetrating
even her own domestic market. So her factories,
designed for the anticipated large market, could not
operate at full capacity. Moreover, Tanzania found that
her membership in the Community was neither economically
nor politically advantageous (Nyerere, 1968, pp. 60-70).

In 1977 Tanzania dropped out of the Community. She
closed her borders with Kenya, but maintained military
presence in Uganda. Meanwhile, falling prices and
decreasing production of traditional exports had brought
the Tanzanian economy to its knees, back to more and
more subsistence production to help support the
country's fast growing population.

A situation like this would have brought chaos to
any country. But Tanzania had - and still has - a
charismatic leader. Mwalimu Julius Nyerere appealed to
nationalism based on socialistic ideals and to the
deep-seated survival instinct of the Tanganyikans and
Zanzibaris in a very harsh economic environment.

This political stroke held the country together.
The people's response was surging nationalism, speeding
up the "Tanzanisation" of government and business. More
Tanzanians replaced expatriates in the public service.
Big private firms were converted to quasi-governmental
agencies or para-statal agencies run by Tanzanians.
These para-statals increased in number and many of them
were active in public services that were rapidly
expanded in line with the socialistic framework of
government.

This created chains of employment opportunities.
The post of an expatriate taken over by a Tanzanian
created a series of promotions from below. A transfer
of a Tanzanian official to a higher-paying post in a
para-statal agency produced similar effects, and the
establishment of more and more para-statals speeded up
this dynamic process. All this, of course, followed
the pre-existing salary structure of the expatriates,
something which officials would not like to revise
downwards.[7] The result was rapid growth of the
bureaucracy, feeding on the supply of university
graduates, secondary school-leavers and inevitably,
taking place at public expense.[8]

The expansion of public services and para-statals
was to some extent a logical necessity, for it was in
the spirit of building the institutional framework for
development along socialist lines. The immediate

impact, however, was the creation of a huge cadre of
civil servants in government employ which in 1966
already accounted for about one-third of total wage
employment in the country (van de Laar, 1972, p. 111).
This proportion, including the employment in
para-statals, had risen to two-thirds by 1976, using
about 70 per cent of what the country spent on wage
employment (Valentine, 1981, p. 42).

Unfortunately, the growth of the bureaucracy was
not accompanied by a corresponding growth in economic
production. With impaired business organisation the
economy was unable to regain its previous levels of
productivity. Marketing was a serious problem, export
earnings were very low and trade was in deep deficit.
The situation was aggravated by the OPEC oil shocks, by
the country's military presence in Uganda, by the
Government's political problems with major foreign-aid
donors, by drought and by development plans that were
heavily dependent on foreign aid and borrowing. Aid
came in trickles, while currency problems and borrowing
quickly exhausted the country's special drawing rights
(SDRs) from the International Monetary Fund (IMF).

The only recourse left was self-reliance. It was
not an easy, or a comfortable choice. Certainly, it
was not easy either for the country's development
planners, whose conceptual apparatus was not prepared
for the zero option.

The planners seem to have been greatly influenced
by the dominant thinking of the time. For instance,
the problem of impaired business organisation was seen
in terms of shortages of skills, especially of the
high-level manpower variety (Tobias, 1963; Thomas,
1965). Thus, manpower planning was pre-eminent in
economic planning. It was of the sort which focused on
public sector employment, that is, on the expansion of
the bureaucracy. The outlook was quantitative and long
term. The immediate concern was to secure what was
regarded as critically needed high-level manpower,
rather than directly to improve the organisation for
production with the existing personnel.

Qualitative factors were overlooked. For
instance, the concept of entrepreneurship - whether at
the individual, communal or state level - was almost
taboo in Tanzania. The proprietary behaviour of Asian
Tanzanians was at best tolerated, while initiative and
achievement motivation were obliterated in communal
ujamaa villages. The attempts to upgrade management
and public administration fell far short of improving
the economic environment and efficiency in the public
sector, despite the increasing supply of educated and

experienced   Tanzanians   from   schools,   training
institutions and public service (Pratt, 1979, p. 228).

All these problems are, of course, not unique to
Tanzania, and indeed they exist in countries that are
relatively better off than Tanzania. The fault lies
largely in undeveloped entrepreneurship. For instance,
if effective state entrepreneurship had existed, new
markets could have been sought vigorously and new
products for domestic and overseas demand produced. But
this is easier said than done. First, demand for
primary products from poor countries was declining
because of world recession. Secondly, new products
demanded by overseas markets implied a technology which
Tanzania did not possess, while on the other hand, the
products available for export, simple processed goods
such as ground coffee and some garments, faced
protectionism overseas. And thirdly, although the
imported capital goods were meant to produce import
substitutes, these domestically produced consumer goods
could not compete - even at home - with products
manufactured elsewhere.

The problem of markets is indeed a formidable
one. This is particularly true for many poor countries
like Tanzania. For instance, tropical products such as
cane sugar and vegetable oils, which in principle
Tanzania can produce cheaply, cannot compete with
similar products of advanced countries. Part of the
reason is that the substitutes tend to be heavily
subsidised by the advanced countries, a situation
causing overproduction and dampening the world market
price of the tropical product. This is, in fact, what
President Nyerere and other leaders of poor countries
pointed out to the international community, during the
so-called North-South Dialogue for fair trade.

Another aspect of the problem of markets, one that
is related to business organisation, is marketing
cost. Tanzania's marketing set-up seems to be riddled
with such inefficiency that its excess cost may well
drive Tanzanian products out of the market (Ellis,
1981). Transport and credit costs are very high, while
the administrative machinery which replaced the
expatriates and small traders has been badly
co-ordinated. The situation has been worsened by the
proliferation and complexity of para-statal agencies
whose functions have not been well defined. According
to a World Bank count in 1981, there were at least 300
para-statals, of which 100 were in agriculture.

So far the problems of economic organisation,
productivity and markets have severely weakened the
economy. They have reduced the capacity to create
gainful work opportunities for the increasing supply of

school-leavers and graduates. At present there are signs that this supply is outstripping the available employment opportunities in Tanzania.

IV. EDUCATIONAL POLICY AND UNEMPLOYMENT

1. Towards education for self-reliance

The above review of the economy may give the impression that Tanzania is teetering on the brink of economic disaster. Per capita income in real terms has remained stagnant, if indeed it has not declined. Thus employment in the real income sense - not in the demographic sense - can hardly be improving. This is not because the country has chosen the socialist path, because other countries which have chosen the road of market economies have fared no better than Tanzania.

Part of the reason for the lack of growth is that on the path to socialism, Tanzania has been laying down an institutional foundation on a scale that cannot be supported by her economy. While some foundation is indispensable, its size has reduced the capacity of the economy for sustained growth, without which further institutional transformation to socialism will inevitably be slowed down and will eventually grind to a complete halt.

Further, employment policies have been focused on high-level manpower, and have paid less attention to workers at the production level. The preoccupation was not with the earning or producing services, but with the "spending services". The inevitable consequence has been that Tanzania's university graduates and upper secondary school-leavers have been comfortably placed in government service of one sort or another. But this has not been true for Tanzanians whose schooling was of a lower standard.

For the less educated there was developed the policy of "education for self-reliance", a policy whose leitmotiv was the use of the educational system for moulding the Tanzanian mind in socialism, "primarily in terms of mental and social attitudes rather than of knowledge and skills" (Dore, 1976, p. 113). Basically the policy was intended to adjust the educational system to the political ideals adopted for the country, a necessity of government throughout history, from ancient Greece and Rome to modern Europe. Its main thrust was political education, not only for the young but also for adults, especially the adults in party cells and in the bureaucracy.

Hand in hand with political education was education for productive work of a nature that would be in keeping with the predominantly rural conditions of Tanzania. Schools were to be transformed into production centres, usually into gardens and farms. Thus the phrase "education for self-reliance" gathered connotations, such as education for farming or education to bring back the school-leavers to the farms.

But the development of the policy of education for self-reliance did not stem from the problem of joblessness as such, but from a series of political events arising out of one school crisis after another. First, there was the primary school-leaver crisis, and second, the university students' revolt against National Service. Additionally, the vocational school students also went on strike. The policy appeared to have been devised to keep the unruly pupils and students busy and out of mischief.

2. The primary school-leaver crisis

This was not only a crisis of joblessness, although gainful jobs would have relieved the crisis. It was also a question of too few secondary school places for too many primary school-leavers. Of course, the demand for secondary schooling was an open manifestation of demand for relatively secure public-sector jobs later.

Since Independence, primary school enrolment had been expanding rapidly. The Government campaigned to put every child of school age in school and to make every adult literate. The Government built schools where there were none before. The campaign caught on, to the extent that many communities actually helped to build schools in places where the official budget could not afford to so do.

But this success sparked off the crisis. In 1965, 46,666 primary school-leavers sat for the Primary Leaving Examination, a requirement for admission to secondary schools after seven or eight years of schooling. Of that number only 6,903 could be admitted to study in Form 1, the first year of high school. This was an admission rate of about 15 per cent, or an exclusion rate of 85 per cent.

This was the breaking point of a tension that had been building up since the start of the massive expansion of primary schools. With 10,316 examinees in 1961, the "failure" rate was 59 per cent; in 1964 the rate was 69 per cent; and in 1965-66, with examinees almost five times as numerous as in 1961, the rate shot up to the 85 per cent mentioned above. In 1967, the year when the Arusha Declaration was promulgated, the

rate was 87 per cent or an admission rate of only 13 per
cent.[9] Their hopes prematurely dashed, many of the
school-leavers felt themselves at a dead end.

This almost exponential rise in failure rates was
not purely a case of lower standards of ability.   It
might be true that as more and more schools were opened,
the quality of supernumerary teachers declined, while
books   and   other   teaching   materials   were   getting
proportionately scarcer.   But even if all examinees had
had   the   achievement   levels   required   to   pass   the
examination,   there   were   not   enough   places   in   the
secondary schools.

Before   schools   opened   for   the   academic   year
1966-67,   the   crisis   reached   political   proportions.
Teachers in primary schools whose pupils fared badly in
the secondary school entrance examination were the
object of abusive remarks, if not physical harm, from
irate parents.   District commissioners were pestered by
long queues of parents of unsuccessful pupils. Likewise,
the party cells of TANU were under pressure from angry
parents to do something.   The Minister of National
Education was in hot water, while President Nyerere
faced hostile audiences inside and outside the National
Assembly.   The criticism was that the Government was
not creating enough places in the secondary schools and
in   vocational   training   programmes,   or   enough   job
opportunites for the primary school-leavers.   The
political pressure was on to force "the Government to
find   suitable   ways   of   eradicating   the   problem"
(Morrison, p. 203).

The Government's options were not easy.   Creating
jobs for the legions of primary school-leavers and
satisfying them all was simply impossible, even though
that would have relieved the pressure on the secondary
schools.   Increasing the number of secondary school
places was perhaps relatively easy, but this had
formidable   implications.   Secondary   schools   are
expensive to establish and maintain.   Further, this
option would swell the ranks of vocal political groups
who would be demanding more places in the University and
highly paid jobs in the government service later.   Each
of these avenues could lead to political disaster, while
other approaches were also equally forbidding.

3. The Students' revolt

In a country in ferment, students as an articulate
and idealistic population group have certain political
uses.   They can, for instance, be instigated to
demonstrate against real or imagined enemies, such as
the colonial or imperial powers.   As a political

instrument this group, however, is not a single-edged
sword, especially when its interests are threatened.

University students in Tanzania represent a very
tiny proportion of the adolescent population. From
high school onwards, their education has been very well
subsidised by the State. Fees are nominal, room and
board are free, while pocket money or allowances are
provided. In return, their only responsibility is
studying. After graduation they walk into highly paid
jobs in the government service. Accordingly they feel
"chartered" as an élite group, a tradition long accepted
since pre-Independence Tanganyika (Nyerere, 1968, p.
276).

This privileged status is the ultimate goal which
all aspiring parents want their children to reach;
parents would break down every barrier that anyone might
put in their children's way. Any slight detour or delay
would be vehemently resisted, not only by the parents of
the students, but also by the students themselves. One
of these detours or delays was National Service, a civic
and para-military service between studies and after
graduation from the University. The students detested
this National Service, and when it was made compulsory
they revolted.

National Service was open to young people of both
sexes, originally on a voluntary basis. The duration
was two years; the first three months were for training
in para-military activities, civics or political
education and in other useful subjects such as
bookkeeping. The next twenty-one months were for
development activities in the villages and youth camps,
which might include service in the armed forces, the
police and in civilian affairs. The trainees or
volunteers, as they were called, were provided with free
board and lodging, uniforms, and pocket money of Tsh.20/
per month. These benefits and the prospect of a
government job after the training period were attractive
to many primary school-leavers, but were not attractive
enough to secondary school-leavers, or to university
students and graduates.

When National Service was made compulsory following
the general election in October 1966, the university
students went on strike; they demonstrated against this
compulsion and defied President Nyerere and his
Government on this issue. In the confrontation that
ensued President Nyerere told the students (and the
public) that the National Service was an opportunity to
serve the peasants and the poor who collectively bore
the burden of expensive university education. The
students replied that they could not be forced to render
this service as a sacrifice to the poor, while

government officials flaunted their "benzies" (Mercedes-Benz cars) and opulent residences at Oyster Bay in Dar es Salaam.

The controversy brought to the surface certain matters which tarnished the images of both the students and the government officials. In its wake President Nyerere renounced 20 per cent of his salary (perhaps expecting the remaining public officials to follow suit). He turned the striking students over to the police and ordered transport warrants for sending the students home.

The confrontation and the strike had a tremendous impact on the President. He was deeply disappointed with the conduct of the students, the product of the Tanzanian educational system. And not long after the students' revolt came the Arusha Declaration (29 January 1967) and the public policy directives called Education for Self-Reliance (9 March 1967).

4. Education for self-reliance

In its essentials the Education for Self-Reliance policy was intended to transform attitudes inherited from the colonial period to the ideas of socialism. Work and study in schools were primarily a means to that attitude transformation; a solution to the problems of poverty and joblessness of primary school-leavers was of secondary importance.

The President's speech on this policy reviewed national progress in schools, such as (i) the abolition of racial distinction, (ii) the expansion of primary school enrolment, and (iii) the Tanzanisation of educational content. But he also pointed out the major fault of the system, which was the allocation of educational opportunities to serve the individual interest of only a few. Accordingly, he presented the need for "design[ing] ... [the] educational system to serve the community as a whole" (Nyerere, 1968, p. 280). Self-reliance had to be seen at a communal, rather than at an individual, level.

In pursuance of this policy, several school reforms were introduced. Development studies, with a particular focus on underdevelopment in Africa, were instituted as a required course in the University. Farming was included as one of the "self-reliant" activities in secondary and teacher-training schools, while a science subject with an agricultural bias was developed and introduced into the primary school curriculum. "Civics" became political education for developing a commitment to socialism, or at least to the party (TANU, now Chama Cha Mapinduzi or CCM) and the Government.

Education for Self-Reliance (or ESR for short) was also addressed – even if rather indirectly – to certain economic and social issues. If the school reforms had the effect of increasing the employment of school-leavers, then pressure on secondary schools and university would be eased and the political estrangement of school-leavers and students from the Government would be reduced.

The basic assumption was that the modern sector was very small, that 95 per cent of the population were in the rural sector, and that 96 per cent of the primary school-leavers would have no places in the secondary schools. Hence, the only possibility for these school-leavers was to return to or remain in the rural areas. The schools should adjust to this reality.

The reforms, if successful, were expected to have a train of effects, first on the pupils and then on their social milieu. The hope was that the pupils would develop the ujamaa attitude of familyhood, that is, the predisposition to work together and share the fruits of the work together. Above all the expectation was that the pupils would return home to improve their villages, thus spreading the effects of the education acquired from schools.

This was the dream, but reality was another matter. Statistics show that the school-leavers were also village leavers! For instance, as noted earlier (Table 8), the proportion of primary school-leavers who remained in the rural areas does not appear to have increased markedly since 1965, despite the dramatic expansion of the primary school system since then, and despite the introduction of extensive school reforms.

To be sure there were serious obstacles to be overcome. First, the reforms called for by ESR were massive and immediate. There was a scarcity of money and personnel to undertake the gigantic task. This scarcity was compounded by the confusion and the communication breakdown within the Ministry of National Education. The policy came from on high and the Ministry was caught unaware, ill-prepared and understaffed to handle the daunting assignment immediately. The result was that the notion of education for self-reliance came to have many interpretations. Parents, teachers and school officials all had different ideas about what it meant, and their ideas were certainly different from what President Nyerere had in mind.

Second, the use of schools to transform attitudes towards the ideals of socialism was premature, being much in advance of the existence of a sufficient economic or material base. It was based on the concept of praxis or work in schools for developing socialistic attitudes, a method of which there are no known examples in countries, even in centrally planned economies whose level of industrialisation is as low as that of Tanzania (Morrison, 1976, pp. 259-266). Moreover, praxis in schools in centrally planned economies was accompanied by coercion, something which President Nyerere was perhaps not prepared to use. Further, it was not accompanied by corresponding changes in the structure of opportunities (Dore, 1976, p. 116).

One also derives the impression that the school reforms were based on a very limited appreciation of what attitudes are, and of how they develop and resist change (Leonor, 1981). The reforms failed to consider that the worst place to start changing attitudes towards socialistic goals could be the schools. In the absence of any substantial improvement in the material base and any positive change in the hierarchical power relationships in school and in government, any attitude change developed by the schools would be immediately neutralised. There is, of course, another possibility, even if it is rather remote, namely that the attitude change that could be developed by schools might impel the school-leavers to enter into a class struggle against certain parts of the bureaucracy which still clung to the attitudes of the colonial past.

Third, there was a flaw in the argument about "self-reliant" activities. The teaching of agriculture in primary schools, and even in secondary schools and the University, does not automatically make farmers out of school-leavers and graduates. Experience in this subject the world over confirms that farm productivity and economic growth in agriculture are very complex issues, far more complex than teaching agriculture in schools.

This was perhaps in the minds of many school officials in the Ministry of Education, when they put up opposition to specific programmes and projects for primary and secondary school pupils. The officials claimed that the pupils in the primary and secondary schools were too young to have any real commitment to farming and that the increasing use of learning time for "self-reliant" activities in practical subjects would stifle the development of innovative and creative imagination, something that Tanzania's long-term development would heavily depend on (Morrison, p. 265, citing Munro). But this opposition went unheeded.[10]

So the Ministry found itself developing and implementing programmes and projects about which it was

not entirely enthusiastic. Nonetheless, after some
personnel changes the implementation moved on rather
briskly. Even so, the transmission of ideas,
especially those on ESR, from the top echelon down to
the classroom underwent many deformations.

What was happening in the classrooms was entirely
different from President Nyerere's concept of education
for self-reliance. To many teachers, ESR "meant little
more than a return to farming" (Morrison, p. 280). The
inference is clear from what one headmaster told a
teacher-trainer: "If you want to watch your students'
lessons, do not come on Wednesday afternoon, because
that is the time we have (sic) education for
self-reliance" (Ndunguru, 1971).

Moreover, the communal idea of working together for
the benefit of all, and having participatory roles in
decision making was quite alien to the essentially
hierarchical structure of the Ministry (and for that
matter, of the Government). This situation was also
true not only in political and social education but also
in agricultural education. Besides, teachers were
simply not prepared to acquire the necessary expertise
not only in the theory but also in the practice of farm
skills. Thus in many cases the returns from farming
programmes in schools were much less than what was spent
on them, (Sheffield, 1979, p. 108), giving the pupils
bad examples and producing negative attitudes towards
farming.

5. The strikes of vocational school students

The strikes were not in connection with compulsory
National Service but for other reasons which at first
sight appear rather mundane and petty. For instance,
in a medical school in Dar es Salaam, " ... Form VI
leavers (or upper secondary school graduates) complained
about unsatisfactory quarters, poor food and dining
facilities, and excessive noise and rowdiness among
lower level school-leavers who were enrolled in medical
assistant and nursing courses (sic). [The complaint
was partly an attempt by the] Form VI leavers to obtain
exclusive dormitories and cafeterias for themselves so
that they would not have to associate with their
educational inferiors" (Morrison, p. 241). In another
instance, " ... students [in] masonry ... refused to
clean their tools at the end of the workshop course.
They refused to accept punishment, and all first and
second year students insisted on leaving ... school ...
[In another school,] most of the students ... stayed
away from classes on the grounds that they were not

willing to work on the gardens and land around dormitories" (Schädler, p. 138).

These strikes occurred in different places and at different times. They arose from specific grievances or reasons which appear to be unrelated. But they sprang from the same profound root causes.

Firstly, schools develop or enhance certain expectations, the so-called "charter effect" of schools. Tanzanian schools are very selective, especially after primary schooling. Selection for further schooling means access to a few – but exclusion to all others. Hence, selection already connotes a distinction, setting the few apart from the rest and creating a sort of élite. This consciousness of being an élite is reinforced by the school itself, that is, by the behaviour of teachers and school officials, by the amenities that are markedly better than those available to the masses, by government officials' exhortations, and the wabenzi mentality of government officials whom students look upon as models. Thus prolonged schooling even in masonry is a preparation for something big, for instance supervisory positions, in government offices or in industry where dirty hands are only for the unschooled, of whom there are plenty. The Form 6 school-leavers felt they were a class of their own, widely apart from the Form 4 school-leavers and from the rest whose schooling was lower, even in the same medical school.

Secondly, vocational instruction has historically been viewed with suspicion by Africans and by Tanzanians in particular. Vocational instruction was imposed, somewhat unadvisedly, by colonial administrators and even by missionaries as something appropriate to the allegedly inferior intelligence of the natives. This imposition was seen by the natives as a means to keep them "down" in manual occupations or subordinate positions in colonial government. (After Independence local officials who used to argue against vocational instruction reversed their arguments, especially after the Arusha Declaration.) These reactions seem to be reflected in the behaviour of the Form 6 leavers, the future medical students, in regarding the Form 4 leavers receiving vocational instruction to become medical assistants and nurses, as inferior not only educationally but also socially. And imposing menial work like cleaning trowels on masonry trainees was to remind them bluntly of their inferior status. They accordingly went on strike.

Thirdly, vocational instruction in the form in which it was carried out in Tanzania was an oversell of an educational ideology whose results belied its supposed merits.

Vocational instruction in schools had been regarded as a necessity to Tanzania's development. Missionaries and colonial administrators saw it as the means to alleviate poverty among the natives. Practical subjects then, were made part of general education. And practical subjects were emphasised more and more when school-leavers could not find urban jobs.

As the supply of school-leavers increased and urban jobs became hard to find, tuition in agriculture or farming was thought to be the solution. Visiting study groups or missions rarely failed to support this solution, even though local officials and parents of schoolchildren looked on it with suspicion, not to say hatred. It was simply that practical exercises in farming were reminiscent of enforced labour, not only in mission schools (Sifuna, pp. 54ff) but also in government schools before Independence. Thus strong emphasis on these subjects was met by equally strong parental opposition. In one instance, irate "villagers ... set fire to a middle school only months after it had opened" (Morrison, p. 85).

Even government officials opposed the widespread introduction of agriculture or farming in the ordinary schools. It was recognised at that time that trying to induce agricultural revolution through schoolboys instead of adults was a fruitless idea. Thus in 1960, the year before Independence, "gardening and farm work were only extra-curricular activities" (ibid.), rather than an integral part of the school curriculum.

It was not a case of the TANU (now the CCM) Party objecting to all forms of vocational instruction, for it supported the expansion of vocational and technical education. At that time TANU and the manpower planners were in accord as to the importance of industrial education for the development of Tanganyika, but both of them thought that industrial education should be imparted separately from the general (i.e. academic) school curriculum in order to produce the thoroughly skilled craftsmen needed by industry. The result was the opening of specialised trade schools — those same schools whose students went on strike.

The theories were not always borne out in practice. Despite the talk of vast shortages of craftsmen, the alumni of the trade schools could hardly find suitable jobs, being viewed by employers either as being "swollen head" and unskilled or simply unfit for the available jobs (Thomas, R.L., pp. 19ff; also Schädler, p. 140). In these schools enrolment dropped; these schools were converted or "upgraded" to become

schools to meet other proclaimed needs, e.g. the
supposed acute shortage of technicians.

A true assessment of the socio-economic impact of
these schools will take a long time, even though some
effort is already under way. The ILO is focusing its
attention on the process of implementation of training
programmes and projects, while the World Bank seeks
evidence on the costs and benefits of vocational school
curricula. Neither looks to the ultimate objective of
alleviating unemployment and speeding up economic
development, or the immediate objective of meeting
shortages of technicians.

Even this specific immediate objective is fraught
with uncertainty, a repetition of the experience with
the schools for craftsmen. Firstly, the supposed
shortage is ill-defined. It is based on projections and
the errors of their assumptions. The projections
follow a conceptual framework which is quite remote from
reality in Tanzania. Worst of all, the projections are
based on ambitious development plans which almost always
fall short of accomplishment. Thus only too often the
supposed acute shortages become surpluses, and
expensively trained technicans find themselves redundant.

Secondly, the training methodology is too lumpy,
that is, it involves long stretches of time, e.g. two to
three years to become a mason, in effect to meet United
Kingdom standards rather than Tanzania's needs. One
result of this methodology is the alleged "swollen-
headedness" of the trainees. Another is the clumsiness
of the schools as a means of providing flexible
vocational instruction (Leonor, 1976). Hence, it would
seem that the methodology tends to worsen rather than
alleviate unemployment.

Thirdly - and more fundamentally - vocational
instruction in schools as the means to meeting the
immediate objective mentioned above, follows the
dominant ethos of development assistance, that of
goading the developing economies like Tanzania into
copying an occupational or skill pattern whose weight
they cannot support. The result is dependency rather
than self-reliance. Above all the ethos tends to weaken
the economy and reduce the prospects of creating truly
gainful work opportunities.

All this is not arguing against the necessity of
vocational instruction, for indeed there is always the
need for it - in its proper form - in Tanzania. In
this regard, there is much to learn from the
long-standing tradition of skill acquisition through the
fundis, the local artisans, and the way in which this
method survives and flourishes despite government
controls and competition from the vocational schools.

V.   LESSONS FROM TANZANIAN EXPERIENCE

A few are already obvious. First, control of the expansion of the school system has associated "bumping effects". For instance, tight control at the university level will reduce the supply of graduates, hence reducing also the demand for jobs. But, especially in a poor, stagnant economy, this solution pushes unemployment to the secondary school-leavers, unless the outturn of secondary schools is also controlled to remain in keeping with the number of job opportunities. Applying the same kind of controls to primary schools in a country committed to socialism and universal primary education would not be politically feasible.

Indeed, Tanzania has tightly controlled the expansion of the University and university-preparatory upper secondary schools. So she has avoided the emergence of educated unemployment at that level. But this solution has shifted the problem to the school-leavers of the lower secondary and primary schools. In addition, this solution is fraught with politics, so there is no telling how long the controls can be kept. At this time (1984) there is strong pressure to expand secondary schools, pressure that is likely to become stronger, as the succeeding cohorts of primary school-leavers become larger and contemplate entering a labour market where there have not been corresponding increases in gainful work opportunities for the school-leavers.

Second, the expansion of schooling as a device to alleviate unemployment postpones unemployment problems and their solution to the future. Tanzania's expansion of high schools as proposed for a World Bank loan may temporarily relieve the unemployment of primary school-leavers, some of whom will go back to school again to prepare for middle-level positions in government or in industry. But this measure will produce a greater number of high school-leavers who will subsequently be demanding either more university places or jobs and pay commensurate with their newly acquired qualifications. This increasing supply of high school-leavers will be extremely difficult to contain later, because once a new school is opened or an old school expanded, closing it or reducing its size will be politically impossible. Hence, present educated unemployment will increase at a higher level, unless the economy improves. Moreover, expansion of schooling is a costly solution, especially if it is fully subsidised by the State as it is at present in Tanzania.

Third, vocational instruction in schools does not automatically solve unemployment. Such instruction does seem to be a promising solution but in the end can be a very expensive palliative. In Tanzania despite expert advice and costly instruction, vocational school-leavers have had difficulty in finding suitable jobs (Sifuna, p. 53; Schädler, op. cit.; Thomas, R.L., op. cit.). In addition, the practical instruction in ESR activities in primary schools seems to have deleterious effects not only in mental attainment but also in the attitude change of pupils. Primary school-leavers still prefer hunting for jobs in towns and cities to going back to ujamaa villages.

Fourth, school solutions to unemployment are ineffective and costly under an economic régime that is not improving. School solutions require a lot of money, men and time before they can be internally coherent and operational. But when the first prototype output, i.e. the school-leavers, enter the labour market, they are either deemed unfit for the jobs they were trained for or unable to find jobs at all. The result is either unemployment or underutilisation of expensively acquired skills.

The vast expense inherent in school solutions has, of course, repercussions on the economy. It reduces investment in the more productive sectors and weakens the economy's capacity to create job opportunities. It is like eating up seed corn so to speak. Moreover, school solutions tend to blur the link between education and productivity, missing the point that the link exists only under dynamic conditions, e.g. when the economy is improving.[11]

Fifth, National Service is an expensive school-like solution whose results are at best uncertain. Whether exposure to National Service will make school-leavers better workers still remains to be proved, and whether any positive result is worth while in relation to the costs borne by the State and by the school-leavers still needs to be assessed. Because of the high financial cost, only a small proportion of school-leavers can be recruited for National Service, and there are also serious problems of implementation. In any case, it would seem that National Service is a temporary political measure rather than a long-term economically sound solution to educated unemployment.

The less obvious lessons are the following. To begin with, school solutions are not substitutes for what should be done in the economy. Economic and school solutions are not mutually exclusive either, even if the former must precede the latter. And if the economic solutions succeed, who needs the latter? In fact school solutions are still needed, but only to speed up or intensify the economic solutions.

In the second place, it is extremely difficult to avoid what might be called a "manpower race" in which poor countries try to follow, as quickly as possible, the manning patterns of rich countries.

In Tanzania the race started with the "Tanzanisation" or the "localisation" of expatriate posts. At Independence only 26 per cent of the middle to senior grade civil servants were Tanzanians; in 1964 the figure was 57 per cent; and in 1968 it was 80 per cent (Helleiner, 1972, p. 186). The manning pattern tended to follow that of the colonial government. Subsequent expansion of government services was along the same lines; it was facilitated by foreign aid which made the manpower supply relatively inexpensive to the Government. The maintenance of the manning pattern was ensured by the structure of opportunities, e.g. the expatriate wage structure, shunting off talent from more productive work. The manning pattern was also reinforced by the Western model of administrative development, a consequence of transplanted models of technology, culture and attitudes (Mbiliṅyi, S.M., 1973, p. 72).

And lastly, the school (and school-like) solutions to unemployment adopted by Tanzania tend to punish the State in general and the school-leavers in particular. On the one hand these solutions have uncertain results, suggesting gross misallocation of very scarce resources for development, thereby stunting the growth of the State's economy. On the other hand, the school solutions, as noted earlier, had adverse effects on the mental attainment of the pupils. These effects could make the school-leavers more costly to train for specific employment opportunities.

Notes

[1] In the British school system and its derivatives, a school-leaver is a pupil who has completed a course of schooling and possesses a school-leaving certificate. The latter is obtained by passing an examination, of which there are three in Tanzania. The first is taken after the seven-year primary school cycle and is known as the primary school-leaving certificate. The second is after completing four-year lower secondary school and is the National School Certificate. The last of these examinations is taken by students who have completed the upper secondary school cycle. It is for the National

Higher School Certificate and is a requirement for university studies.

[2] It may be noted that the population figures cited in this section, principally in Tables 1 to 4, are from the 1965 Labour Force Survey whose published results are more detailed and useful than those of the 1967 Population Census. Further, the two sources have different population estimates, but this difference between totals may not heavily influence the proportions, i.e. the percentages, on which the discussion is based.

[3] Underemployment falls into two categories, visible and invisible. The first is measured on the basis of the duration of unemployment in a work-week, while the second is calculated on the basis of the earnings from the work-week. See "Measuring employment, unemployment and underemployment", MEHS/1981/D.1, Geneva, ILO, 1981, particularly paras. 122-172.

[4] The Arusha Declaration is the declaration of principles of socialism and self-reliance, adopted by the TANU Party on 29 January 1967 in Arusha, Tanzania.

[5] The administration of Tanganyika passed to Britain from Germany in 1919 by Mandatory Power under the Charter of the League of Nations. "... in 1922, Britain was enjoined to promote the material and moral well-being and social progress of the inhabitants ... From then on [Tanganyika] was a Class B Mandate, that is, one with an overseas national administration under international supervision" (Cameron and Dodd, 1970, p. 38).

[6] Section (a) of the Arusha Resolution states the following:

1. Every TANU and Government leader must be either a peasant or a worker, and should in no way be associated with the practices of capitalism or feudalism.

2. No TANU or Government leader should hold shares in any company.

3. No TANU or Government leader should hold directorships in any privately owned enterprise.

4. No TANU or Government leader should receive two or more salaries.

5. No TANU or Government leader should own houses which he rents to others.

6. For the purpose of this Resolution the term 'leader' should comprise the following: Members of the TANU National Executive Committee; Ministers; Members of Parliament; senior officials of Organisations affiliated to TANU; senior officials of para-statal organisations; all those appointed or elected under any clause of the TANU Constitution; councillors; and civil servants in the high and middle cadres. (In this context 'leader' means a man, or a man and his wife; a woman, or a woman and her husband.) (See Nyerere, 1968, p. 249.)

7 Attempts to cut down the salaries of officials by revising the salary scale were foiled by promotion either in the civil service or in the para-statal agencies.

8 Perhaps the phrase "at public expense" is not strictly correct. But it is exactly what an African poet meant in the following passage:

... Our university and schools are nests in which black exploiters are hatched and bred, at the expense of taxpayers, or perhaps heartpayers.

And when they have fallen into things
They eat the meat of the chest of the bulls
And their wives grow larger buttocks
And their skins shine in health
They throw themselves into soft beds
But the hip bones of the voters
Grow painful sleeping on the same earth
They slept before Uhuru (or Independence)

(Okot p'bitek: "indigenous ills", in Cliffe and Saul, op. cit., Vol. 2, p. 293).

9 Available data from 1977 to 1980 show that the uptake of Form 1 was maintained at 9 to 10 per cent of Standard 7 enrolment of the year before.

[10] The opposition was later on vindicated by a World Bank report citing "... widespread public concern (over) ... any deterioration in cognitive attainment (of pupils in the wake of) unprecedented educational innovations ..." and calling for qualitative improvement of schools and educational programmes to reverse the trend (IBRD, 1980, p.7).

[11] See Leonor, 1976b; Chaudhri, 1979; and Lockhead, et al., 1980.

BIBLIOGRAPHY

Barkan J.D.; Okumu J.J. (eds.). Politics and public
policy in Kenya and Tanzania. New York, Praeger
Publishers, 1979.

Barnum, H.M.; Sabot, R.H. Migration, education and urban
surplus labour: The case of Tanzania. Paris, OECD,
1976.

Blue, R.N.; Weaver, J.H. "A critical assessment of the
Tanzanian model of development", Paper No. 30. New
York, Agricultural Development Council, July 1977.

Cameron, J.; Dodd, M.A. Society, schools and progress in
Tanzania. Oxford, Pergamon Press, 1970.

Centre for Study of Education in Changing Societies.
Primary education in Sukumaland, Tanzania. The Hague,
Wolters-Noordhoff, 1969.

Chaudhri, D.P. Education, innovation and agricultural
development. London, Croom Helm, 1979.

Cliffe, L.; Saul, J. (eds.). Socialism in Tanzania,
Vol. 1 Politics, Vol. 2 Policies. Nairobi (Kenya),
East African Publishing House, 1972 and 1973 for Vols.
1 and 2 respectively.

Collier, P. "Migration and unemployment: A dynamic
general equilibrium analysis applied to Tanzania", in
Oxford Economic Papers (New Series), Vol. 31(2), July
1979, pp. 205-236.

---; Radwan, S.; Wagner, A.; and Wangwe, S. "Ujamaa
and rural development: Labour and poverty in rural
Tanzania". Geneva, ILO, forthcoming.

Court, D. "The education system as a response to
inequality", in Barkan and Okumo (eds.), pp. 200-238,
q.v.

Dore, R. The diploma disease: Education, qualifications
and development. London, George Allen and Unwin, 1976.

Dumont, R. False start in Africa. London, Andre Deutsch,
1966.

Ellis, F. "Agricultural pricing policy in Tanzania,
1970-1979: Implications for agricultural output,

rural incomes, and crop marketing costs", in ILO/JASPA National Seminar, 1981, q.v.

Guruli, K. "Towards an independent and equal East African common market", in Cliffe and Saul (eds.), Vol. 1, q.v.

Heijnen, J.D. Development and education in the Mwansa District, Tanzania: A case study of migration and peasant farming. Rotterdam, Bronder-offset, 1968.

Helleiner, G.K. "Socialism and economic development in Tanzania", in Journal of Development Studies (Brighton, U.K.), Vol. 8, No. 2, Jan. 1972.

Hunter, G. Manpower, employment and education in the rural economy of Tanzania. Paris, UNESCO/IIEP, 1966.

IBRD. "Economic memorandum on Tanzania", Report No. 3086-TA. Washington, January 1981.

--- . "Staff appraisal report of the seventh education project in the United Republic of Tanzania", Report No. 2782-TA. Washington, 2 June 1980.

ILO. Measuring employment, unemployment and under-employment. Geneva, doc. MEHS/1981/D.1, 1981.

--- . Towards self-reliance, Report to the Government of Tanzania by Jobs and Skills Programme for Africa (JASPA) Employment Advisory Mission (Addis Ababa, 1978).

ILO/JASPA. "Development, employment and equity issues in Tanzania", Report of national seminar held in Dar es Salaam from 21 to 25 July 1980 by Jobs and Skills Programme for Africa (JASPA) (Addis Ababa, 1981).

Jamal, V. Rural-urban gap in Tanzania. Addis Ababa, ILO/JASPA, 1981, mimeographed JASPA research working paper; restricted.

Jedruszek, J. "Policy implications of the development in productivity of labour in Tanzania", in ILO/JASPA National Seminar, 1981, q.v.

Kim, K.S., et al. (eds.). Papers on the political economy of Tanzania. Nairobi, Heinemann Educational Books Ltd., 1979.

Kinunda, M.J. The Tanzanian primary school reform-

expectations and realities. Paris, IIEP Working
Document No. 556/20A, 19 Nov. 1979.

Leonor, M.D. Duration of unemployment and first job
earnings, I. Upper secondary vocational school
graduates, Ayuthya, Thailand, 1970-74. Geneva, ILO,
1976; mimeographed World Employment Programme
research working paper; restricted.

--- . Education and productivity: Some evidences and
implications. Geneva, ILO, 1976b; mimeographed World
Employment Programme research working paper;
restricted.

--- . "How attitudes towards work develop: Evidence
from Project Soutele, Philippines, 1975". Geneva,
ILO, 1981 typescript.

Lockhead, E.; Jamison, T.; Lau, J. "Farmer education
and farm efficiency: A survey" in Timothy King
(ed.): Education and income. Washington, DC, IBRD,
1980.

Mascarenhas, A.C.; Skutsch, M. Tanzania country study
on rural employment promotion. Geneva, ILO, 1976;
mimeographed research working paper; restricted.

Mbilinyi, M.J. Attitudes, expectations and the decision
to educate in rural Tanzania. Research Report No.
3/1, Bureau of Resource Assessment and Land Use
Planning, University of Dar es Salaam, November 1973.

--- . "Education and productive work, productive work
and education: The development of Tanzanian education
reform", in Final Report of the International Meeting
of Experts on the Promotion of Productive Work in
Education. Paris, UNESCO, Nov. 1980, Chapter X, pp.
47-59.

Mbilinyi, S.M. "Rural development and rural employment
generation: Lessons from experimentation in Tanzania"
in Rural Africana, Vol. 19, Winter 1973, pp. 67-85.

Morrison, D.R. Education and politics in Africa: The
Tanzania case. London, Heinemann, 1976.

Munch-Petersen, P.M. "Final report on the labour market
information consultancy of the project on manpower and
employment planning, training, programming and
manpower utilisation". Geneva, ILO, 1982.

Mwansasu, B.U.; Pratt, C. (eds.). Towards socialism in Tanzania. Dar es Salaam, Tanzania Publishing House, 1979.

Ndunguru, S. "Education for self-reliance and the curriculum", in East Africa Journal, Vol. 8, No. 2, Feb. 1971, pp. 13-16.

Nyerere, K. Freedom and socialism. Oxford University Press, 1968.

Pratt, C. "Tanzania's transition to socialism: Reflections of a democratic socialist", in Mwansasu and Pratt, Towards socialism in Tanzania, q.v.

Ray, R.S. Labour force survey of Tanzania. Dar es Salaam, Ministry of Economic Affairs and Development Planning, Jan. 1966.

Rweyemamu, J.F. "The structure of Tanzania industry". ERB Paper No. 71.2, University of Dar es Salaam, 1971.

Sabot, R.H. Economic development and urban migration, Tanzania, 1900-1971. Oxford, Clarendon Press, 1979.

Sanyal, B.C.; Kinunda, M.J. Higher education for self-reliance: The Tanzanian experience. Paris, IIEP/UNESCO, 1977.

Schädler, K. Crafts, small-scale industries, and industrial education in Tanzania. München, Weltforum Verlag, 1968.

Sheffield, J.R. "Basic education for the rural poor", in Journal of Developing Areas, Vol. 14:1 (October, 1979), pp. 99-110.

Sifuna, D.N. Vocational education in schools: A historical survey of Kenya and Tanzania. Dar es Salaam, East African Literature Bureau, 1976.

Smith, W.E. Nyerere of Tanzania. London, Victor Gollancz Ltd., 1973.

Thomas, C.Y. Dependence and transformation: The economics of transition to socialism. New York, Monthly Review Press, 1974.

Thomas, R.L. Survey of the high-level manpower requirements and resources for the five-year development

plan, 1964–65 to 1968–69. Dar es Salaam (Tanzania),
Directorate of Development Planning, 1965.

Tobias, G. High-level manpower requirements and resources
in Tanzania. Dar es Salaam, Government Paper No. 2,
1963.

Valentine, T. "Wage policy in Tanzania since Independence - Trends and perceptions", in ILO/JASPA National
Seminar, 1981, q.v.

Van de Laar, A. "Growth and income distribution in
Tanzania since Independence", in Cliffe and Saul,
Socialism in Tanzania, Vol. 1.

3 EGYPT

I. OVERVIEW

This study of Egypt presents a case in which the following policies were applied: a free-tuition policy, a policy of guaranteed employment for technical school-leavers and university graduates, a liberal emigration policy, and a policy of increasing the practical and vocational content of instruction in schools. There were also other policies, e.g. a shortened work-week in public enterprises and a prolonged period of military conscription, that were addressed to certain objectives, including the alleviation of unemployment and underemployment.

The policies were applied in an economy which was at first market oriented, which then veered towards socialist planning, and which returned later to its previous orientation. This was in an Arab country whose increasing income from oil, the Suez Canal and other sources has now placed the country among the middle-income economies, with a gross national product (GNP) per capita of about $540 in 1981, as against only $260 in 1973.

The time-frame of the study is the inter-census interval between 1960 and 1976, a choice dictated by the availability of most of the data. This period was characterised by political change. It was just a few years from the revolution and change of regime in 1952 and the conflict between Egypt and the United Kingdom and France in 1956 over the jurisdiction and control of the Suez Canal. It was a time when the country was in the process of redressing her relations with her neighbour countries. It was also a period of internal strife, especially after the death of President Nasser in 1970 and during the early years of President Sadat's government. It was, therefore, a period of uphill struggle during which the primary task of the government was to consolidate its power so as to be able to establish law and order before coping with the other pressing problems of the country.

After the revolution the new leaders had inherited a run-down economy which was difficult to restore to

normalcy by post-revolutionary socialistic experiments
that were interrupted by wars.

It is this background that the reader should keep
in mind when appreciating the effects of certain
employment policies and the lessons that can be learned
from them. The policies in question were not destined
for a textbook economy; they were in fact ad hoc
measures by a government which was trying to play for
time before the next crisis materialised. It should not
be forgotten that the government was fighting what were
often collectively called in certain quarters "the
external forces of domination". Part of the trouble was
that the measures outlived their temporary object and
became to all intents and purposes permanent, as
unemployment became chronic and as the policies became
politically too difficult to abrogate.

This background seems to have had much less effect
on education and training policies whose origins are
rather older. In their contemporary form, the policies
appeared to be complementary measures, because they did
not alter the basic design of general education
programmes. They did, however, reflect the idea of
increasing the practical and vocational content of
curricula when unemployment became worse.

Nevertheless, the background is relevant to the
rapid expansion of secondary and higher education, which
took the form, inter alia, of the conversion and
transformation of practical and vocational schools into
technical institutes for higher studies. The apparently
natural purpose of this development was to serve a
labour market much larger than that of Egypt alone and
including that of other Arab countries.

During the reference period of the study
(1960-1976), Egypt had the 6-3-3 system of
pre-university schooling. Primary schooling was 6 years
of free and compulsory basic education for boys and
girls. This level was followed by two cycles of
secondary schooling. The first cycle of 3 years was
called the preparatory cycle or lower secondary school,
after which the pupils sat for an examination. Passing
this examination was a requirement for admission to the
next 3-year cycle, or upper secondary school.

This last cycle consisted of two curricular
streams, namely, the academic and the practical. The
academic stream prepared students for further studies in
the university, while the practical stream trained
students either for immediate employment or for
specialised training in technical institutes. Upon
completing the secondary school, the students sat for
their separate school-leaving examinations. The marks
or results of these examinations largely determined the

students' access to the pattern of opportunities that is
familiar in many countries: high marks usually afforded
access to further studies and subsequently led to good
positions in government offices.

The primary school enrolment rates in Egypt have
changed very slowly since the 1930s. From 1937 to 1960,
the proportion of persons with primary education in the
country's population (10 years and over) increased only
from 1.1 per cent to 1.7 per cent,[1] while the general
trend of primary school enrolment rates, i.e. the
proportion of enrolment to the population in the 6-11
age group, even fell off from 77 per cent in 1960 to 74
per cent in 1978.

The expansion of primary schooling was, however,
uneven. It was indeed very slow in rural areas but
comparatively fast in towns and cities, as shown by
uneven enrolment rates. For instance, in 1978 the
primary enrolment rates were 47 per cent in Fayoum,
Upper Egypt and 95 per cent in Port Said.

This was not due to an overall lack of teachers
because, according to a report, there were more
personnel with teaching qualifications on the government
payroll than there were classrooms available.[2]
Apparently the conditions in the rural areas hardly
encouraged teachers to go there and the remuneration for
teachers working under those conditions was not
attractive enough. Above all, there was a bias in the
allocation of resources in favour of post-primary
schools in cities.

Meanwhile, secondary schools and higher education
expanded quickly in towns and cities, but stopped short
of spreading their benefits beyond these areas.
Accordingly, selection for secondary schooling and
progression to higher education and then on to civil
service jobs guaranteed by the Government were quite
beyond the reach of the masses in the villages.

Such a situation was not new, for it had its roots
in the long-established dualism of Egyptian education
which separated one sort of schooling for the rich and
those destined for government service from another sort
for the masses. But after the revolution and the end of
monarchic rule in 1952, access to the educational
facilities previously only open to the upper class was
widened and made available to a large part of the
population. The same applied to job opportunities that
were open in principle to all.

This progress should have become stabilised a few
years after the revolution. However, there was the
Anglo-French conflict with Egypt in 1956, followed by
the wars with Israel. At that time the revolutionaries
had to consolidate their power, while the students and

intellectuals were bent on accelerating political change
towards socialism. It was no time to leave a sizeable
and articulate minority unemployed.

Thus it would seem that the guaranteed jobs policy
introduced in 1961 was calculated to reduce the risk of
widespread internal conflict and hasten socialistic
development. The implementation of this policy was
greatly facilitated by the nationalisation and
sequestration of private property, especially that of
the ancien régime and also of some European countries
that were at the opposite end of the political spectrum.

But the guaranteed jobs policy quickly lost its
effectiveness, because not enough jobs were available
for all. Besides, the policy spawned new problems. It
inflated employment in government (according to one
estimate, by about 40 per cent overstaffing)[3] by
creating a large demand for such employment, while the
schools produced more graduates than could be absorbed
by the economy. Unemployment in the educated labour
force increased and waiting lists for government jobs
became extraordinarily long, both in terms of numbers
and waiting time.

According to official estimates, aggregate
unemployment in Egypt was only 2.2 per cent in 1960 and
7.7 per cent in 1976. These are figures which, in
conventional terms, are within the range of what might
be called frictional unemployment in a full employment
economy. But conventional estimates do not capture
other nuances of employment, especially those of
underemployment. Thus, these estimates are part of the
truth rather than the whole truth.

The available unemployment figures for workers with
secondary school and university qualifications were 8.4
per cent and 4.3 per cent, respectively, in 1960. But
the corresponding figures were 19.9 per cent and 10.8
per cent in 1976. The last two figures denote something
much greater than frictional unemployment. In fact,
they are in the range of structural unemployment, as if
the Egyptian economy were in a state of rapid technical
change, forcing workers to remain unemployed for a while
until they could readjust to the new skill
requirements. But this was not the case. The educated
labour force was simply greater than could be
effectively absorbed by the economy, in addition to
those who were already underutilised in overstaffed
agencies in the public sector.

Closer scrutiny indicates that, even with
conventional estimates, unemployment in Egypt was rather
severe and showed no signs of abating during the
reference period. It was more of an urban disease than
a rural one, and it was more prevalent among the young

and female workers looking for work to augment the family's income - in an economy beset by inflation and a soaring cost of living - than among established primary workers. It was particularly widespread in the ranks of the educated labour force, especially those who had a secondary school or university qualification.

In order to absorb this plethora of educated manpower the Government devised a number of labour market policies, as well as educational policies designed to modify the supply. The policies were not sufficient to contain educated unemployment, but they did help to alleviate the problem, even though in some instances their unintended side-effects seemed to have made the situation worse.

Free tuition, for example, may have increased enrolment and absorbed part of the unemployed in a move back to school. But more schooling as a policy simply shifted the problem and cumulated a small part of present unemployment into a larger mass of educated unemployment later.

The short work-week policy in public enterprise was a redistributive device. It was a means of spreading the bounty of public sector wages and sharing the burden of unemployment evenly and in a relatively painless manner. The policy increased the sector's capacity to absorb unemployment, albeit artificially, to make way for the guaranteed jobs policy.

The guaranteed jobs policy was conceived as a means to mop up educated unemployment, but the guarantee petered out because jobs simply could not be created as fast as they were claimed. Given the favourable wage levels of the public sector, the policy stimulated the demand for higher education tremendously, thereby rapidly increasing the supply of educated workers demanding government jobs. The result was overstaffing and underemployment, but with an ever-growing pool of educated unemployed.

Prolonging the period of military conscription between the wars of 1967 and 1973 had of course a purpose of its own. But it also had side-effects: it reduced the demand for civilian jobs and helped to keep unemployed workers out of the unemployment statistics. Besides, the workers in uniform would acquire not only military experience and discipline but also some skills that could be useful in civilian life. However, the low pay of the conscripts forced secondary workers in their families to look for work. This additional demand for employment again boosted the unemployment statistics by introducing new entrants to the labour market who would otherwise not have been counted in the labour force.

Liberal emigration as a policy was inevitable in Egypt. Unemployment or underemployment and low incomes were powerful forces which drove more than one million Egyptians to work outside their country. The policy was a necessity for a country harassed by trade deficits, food shortages and war. Restricting emigration would have risked political upheaval, offset against which the loss of the potential output of the migrant workers was not of greater immediate consequence. Some of them were unemployed or underemployed anyway, but their remittances from abroad would be large enough to help pay for Egypt's food imports. However, the policy had an unforeseen effect, namely, a qualitative deterioration of the country's available manpower supply, because the skilled workers who emigrated tended to be replaced by less skilled ones.

All this took place in a socio-economic régime dominated by a very large centrally planned public sector whose investment policies favoured capital-intensive industries, whose wage scale was rather rigid, and whose wages were also high in relation to labour earnings in the traditional sector. Hence, the appearance of a large body of educated workers who were demanding public sector employment.

Tuition in academic disciplines was in much greater demand than technical and practical training mainly on account of the greater rewards that were believed to attach to academic qualifications in the public mind. Efforts to reverse this trend in favour of technical education encountered great resistance, so much so that some existing technical and practical schools were converted into academic or other schools preparing students for university studies. And universities were churning out an increasing number of graduates, while chronic unemployment of young educated Egyptians was creating serious problems of alienation, aggression and revolt.

Against this trend, however, it was noted that increasing numbers of university graduates were taking out-of-school vocational training to increase their employability - after long years of study and vainly waiting for jobs that were supposedly guaranteed by the Government.

II. UNEMPLOYMENT AND LABOUR MARKET POLICIES

A. Unemployment

Information about unemployment in Egypt is confusing. While labour force surveys showed that unemployment was decreasing from 4.8 per cent in 1960 to

2.8 per cent in 1976, population censuses revealed that
the trend had been in the opposite direction, that is,
from 2.2 per cent to 7.7 per cent in the same period.
This study uses the population census figures in
preference to those of the labour force surveys for the
simple reason that the latter were based on samples
rather than on the population itself and that sample
statistics cannot be better than population
parameters.[4] According to the census, aggregate
unemployment rose from 174,940 in 1960 to 850,432 in
1976, an increase of almost five times! The 1976 figure
is from a labour force of about 11 million and a
population of 37 million.

1.   Rural/urban unemployment

The census estimates in Table 9 show that the
majority of the unemployed during the census years were
in the urban sector. Urban unemployment in those two
census years was estimated at 4.3 per cent and 9.5 per
cent, while that of the rural sector was only 1.1 per
cent and 6.4 per cent respectively.
These figures, however, are not precise because
there are statistical artifacts in them in the form of
seasonal effects. For example, the 1960 census was
carried out in September, the peak month of agricultural
activity; hence, rural unemployment was almost
unbelievably low at 1.1 per cent. But the 1976 census
was conducted in November, the slack month in
agriculture, a fact which could well account for the 6.4
per cent rural unemployment.
The changes in the unemployment figures for the
urban areas, however, were caused by factors that are
different from the seasonal fluctuations in agricultural
employment. They were influenced by such factors as the
banning of the expansion of the private sector and later
the lifting of this ban by the "open door" (infitah)
policy. Spurts to growth caused by this policy
increased the employment of primary workers. But this
growth has also encouraged secondary workers (defined as
women, children and the elderly) to look for work, and
thus be counted as unemployed.

2.   Age and sex of the unemployed

The estimates in Table 10(b) show that the
unemployed primary workers, defined as male workers
between ages 15 and 60, increased from 109,000 in 1960
to 299,000 in 1976, but their relative share in total
unemployment decreased from 62.8 per cent to 35.3 per

Table 9:   Unemployment by sectors in Egypt, 1960 and 1976 (6 years and over)

Unemployment by sex	Urban	%	Rural	%	Total	%
1960 Census						
Unemployed[1]						
1. Male	93 293	67.0	45 856	33.0	139 149	100.0
2. Female	25 549	71.4	10 243	28.6	35 791	100.0
3. Sub-total (1 + 2)	118 842	67.9	56 099	32.1	174 940	100.0
4. Total labour force[2]	2 737 661	35.0	5 081 250	65.0	7 818 911	100.0
5. Unemployment rate (=3/4)%		4.3		1.1		2.2
1976 Census						
Unemployed with Previous experience						
6. Male	22 172	63.2	12 918	36.8	35 090	100.0
7. Female	3 362	58.9	2 349	41.1	5 711	100.0
8. Sub-total (6 + 7)	25 534	62.6	15 267	37.4	40 801	100.0

Newly unemployed, 1976

9. Male	275 104	52.6	247 633	47.4	522 737	100.0
10. Female	153 658	53.6	133 236	46.4	286 894	100.0
11. Sub-total (9 + 10)	428 762	53.0	380 869	47.0	809 631	100.0
12. Sub-total (8 + 11)	454 296	53.4	396 136	46.6	850 432	100.0
13. Total labour force[2]	4 770 225	43.4	6 211 310	56.6	10 981 535	100.0
14. Unemployment rate (=12/13)%	9.5		6.4		7.7	

[1] The unemployed with previous experience and the newly unemployed were not separated in the 1960 census.

[2] The labour force consists of the unemployed and the employed labour.

Sources: CAPMAS: The Population Census, 1960, Table 5 and The Population Census, 1976, Table 4, pp. 97–108.

Table 10(a): Distribution of the unemployed labour force by age and sex in 1960 and 1976

Unemployment by sex	Age 6 to 15 No.	%	Age 15 to 30 No.	%	Age 30 to 60 No.	%	Age 60+ No.	%	Total[1] No.	%
1960 Census										
Unemployed[2]										
1. Male	25 309	18.3	78 320	56.7	30 791	22.3	3 714	2.7	138 134	100.0
2. Female	6 106	17.2	17 657	49.7	11 333	31.9	396	1.1	35 492	100.0
3. Total (1 + 2)	31 415	18.1	95 977	55.3	42 124	24.3	4 110	2.4	173 626	100.0
1976 Census										
Unemployed with previous experience										
4. Male	4 118	12.0	1 358	3.9	26 969	78.3	1 973	5.7	34 418	100.0
5. Female	1 617	28.7	180	3.2	3 546	62.8	296	5.2	5 639	100.0
6. Subtotal (4 + 5)	5 735	14.3	1 538	3.8	30 515	76.1	2 269	5.2	40 057	100.0
Newly unemployed										
7. Male	250 049	48.0	271 007	52.0	–	–	–	–	521 056	100.0
8. Female	181 709	63.5	104 479	36.5	–	–	–	–	286 188	100.0
9. Subtotal (7 + 8)	431 758	53.5	375 486	46.5	–	–	–	–	807 244	100.0
TOTAL (6 + 9)	437 493	51.6	376 924	44.5	30 515	3.6	2 269	0.3	847 301	100.0

1 Excludes "unspecified".
2 Unemployed with previous experience and the newly unemployed were not separated in the 1960 census.

Sources: Population Census, 1960, Table 35, pp. 220-221; and Population Census, 1976, Table 8, pp. 137-138.

Table 10(b): Distribution of unemployed labour, by age, sex and type of workers, 1960 and 1976

	Age of primary workers			Age of secondary workers				
	15-29	30-60	Subtotal	6-14	15-29	30-60	60+	Subtotal
1960								
Male	78 320	30 791	109 111	25 309	17 657	–	3 714	29 023
Female	–	–	–	6 106	–	11 333	396	35 492
Total	78 320	30 791	109 111	31 415	17 657	11 333	4 110	64 515
	(45.1)*	(17.7)	(62.8)	(18.1)	(10.2)	(6.5)	(2.4)	(37.2)
1976								
Male	272 365	26 969	299 334	254 167	–	–	1 973	256 140
Female	–	–	–	183 326	104 659	3 546	296	291 827
Total	272 365	26 969	299 334	437 493	104 659	3 546	2 269	547 967
	(32.1)	(3.2)	(35.3)	(51.6)	(12.4)	(0.4)	(0.3)	(64.7)
With experience								
Male	1 358	26 969	28 327	4 118	–	–	1 973	6 091
Female	–	–	–	1 617	180	3 546	296	5 639
Total	1 358	26 969	28 327	5 735	180	3 546	2 269	11 730
Without experience								
Male	271 007	–	271 007	250 049	–	–	–	250 049
Female	–	–	–	181 709	104 479	–	–	286 188
Total	271 007	–	271 007	431 758	104 479	–	–	536 237

* Numbers in parentheses are row percentages whose subtotals add up to 100.

Source: CAPMAS: The Population Censuses of 1960 and 1976.

cent during the period between the census years. Out of
the figure for 1976, 90.5 per cent or 31.9 percentage
points (i.e. 35.3 x 90.5) were new, inexperienced
workers in the age group 15 to 30 years old.

This estimate is perhaps on the high side, perhaps
even an overestimate, because many graduates who were
working in the private sector preferred not to report
their employment as this would disqualify them for the
government jobs for which they had applied. This
non-reporting of private sector employment kept these
graduates in the queue for government jobs, but of
course it inflated the unemployment figures.

The large drop in the share of jobless primary
workers was due to the large increase in the share of
unemployed secondary workers. The latter increased from
64,515 in 1960 to 547,967 in 1976, and their share in
total unemployment rose from 37.2 per cent to 64.7 per
cent during the same period. In 1976 the secondary
workers were mostly young boys (30 per cent) and girls
(21.6 per cent), which together make up 51.6 per cent of
the unemployed. Besides children, female workers from
15-year-old girls to women over 60 accounted for about
13 per cent of the idle manpower. These secondary
workers joined the labour force possibly because of a
loss of adult male members of their families to the army
or the migration of one or more members of their
families to the cities or to other Arab states. But it
is likely that low income, made worse by inflation and
the rapid rise in the cost of living, was an important
factor behind the entry of secondary workers to the
labour force.[5] In addition, improved education for
girls increased the participation rates of females in
the labour force.

3.   Educational attainment of
      unemployed workers

The population census shows that the proportion of
illiterates, including those who could barely read and
write, in the total unemployed labour force (age 10
years and over) decreased from 62.82 per cent in 1960 to
26.25 per cent in 1976 (calculated from Table 11). This
implies that unemployment was increasingly that of at
least partly educated labour, i.e. from about 37 per
cent in 1960 to about 74 per cent in 1976.[6]

However, these figures may be overestimates, in the
sense that they do not account for the age group 6 to 10
years old. Whether or not this age group should be
included in the estimates is, of course, a moot point,
but since they are included in the census employment
data, they should be accounted for in the unemployment

Table 11: Unemployment by educational level, 1960 and 1976 (10 years old and over)

	1960			1976		
	Unemploy-ment	Labour force	Rate %	Unemploy-ment	Labour force	Rate %
Illiterate	76 687	4 767 048	1.61)	138 997	5 520 203	2.52)
Read and Write	49 623	2 064 876	2.40)1.85	64 863	2 629 108	2.47) 2.50
Primary	5 729	141 906	4.04)	46 374	671 470	6.91)
Secondary	29 107	347 374	8.38)	206 484	1 037 661	19.90)
University	5 405	126 854	4.26)6.53	56 693	524 773	10.80)13.80
Secondary and University	34 512	474 228	7.28	263 177	1 562 434	16.84

Sources: Figures on unemployment are from The Population Census, 1960, Table 36, pp. 222-223 and from The Population Census, 1976, Table 11, pp. 145-146.

figures as well. With this adjustment the relative share of the non-educated unemployment would decrease from 76.5 per cent in 1960 to 54.4 per cent in 1976 (see Table 12). The proportion of the educated labour would then rise only from 23.5 per cent to 45.6 per cent during the same period.

In absolute numbers, the unemployed secondary school-leavers[7] rose from 29,107 in 1960 to 206,484 in 1976. The unemployed workers with higher education (university and post-university graduates) increased tenfold from 5,400 to 56,700 during the 17-year inter-census period. However, the share of this group in total unemployment only doubled from 3.1 per cent to 6.7 per cent, because the total of unemployed labour was heavily inflated by the large inflow of children to the labour force (see Table 12). But in terms of unemployment rates, unemployment of university graduates rose from 4.3 per cent in 1960 to 10.8 per cent in 1976, as shown in Table 11, while the rates for secondary school-leavers soared even higher, from 8.4 per cent to 19.9 per cent during the same period. These figures suggest the existence of open unemployment comparable to recent levels in advanced countries.

B.   Labour market policies

This section tries to trace the progression of educated unemployment in Egypt through labour market policies. The first part describes the policies that had a direct impact on the labour market. The second part describes those that influenced the labour market rather indirectly. The third and fourth parts discuss the impact of these policies on wages and unemployment, respectively.

1.   Direct policies

The direct policies were the following: (i) free university tuition, (ii) reducing the work-week from 48 to 42 hours in public enterprises, (iii) guaranteed jobs for technical secondary school-leavers and university graduates, (iv) lengthening the period of military conscription between the 1967 and 1973 Arab-Israeli wars and (v) untrammelled emigration of Egyptians after 1973.

Free-tuition policy

This was part of the socialistic policies in the 1960s. Before this period, elementary schools had been free and compulsory since 1925[8] and secondary schools had been free since 1952. In 1962 the free-tuition policy was extended to all levels of education.

Table 12:   Distribution of the unemployed labour force by educational level in 1960 and 1976
(6 years and over)

Educational Level	1960		1976 With previous experience		Newly unemployed		Total	
	Number	%	Number	%	Number	%	Number	%
1. Illiterate	76 687	44.2	21 805	54.4	117 192	14.5	138 997	16.4
2. Read and write[1]	49 623	28.6	7 959	19.9	56 904	7.0	64 863	7.7
3. 6 - <10 years	6 357	3.7	-	-	257 403	31.9	257 403	30.4
4. Subtotal (1+2+3)	132 667	76.4	29 764	74.3	431 499	53.5	461 263	54.4
5. Primary and less than intermediate	5 729	3.3	2 549	6.4	43 825	5.4	46 374	5.5
6. Intermediate and less than university	29 107	16.8	3 824	9.5	202 660	25.1	206 484	24.4
7. University and post-graduate	5 405	3.1	2 875	7.2	53 818	6.7	56 693	6.7
8. Unspecified	718	0.4	1 045	2.6	75 442	9.3	76 487	9.0
9. Total (4+5+6+7+8)	173 626	100.0	40 057	100.0	807 244	100.0	847 301	100.0

1 Includes also those who can read only.

Source: Except for line 3, see: The Population Census, 1960, Table 36, pp. 222-223, and The Population
Census, 1976, Table 11, pp. 145-146. The census tables include the unemployed of 10 years of
age and over. Line 3 – those in the age group 6 – <10 years – is estimated as the difference
between the total unemployed of 6 years of age and over (taken from Table 10(a) in the text) and
the total unemployed of 10 years of age and over (taken from Table 36 in the 1960 Population
Census, and Table 11 in the 1976 Population Census).

This policy certainly increased school enrolment, as shown in Table 13.

Two points, however, should be noted here. First, in a country where family income is low, free tuition is a necessary but not a sufficient condition for keeping children and school-leavers in school, as tuition fees are only a small part of the private cost of schooling. By far the greater part is the income forgone when young people go to school instead of to work – assuming of course that there are employment opportunities. In poor families this forgone income weighs heavily in the family decision as to whether or not children should continue their schooling. Secondly, the free tuition policy led to increased enrolment and consequent overcrowding of schools which in turn brought about a deterioration in the quality of instruction and increased the direct private cost of education. Taking private lessons became a must for many students if they were to pass their examinations.

Short work-week in public enterprises

By today's standards a 48-hour work-week is rather long; for that matter, so is 42 hours. But the reduction was a hefty one of 12.5 per cent! This reduced schedule was followed by the recruitment of new employees to the point of overstaffing public enterprises (nationalised private firms and corporations operating as quasi-government establishments). This was done through a special public employment campaign which started after the Nationalisation Acts of 1961 and through the guaranteed jobs policy.

Guaranteed jobs

This policy of guaranteeing jobs for technical school-leavers and university graduates[9] was formalised by the passing of Law No. 14 in 1964, which was followed by Law No. 85 in 1973. These laws gave school-leavers and graduates the right to apply for government jobs. When this policy started after 1961, unemployed graduates were given guarantees of jobs in the public sector. This right was modified later to apply to new graduates only.

In implementing these laws, the Ministry of Manpower and Training operated a system of placement services. The Ministry collected information on manpower needs of public enterprises and government offices and used the information for placing applicants in jobs. The system operated well as long as the alleged manpower needs were converted into actual jobs.

Table 13:   Educational expansion in Egypt

Year	Population with primary education %	Enrolment rates				University enrolment number	University graduates number
		Primary	Secondary		Upper		
			Prep.				
1937	1.1	...	...		...	...	...
1947	1.6	...	...		...	...	...
1960	1.7	77	15.8		16.3	...	...
1965	...	78	29.3		17.5	...	...
1970	...	70	39.5		27.9	176 023	...
1971	...	71	41.2		28.8	199 074	31 634
1972	...	69	42.2		29.8	...	8 913
1973	...	71	43.1		29.9	...	42 295
1974	...	72	46.1		30.6	...	46 783
1975	...	73	50.2		30.5	...	55 430
1976	13.2	74	53.2		31.4	453 696	63 853
1977	...		54.4		32.8	...	...

Sources: Ministry of Education and CAPMAS Statistical Yearbooks of 1975 and 1978, cited by IBRD, 1981.

In this, there was no difficulty because budget items for personnel salaries were almost automatically provided for, in line with the employment policy of the Government. In fact, the allocation of budgetary resources for more personnel was a means of upgrading positions and salaries in an expanding bureaucracy. It was a system that served its purpose well while budgetary funds for job creation lasted.

The immediate result was the increased hiring of educated personnel in the public sector, even to the point of overstaffing. According to an estimate made by the ILO Mission to Egypt, this overstaffing amounted to as much as 40 per cent in 1976.[10] This result altered the supply in a complex way. At first the policy increased the demand for educated labour, thereby mopping up much educated unemployment. In addition, the policy increased the demand for further schooling, the immediate effect of which also reduced unemployment – but only temporarily. Schooling simply converted unemployed school-leavers now into unemployed university graduates later, by shifting a large supply of educated workers to a later period during which demand was not as large. This is because the Government was unable to create enough jobs for graduates soon after graduation, as it had managed to do in the 1960s. In 1981, for example, only the school-leavers of 1977 and university graduates of 1978 were offered jobs.

The gradual lengthening of the waiting period increased the unemployment of new graduates. When the policy began, new graduates were found posts within a year of graduation, but by 1982 the "hiring delay" was one of four years for secondary school-leavers and three years for university graduates. Consequently, despite, or possibly because of the guaranteed jobs policy, unemployment of the educated labour force increased.

Lengthening the period of military conscription

The lengthening of the period of military conscription from three years (one-and-a-half years for university graduates) to five years or six years in some cases, after the 1967 war until the following war in 1973, definitely decreased the supply of primary workers, by delaying the entry or re-entry of the draftees to the labour market. However, this policy probably increased the supply of secondary workers, since many females, older workers and children seem to have entered the labour market in the 1960s and in the early part of the 1970s, because the male workers who were drafted into the army received only nominal pay.[11] The net result would depend on which of the following was larger: the decrease in primary workers or the increase in secondary workers. This, however, is difficult to determine because of the lack of precise information.

Untrammelled emigration

Emigration was obviously a private decision for individuals wishing to increase their, or their family's, income. It was not a deliberate government policy to export skilled labour. At the same time, a country with extensive unpoliced borders could hardly prevent such migration. The push of unemployment and low income in the country and the pull of jobs and high wages in the receiving countries were so powerful that regulating the flow of Egyptian migrant workers was difficult. As a result, in 1976 about 1.4 million Egyptians were resident abroad. Egyptian migrant workers increased from under 1 million to over 2 million in that year, of which the great bulk went to other Arab countries, as they had generally done after the 1973 war with Israel.[12]

This migration had positive and negative effects. By allowing labour to migrate the country thinned the ranks of its unemployed by at least 1 million, according to conservative estimates, though the net size of this positive effect depended on whether those who migrated were unemployed in the first place. Secondly, the workers' remittances - about $58 million in 1969 and $514 million in 1977 (or $1425 million, according to some estimates) - were so substantial as to pay for almost all food imports and counterbalance the trade deficits of a war-torn country such as Egypt.[13] The negative effect was that the better workers were the first ones to go. There is evidence that the migration was educationally selective,[14] as large numbers of migrants were qualified and highly skilled tradesmen most of whom were employed in Egypt and for whom replacements could not be found immediately. If found, the replacements were usually of inferior quality. In this case, migration led to a dip in the quality of available labour.

2.   Indirect policies

Two policies had significant, albeit indirect, effects on the labour market in Egypt. The first was the centralised planning policy adopted in the early 1960s, and the second was the so-called "open door" (al-infitah) policy for the expansion of the private

sector.   Both policies altered the sectoral composition
and labour demand of the economy.

Central planning policy

In the early 1960s the Egyptian economy veered from
market   orientation   towards   tight   controls   by
government.   Before then only a few means of production
had been in the hands of the State.   But sequestration
of private property – which followed the revolution in
1952 when the Free Officers came to power – increased
public   ownership.   British and French assets in the
country were nationalised in 1956; this was followed by
what was called the "Egyptianisation" measures embodied
in Laws Nos. 22-24 of January 1957 which required
financial institutions to change their legal status and
ownership and entrust their management to Egyptians.   In
1960 the Bank Misr was nationalised and a year later,
Belgian   assets   were   sequestrated.   Then Laws Nos.
117-119 of July 1961 nationalised all private banks and
insurance companies, while Laws Nos. 122-123 transferred
the   franchise   of   public   utilities   in Alexandria
(electricity) and in Cairo (tramways) from private hands
to the State.[15]

By   1963,   public   ownership   was   extensive.   It
covered financial institutions, public utilities, large
industrial   enterprises,   department   stores   and   even
hotels.   This coverage was extended to the import and
export trade, especially of the country's main export
crop, cotton.   This growing public ownership and control
of the means of production foreshadowed the need for
comprehensive   planning   which   became   more   and   more
centralised.

By   deliberate   government   decision,   the   first
five-year plan (1960/61-1964/65) emphasised industrial
development.   One year after the five-year plan began,
the Nationalisation Acts were announced.   Under these
Acts a large public sector was created, through which
the plan was to be implemented and through which the
Government was to give effect to its guaranteed jobs
policy.

After the first plan, the second five-year plan was
scheduled to start in 1965, but was postponed for two
years to allow, according to an official announcement,
for the completion of projects that had not been
finished   during   the   first   plan.   In   1967   the
Arab-Israeli war broke out and the second five-year plan
was never started.   Instead there were "annual plans"
which continued the transformation of the Egyptian
economy, according to official circles, into a centrally
planned economy.

The growth rates of the gross domestic product (GDP), according to the ILO Mission in 1980, were about 6 per cent yearly from 1959-60 to 1964-65 and about 3 per cent yearly from 1964-65 to 1973. From 1973 onwards the GDP growth rate was about 8 to 9 per cent yearly, of which a large part was nominal, mainly due to a "considerable increase in unproductive government employment" (ILO Mission Report, p. 29). The growth of real GDP per head may only have been about 2 to 3 per cent yearly from 1959 to 1965, virtually nothing from 1965 to 1974, and about 5 per cent yearly from 1974 onwards (to 1980). In terms of real income per head, the growth rate was about 7 per cent from 1973 up to 1980 (ibid.).

Naturally, public sector dominance was evident in employment. The guaranteed jobs policy ensured the further overstaffing of public enterprises and government offices. Its wage scale, high and rigid, was also dominant, attracting the educated labour force. Excluding the army, government employees numbered 310,000 in 1947, 770,000 in 1960, 1,035,000 in 1966, and 1.5 million or about 80 per cent of employed educated labour and about 16.4 per cent of total employment in 1976. During this year, government offices and public enterprises together absorbed about 29.5 per cent of total employment or about 25 per cent of the labour force.

Open-door policy

After massive sequestration of private property, only small firms remained in private hands. These were small shops, some repair shops and small commercial institutions, mostly in retail trade, and informal sector enterprises in urban areas. They produced handicrafts, leather products, fruits and vegetables.

By 1972 the sequestrations had stopped and private investments were allowed in certain industries. The investment climate changed from tight government control to a liberal, open-door policy. Indeed, Law No. 43 of 1974 which prescribed the policy, provided for tax concessions to joint ventures between Egyptian and foreign capital. Most of these ventures, however, were in free trade zones and in rather capital-intensive technologies, generating 36,500 jobs in 1979 from a capital investment which represented about 15 per cent of total investment in that year.[16]

3.   Impact on wage scale

After the Nationalisation Acts of 1961, a large
public sector emerged, where wages were determined by a
grade system based on formal schooling. Each grade in
the wage scale had a corresponding basic wage. In
addition, there were overtime payments, bonuses and
incentives, all of which could add up to a maximum of 50
per cent of the basic wage in civil service or up to 100
per cent of the basic wage in public enterprises.

There were 14 grades in the wage scale during the
early 1960s, but this number was reduced to 12 in 1971
and to 9 in 1978. This decreased the spread of the
basic wage levels, and the ratios between the starting
wages of the lowest and the highest grades changed from
1:30 in 1964 to 1:11 in 1978.[17] Nonetheless, wages in
the public sector were still much higher than wages in
the unprotected traditional segments of the private
sector.

The vast centrally planned public sector was
naturally dominant in wage determination. The public
sector virtually set the wage floor for large
enterprises and prevented wages for very scarce skills
from soaring. It had also its effects on the economic
climate, on investment policies which placed emphasis on
industrialisation, and on the sort of employment and
expectations of employment which these policies created.

In the private sector, wage determination was
theoretically based on market forces, but direct and
indirect government influence was always there. The
direct influence was exerted through wage legislation
which in 1962 set statutory minimum wages for industry
and agriculture, and which in 1974 extended the coverage
of the statutes to all private employment. From 1975
onwards, cost of living allowances were imposed by law
on large private enterprises.

The indirect influence was the competition of the
public sector wage scales. The private sector could
attract labour of a certain quality only if its wages
were at least equal to public sector wages (with all
fringe benefits included, of course). Otherwise, only
when a surplus existed could the private sector get its
labour requirements at lower wages. However, this
situation did not apply to skilled labour because
skilled tradesmen were in short supply, nor to educated
labour because of the guaranteed jobs policy. Under
these conditions, however, unemployed educated workers
might accept low wages temporarily while waiting – up to
three or four years – for government jobs.

Further, the influence of public sector wages was
not confined to setting the wage floor; it extended to

wage determination at different levels of jobs as well,
because private enterprises set their wage schedules to
be comparable to that of the public sector. Otherwise
the range of wages in the private sector would have been
much wider, higher in the relatively scarce skills and
lower in the abundant ones than the official rates.

The existence of unemployment in the economy might
be taken as evidence that wages were "downwards rigid"
in the private sector. Thus it would seem that if wages
had been flexible enough to move downwards, this sector
would have been able to absorb, within its capacity, the
labour in excess ot public sector requirements.[18]
However, the degree of wage rigidity varied from one
segment of the labour market to another. For instance,
among labour with secondary or higher levels of
schooling who were guaranteed jobs, the wage rigidity
could be high. But among the illiterate and those with
low levels of schooling, representing the great bulk of
the labour force, the wages might be less rigid and
indeed somewhat flexible. This was especially true
among adults with dependants because they could not
afford to be openly unemployed for a long time; they
must find work to be able to support their families
financially.[19]

Evidence for this hypothesis on wage rigidity
showed that in 1976 the unemployment rate among the
first group was 16.8 per cent, while that of the second
(children and adults) was 5.8 per cent. However, that
of adults in the second was only 1.3 per cent.[20] It
would seem then that the downward rigidity of wages was
high among workers with intermediate and higher
qualifications[21] and very low among illiterate adults,
including those with low levels of schooling.

4.   Impact on employment structure

The labour market policies seem to have led to
substantial changes in the structure of employment.
Employment became increasingly urban as the workers
moved away from farms towards work in the cities and
towards work in other Arab countries. In Table 14 this
change can be observed in the decreasing share of rural
employment in total employment from 65.4 per cent in
1960 to 57.2 per cent in 1976, and in the decreasing
share of employment in agriculture from 57 per cent to
47.6 per cent over the same period.

In the urban sector, the shifts were towards
manufacturing (from 19.7 in 1960 to 23.9 per cent in
1976), away from services, trade and agriculture. This
result is perhaps related to the special emphasis on

Table 14: Distribution of the employed by economic activities in 1960 and 1976
(6 years and over)

Economic Activity	1960					
	Urban (000)	%	Rural (000)	%	Total (000)	%
Agriculture	327.0	12.23	4 079.4	80.75	4 406.4	57.03
Mining and quarrying	15.6	0.58	5.4	0.11	21.1	0.27
Manufacturing	525.5	19.65	187.6	3.71	713.1	9.23
Electricity, gas and water	29.5	1.10	7.3	0.14	36.8	0.48
Construction	107.2	4.01	51.6	1.02	158.8	2.06
Transport and communication	200.4	7.49	59.8	1.18	260.2	3.37
Trade, restaurants and hotels	416.4	15.57	225.0	4.45	641.4	8.30
Services	970.7	36.29	398.8	7.89	1 369.5	17.72
Unspecified activities	82.4	3.08	36.9	0.73	119.3	1.54
Total employment	2 674.7	100.00 (34.6)	5 051.8	100.00 (65.4)	7 726.6	100.00 (100.0)

1976

Agriculture	454.6	10.36	4 426.4	75.39	4 881.0	47.58
Mining and quarrying	21.8	0.50	12.0	0.20	33.8	0.33
Manufacturing	1 046.8	23.87	322.7	5.50	1 369.5	13.35
Electricity, gas and water	44.4	1.01	17.4	0.30	61.8	0.60
Construction	301.3	6.87	123.7	2.11	425.0	4.14
Transport and communication	371.9	8.48	110.3	1.88	482.2	4.70
Trade, restaurants and hotels	616.4	14.05	244.9	4.17	861.3	8.40
Services	1 420.9[1]	32.4	535.8[1]	9.12	1 956.7	19.08
Unspecified activities	107.9	2.46	78.5	1.34	186.4	1.82
Total employment	4 386.0	100.00 (42.8)	5 871.7	100.00 (57.2)	10 257.7	100.00 (100.0)

1 Includes finance and insurance.

Sources: CAPMAS, The Population Census, 1960, Table 4; and CAPMAS, The Population Census, 1976, Table 3, pp. 85-96.

manufacturing in the first five-year plan and in the investment policies in the 1960s and 1970s.

Policies such as the lengthening of the military conscription period altered the composition of the labour force in terms of primary and secondary workers (women, children and the elderly). The shift was towards more secondary workers who were mostly children (44.8 per cent in 1976), despite the policy of free schooling and other policies to encourage school attendance.

Further, as shown in Tables 15 and 16, the shifts in the educational composition of employment were towards more educated workers, viz. from 7.9 per cent of the employed labour force in 1960 to 19.5 per cent in 1976, and towards the manufacturing sector, which increased its share of these workers from 9.7 to 15.7 per cent during the reference period.

Moreover, the educated workers moved away from the private towards the public sector, which in 1976 employed about 79.7 per cent of those with at least primary schooling and about 86.2 per cent of those with at least intermediate school qualifications as shown in Table 17.

III. MIS-EDUCATION AND ITS SUPPOSED REMEDIES

Besides economic causes, mis-education is a prominent alleged cause of the high rate of educated unemployment in Egypt. This is described below, starting with the historical background and continuing with contemporary observations on aspects of mis-education, quantitative imbalances and supposed remedies.

1. Historical background

Long before the nineteenth century Cairo already had Koranic elementary schools and the thousand-year-old University of Al-Azhar. These schools were influenced by the French towards the end of the eighteenth century when Napoleon's army ruled Egypt for four years, starting in 1798. After Napoleon's rule the French influence continued through Mohamed Ali (1769-1849), the ruler of Egypt from 1804 to 1849.

Mohamed Ali was keenly interested in establishing schools to train people for technical and administrative duties in his army and government service.[22] He established special schools to train engineers, doctors, accountants, translators, army officers and other staff. Under his rule secondary schools were established to supply students for these special and higher schools. Primary schools of the modern European type were in turn established to provide the secondary schools with students. All these schools were then attached to the War Department to ensure that the army's personnel requirements were met, until 1837 when a special department called the Schools Department was established. In addition, apprenticeship and other forms of practical training were instituted to produce the technicians, engineers and other officials who were needed in building roads, bridges, barrages, irrigation canals and other projects. Accordingly, the number of schools increased or decreased with the expected number of vacant posts in the government service and in the army.

While these projects were developing, Mohamed Ali selected a number of graduates of Al-Azhar University to study in France. With these trained graduates he organised an efficient administrative machine.

Until the middle of the century the aim of modern education was mainly to produce government officials, who were accorded high social status and regular salaries. Apprenticeship and out-of-school training were regarded as sufficient for workers in agriculture and the crafts.

When the British occupied Egypt in 1882, they took full control of the educational system, including the traditional Koranic schools. English became the medium of instruction in state primary schools and textbooks were not only written in English but were also printed and bound in England. Foreign thought and opinion became economically and socially important. Consumption of foreign goods was a status symbol, while foreign languages such as English and French were the vehicle of communication in business and government. This trend continued until 1907 when, as a result of public revolt under the leadership of Saad Zaghloul, Arabic replaced English as the medium of instruction.

Under British rule, Egypt had three streams of education, namely, the foreign, the modern and the traditional schools. The British encouraged the establishment of the foreign schools which supplied qualified personnel to foreign trade, banking and modern sector industries. The emphasis of these schools was on European languages, secretarial skills, accountancy and the foundations of business management.

The second stream of education was the modern primary schools. These schools were fee-paying and had English as a subject in their curriculum. Their pupils could proceed to the highest level of education in the country, the access to which was not accorded to pupils in the traditional schools.

Table 15: Distribution of the employed by educational level in the different economic activities in 1960 (10 years and over) (in percentages)

Educational level / Economic activity	Illiterate (1)	Read and write (2)	Non-educated labour (1+2) (3)	Primary & less than inter-mediate (4)	Inter-mediate % less than univer-sity (5)	Univer-sity and post-graduate (6)	Educated labour (4+5+6) (7)	Unspe-cified (8)	Total (3+7+8) (9)
1. Agriculture	70.1	40.2	61.2	10.7	4.2	2.1	5.3	47.8	56.7
2. Mining and quarrying	0.3	0.3	0.3	0.3	0.4	0.6	0.3	0.1	0.3
3. Manufacturing	7.1	15.3	9.6	14.5	9.5	4.9	9.7	7.5	9.6
4. Electricity, gas and water	0.4	0.7	0.5	0.8	1.0	0.6	0.9	0.2	0.5
5. Construction	2.1	2.6	2.2	1.5	0.9	1.6	1.2	1.5	2.2
6. Trade, finance and insurance	6.4	13.0	8.4	15.2	10.0	7.8	10.8	5.0	8.6

	(1)	(2)						
7. Transport and communication	2.2	5.2	3.1	14.1	6.9	3.3	7.8	1.9	3.5
8. Services	11.1	22.0	14.4	40.8	65.5	78.1	62.3	34.6	18.2
9. Unspecified activities	0.3	0.7	0.4	2.0	1.7	1.2	1.7	1.4	0.5
10. Total	100.0	100.0	100.0	100.0	100.0	100.0	100.0	100.0	100.0
Number	4 690 361	2 015 253	6 705 614 (92.1%)	136 177	318 267	121 449	575 893 (7.9%)	28 909	7 310 416

Col. (2) also includes those who can read only; they represent a small percentage of those who can read and write.

Source: CAPMAS, The Population Census, 1960, Table 31, pp. 130-135.

Table 16: Distribution of the employed by educational level in the different economic activities in 1976 (10 years and over) (in percentages)

Educational level / Economic activity	Illiterate	Read and write	Non-educated labour (1+2)	Primary & less than intermediate	Intermediate % less than university	University and post-graduate	Educated labour (4+5+6)	Unspecified	Total (3+7+8)
	(1)	(2)	(3)	(4)	(5)	(6)	(7)	(8)	(9)
1. Agriculture	69.7	29.0	56.5	7.9	4.2	2.8	5.1	54.4	46.6
2. Mining and quarrying	0.0	0.4	0.3	0.5	0.4	0.6	0.5	0.3	0.3
3. Manufacturing	10.3	19.3	13.2	23.3	13.3	9.7	15.7	9.7	13.6
4. Electricity, gas and water	0.0	0.7	0.4	1.0	2.1	1.1	1.5	0.3	0.6
5. Construction	4.2	5.0	4.4	4.7	2.3	2.8	3.2	8.6	4.2

6. Trade, Finance and Insurance[1]	3.8	20.9	9.3	11.6	8.7	10.3	10.0	8.1	9.4
7. Transport and Communcation	2.8	6.7	4.1	14.5	5.6	3.5	8.0	2.6	4.8
8. Services	7.3	16.4	10.2	34.1	61.1	66.8	53.7	10.4	18.6
9. Unspecified	1.5	1.6	1.5	2.4	2.3	2.4	2.4	5.7	1.7
10. Total	100.0	100.0	100.0	100.0	100.0	100.0	100.0	100.0	100.0
Number	5 381 206	2 564 245	7 945 451 (80.5%)	625 096	831 177	468 080	1 924 353 (19.5%)	95 913	9 965 717

0.0 indicates less than 0.1% after rounding

1 This category is composed of "trade, restaurants and hotels" and "finance and insurance".

Source: CAPMAS, The Population Census, 1976, Table 17, pp. 174-181.

Table 17: Distribution of the employed labour by educational level and by public and private institutions in 1976 (15 years and over)

Educational level	Public sector[1] Number	%	Private sector[2] Number	%	Total
1. Illiterate	475 063	17.3	4 286 833	65.3	4 761 896
2. Read and write	729 204	26.5	1 754 127	26.7	2 483 331
3. The non-educated (1+2)	1 204 267 (16.6%)	43.8	6 040 960 (83.4%)	92.0	7 245 227 (100.0%)
4. Primary and less than intermediate	406 537	14.8	209 353	3.2	615 890
5. Intermediate and less than university	717 552	26.1	113 750	1.7	831 302
6. University and post-graduate	402 460	14.6	65 628	1.0	468 088

7. The educated (4+5+6)	1 526 549 (79.7%)	55.5	388 731 (20.3%)	5.9	1 915 280 (100.0%)
(5+6)	1 120 012 (89.6%)		129 378 (10.4%)		1 249 390 (100.0%)
(6)	402 460 (86.0%)		65 628 (14.0%)		468 088 (100.0%)
8. Total (3+7)[3]	2 750 091 (29.5%)	100.0	6 566 168 (70.5%)	100.0	9 316 259 (100.0%)

1 Government and public institutions and enterprises.

2 Private, co-operative, foreign, international and "unspecificed" institutions.

3 Includes the "unspecified" category.

Source: Calculated from CAPMAS: The Population Census, 1976, Table 12, pp. 239-321.

The third educational stream was composed of the
Koranic and traditional primary schools, teaching
Arabic, reading, writing, arithmetic and general
knowledge. These schools prepared their pupils for
agricultural, commercial and low-level industrial
activities that were previously performed by illiterates
and semi-literates.

These three educational streams served different
labour markets. The foreign schools catered for the
European private sector; the modern schools were for
employment in the government service, while the
traditional elementary schools were for employment in
low-level trades, agriculture and traditional crafts.

Towards the end of the nineteenth century
employment in the foreign private sector and in
government flourished, but work in agricultural and
traditional handicraft activities lost its
attractiveness. This development determined the demand
for educational opportunities. Demand for entry to
foreign and modern schools was high, while aversion
developed to traditional schools that led only to poorly
rewarded manual work.

The situation produced another dualism in
education: one form of education, the verbal and
academic, was for the rich, while another form, the
manual and vocational, was for the poor. Public
pressure, however, gave rise to the establishment of a
number of private modern schools for poor pupils, at
which attendance was either free or at nominal fees. In
1920 these private schools outnumbered the public
schools established by the Ministry of Education.

After independence from Britain in 1922, the
Government responded to public demand by taking on the
responsibility of supporting modern (academic) education
even in private schools. Higher education was also
expanded. Technical faculties in veterinary medicine,
engineering, commerce and agriculture were elevated to
university status, along with the faculties of arts,
science, law and medicine. Many institutes which had
been established for specific manpower needs were
likewise elevated to become integral parts of new
universities established at the regional level. For
instance, the institutes of tourism and hotel-keeping,
physical education, and social work were constituted
under the University of Helwan. With the multiplication
of universities and institutes, the Department of Higher
Education was elevated in 1961 to the rank of a
Ministry, distinct and separate from the Ministry of
Education. Likewise, the Supreme Council of
Universities was created.

The speed of this development outstripped the increased resources made available to the authorities, and produced difficult transitional problems. Further, as the number of schools increased, enrolment and the output of graduates increased, too, and at a pace much faster than the employment opportunities that were created.

In a parallel development, public demand for academic-type education militated against the continued existence of trade and technical schools. These schools had been either neutralised by the prevailing system of verbal, dictative education or were simply exterminated altogether by other factors. The School of Arts and Industries became part of the Faculty of Engineering of Ain Shams University. Post-elementary schools for manual subjects, such as carpentry and metal work for boys and embroidery and home arts for girls, were converted into training colleges for elementary teachers. Schools for gardeners were closed down and so were the schools for home arts (domestic science) and evening commercial schools for training clerks.

Moreover, institutions which had been created to respond flexibly to new manpower needs acquired certain of the aspects of inflexibility of established universities. The National Egyptian University, an open university in 1908, became governmental in 1925 with all the laws and regulations that closed its original open-door system. Al-Azhar, the oldest open university in the world, was subjected to systematisation and regulation until it displayed almost the same inflexible features as all the other universities in Egypt.

2. Aspects of mis-education

The rigidities in the school system were not calculated to correct the imbalances of education in Egypt. In the qualitative sense, the students' capacity to use what had been learned was weak in both theoretical and practical subjects. Communication skills both in language and mathematics were also weak because learning had been focused on rules to be memorised and reproduced in examinations rather than to be applied in the real world. This observation is true not only in academic schools but also even in technical and vocational schools.

Education in Egyptian schools is mainly verbal and mentally passive. The students are gathered together in a classroom with one teacher spending most of his time reciting the day's lesson. The pupils listen to the teacher or watch what is written or drawn on the blackboard. All the pupils have to do is to memorise

the lesson from textbooks or from notes and reproduce it
later in examinations. The more the pupils keep their
answers in conformity with textbook information, the
higher will the marks be.

What happens in the classroom is made no better by
overcrowded curricula. The number of subjects is simply
too great: 9 in primary schools, 11 in preparatory
schools and more than this number in secondary general,
technical and teacher training schools. Besides, the
course content is often beyond the mental preparedness
of pupils or is simply unrelated to everyday life,
inducing the pupils' minds to wander or encouraging them
to play truant.

Certain contradictions and conflicts between the
school system and society only compound the problem.
For instance, school officials regard manual training
given by communities as wasteful, while community
dwellers tend to see school education as unnecessarily
theoretical and unrelated to labour market needs.
Besides, the intellectual and spiritual aims of
education are neutralised by schools, first of all by
excessive emphasis on memorising, mentioned earlier, and
by examinations that disregard ingenuity and
problem-solving but reward simple recall and rote
memory. Moreover, the public scale of values declares
work to be a source of honour and pride, a right and
duty, while idle hands breed mischief. Yet schools in
Egypt teach the opposite. Practical subjects are given
less emphasis than verbal subjects at all school
levels. Practical subjects have less qualified
teachers, less attention and even less time than verbal
subjects. Most of all, practical and vocational schools
were transformed into general preparatory schools, while
technical institutes were made into colleges and
universities with an academic bias.

3. Quantitative imbalances

Mis-education also has its quantitative aspects.
The labour force is not only badly educated but it is
also receiving education and training that fail to match
the quantitative requirements of the economy.

The educational profile of the labour force is far
from desirable. Overall illiteracy in the labour force
is still very high; in 1976 it was 50.1 per cent. This
constitutes a serious obstacle to technological
innovation, especially in the traditional sectors of the
economy. At the higher level, later data show that
professional, managerial and administrative personnel
(9.1 per cent in 1977) outnumbered clerical workers (6.6
per cent, also in 1977), suggesting that personnel at

the highest occupational level were doing the work of
subordinates, although the latter might actually be
doing the work of the former.

This general picture, however, differs from one
sector to another. In the public sector, composed of
central and local government and the quasi-public
enterprises, about 26.7 per cent of the personnel were
either illiterates (4.3 per cent) or semi-literates
(22.4 per cent). Only about 6.3 per cent had primary
education. However, about 33.2 per cent were holders of
intermediate (lower secondary school) qualifications and
33.8 per cent possessed university degrees. These
proportions suggest almost equal ratios i.e. 33:33:33,
implying a profile that is top-heavy, as exhibited by
government offices that are overcrowded with employees
who seem to be doing next to nothing.

This may have been made worse by the expansion of
employment in the government service. From 1965 to 1975
government employment increased by 137 per cent,
although over the same period the population increased
by only 35 per cent. This "over-appointment", as it is
called in Egypt, was particularly high in certain fields
such as insurance (about 146.7 per cent), defence,
security, justice, trade, local councils, health and
social and religious services, but not in other domains
such as energy (61.4 per cent), industry, oil,
transport, communication, tourism and aviation.

In the private sector the educational profile was
even less appropriate. About 94 per cent of the workers
were illiterate or semi-literate, and only some 4 per
cent had primary to secondary school qualifications,
leaving only 2 per cent with better than secondary
school education. Moreover, more than half of the
personnel in administrative and management posts were
illiterate or semi-literate, as were the clerical
workers.

What seemed to be worst was the maldistribution of
occupational classes. In the private sector there were
more professional, technical and administrative
personnel than clerical workers, implying that
high-level personnel were doing clerical and accounting
work. In the medical field, again in the private
sector, there seemed to be more doctors (13.2 per cent)
than qualified nurses (1.1 per cent).

4.   Educational remedies

Egypt's response to worsening unemployment was
rather sweeping, following a diagnosis of mis-education
in ¯both quality and quantity. Curiously enough the
response was not in reducing the supply but in

increasing the practical and vocational content of
curricula as the means of linking education to
employment and productive work.

Attempts to relate general education to employment

Over the years a number of attempts had been made
to make the general educational curricula more relevant
to employment and available job openings in the economy,
though without much popular support. Since the
introduction of modern education to Egypt at the
beginning of the nineteenth century, it had been felt
that students were not being trained for the labour
market. School education was, in fact, not directed to
producing workers but rather to training civil servants
or government officials. The object was to produce
educated mediators between the ruling authorities and
the governed masses of the public. The academic verbal
talk-and-chalk medium was dominant in schools, while
practical training was almost non-existent.

Under public pressure, schools began to provide
practical, manual and physical instruction to their
pupils. Arts and crafts were taught in primary
schools. In the 1920s the pupils attended school during
half of the day and were let free during the other half
to work either at home or elsewhere. The pupils thus
combined schooling and working. However, this excellent
idea did not prosper.

Later, many modern primary schools taught
carpentry, metal work and other skills. Some of these
schools taught advanced courses in these skills and were
called advanced or higher elementary schools. These
schools, however, were transformed into teacher-training
schools.

After the revolution and the end of royal rule in
1952, a large number of reforms were envisaged. One
educational leader undertook the establishment of what
was called the "combined units", which were intended to
be the pivots for village development. A combined unit
was made up of three sub-units, namely, one for social
welfare, another for health, and another for education.
The educational sub-unit had one or more workshops for
making what was needed in village life and work. The
idea was certainly a good one but there were
difficulties of administration that impaired its
development.

In the late fifties, an experiment in practical
training was carried out in five secondary shools, one
for girls and four for boys. The purpose was to
introduce vocational training in such trades as

carpentry, bricklaying, metal work and mechanical skills into the ordinary general secondary schools. This experiment did not succeed because the training was completely isolated from other school instruction; most of all, it was not accepted by the people.

It may be said too that the practical courses taught in some schools were not related to the skill needs - or desires - of the Egyptian community. For instance, with assistance from the German Democratic Republic, Egypt tried to establish in the early 1970s a polytechnic school for 6- to 14-year-old pupils. The curriculum contained academic and practical subjects. The academic subjects were like those taught in the ordinary primary and preparatory schools. After eight years of studies, the pupils were supposed to continue their education in higher secondary technical schools. But to the amazement of everyone, none of the pupils entered the technical schools, their intended destination; all of them went to the academic secondary schools. This result shows the attractiveness of academic education leading to white-collar jobs and the aversion to technical education that leads to manual and practical work.

In addition to the experiments mentioned above, Egypt has also tried a basic education scheme. The idea is to equip the pupils with the knowledge, skills and attitudes necessary for living in their communities. Briefly the scheme begins with arts and crafts, together with physical training, singing and music in grade 1, until grade 5 when prevocational studies start. This training continues until grade 9, thereby extending compulsory schooling up to the preparatory level. How successful this scheme has been is not definitely known but its spread from 150 primary and preparatory schools in 1977 to 1000 in the 1980-81 school year certainly indicates its acceptability.

In yet another effort to relate education to employment Egypt has been trying to reform higher secondary schools to lead either to the university or to further schooling for direct work in the community. This idea is being tested in two pilot comprehensive secondary schools.

Modern secondary education is planned to have one or two practical subjects in its curriculum. Along with linguistic, social, scientific, and mathematical subjects, students can choose one or two of the following practical areas, namely, agricultural, industrial and commercial training. Thus the philosophy of basic education that integrates varied school activities on the one hand with the community on the other hand is continued. The student can be equipped with abilities that will prepare him or her for directly productive work in the community or for pursuing higher education. This plan is intended to increase the number of students who would choose technical and practical training needed for immediate employment, which would then in turn reduce overcrowding in university studies.

However, no matter how good this plan may seem to be, there have been indications that the results will be uncertain. For instance, the streaming of students at the beginning of the higher secondary school carried 56 per cent to the technical and 44 per cent to the academic streams, but there had been great pressure from students and their parents to reverse the proportion towards increasing admission to the academic stream.

Attempts in vocational training

At the beginning of the twentieth century, Egypt established elementary schools in agriculture and industry. The schools in agriculture accepted young boys of about 10 years or older and taught them the elements of reading, writing, arithmetic and some theoretical and practical knowledge about agriculture in Egypt. After three or four years of studies the boys were supposed to become farmers or junior officials in the Ministries of Irrigation and Agriculture, while the boys who studied in the industrial elementary schools were to become employees of the Ministries of Industry and Public Works.

Later, these elementary schools became junior secondary schools. In addition, a number of intermediate schools accepting students with primary certificates were established. These schools were the intermediate schools of arts and industries, agriculture, commerce and home economics. After completing their studies the students were expected to work in the private sector or in junior posts in the civil service. However, the students pressed for the same opportunities, i.e. access to the university, which were accorded to students of academic secondary schools. The overall result was that the large number of institutions for practical, non-academic training were somehow transformed into academic schools preparing students for university studies.

In the 1950s the Ministry of Education established a number of preparatory vocational schools which were equipped with the most modern facilities and the latest curricula. They accepted pupils who were rather young (12 to 15 years old) to receive vocational instruction and were a failure for this reason. As a consequence these schools were upgraded to become secondary technical schools.

At present the Ministry of Education trains workers and technicians in secondary or intermediate schools. The training lasts three years for skilled workers or five years for technicians. The purpose is to achieve a 60:40 ratio of enrolment as between the technical secondary schools and the general secondary schools. In 1980-81 the ratio was already 56:44, but public pressure to reverse this proportion is still strong. Many students in technical schools sit and pass the General Secondary School Examination for entrance to the university. This tends to increase the number of technical school-leavers who choose to go on to the university.

There were also elementary schools for gardeners and farmers near the barrage where the two branches of the Nile begin. Again these schools were upgraded to higher schools, thus losing their original function of providing the country with educated farmers, gardeners and agriculturalists.

In the same way, the intermediate schools of agriculture, industry, commerce, home economics and applied arts were transformed into colleges and became parts of universities. These intermediate schools had to abandon their objective of producing leading technicians and take on the new function of increasing the number of bearers of university diplomas.

Other schools were established to supply the country with trained post office officials and workers, surveyors, and workers in seafood industries. These schools covered more than 90 trades (occupational titles) in an effort to relate schools to the needs of the labour market. However, a great deal has yet to be done in these schools.

Higher education in Egypt comprises 32 two-year technical institutes related to commerce and industry. Enrolment in these institutions in 1980-81 was about 50,000, spread over 12 commercial and industrial specialisations. With loans from the World Bank, Egypt has also established 18 higher institutes in agriculture, industry, commerce, social service, cooperative and administrative studies. The students of these institutes, especially those who distinguish themselves in their studies, have access to further studies in their specialisations in the university.

These institutions and the universities are linked to the labour market by the employers of university graduates who are now represented in the various sectors of the Supreme Council of Universities. The employers, together with officials of the universities and

ministries, meet to discuss manpower needs and how these
needs can be met by educational institutions.

Attempts in non-formal education

It is difficult to encompass the vast non-formal
education activities of the various ministries,
institutions and organisations in Egypt. A number of
voluntary agencies and associations provide evening
classes for workers as well as day training programmes
in industrial schools for orphans and poor children.
These associations also run schools for nurses and
training centres in sewing, knitting, tailoring,
carpet-making and home economics. A big business
institution called Arab Contractors has a well developed
training programme for architectural skills, at-home
repairs, carpentry and many other practical subjects.
In addition, the American University in Cairo operates a
training programme in languages, shorthand, typing and
secretarial work.

Training is also carried out by public
institutions. The national organisation for land
reclamation has developed a number of training courses
for improving the earning ability of peasant children
and raising the standard of living of the peasant family
in sewing, embroidery, tailoring, bee-keeping, crop
preservation, and many other subjects. In addition,
most ministries carry out their own training
programmes. For instance, the Ministry of Labour has a
vocational training programme lasting for nine months in
the rural as well as in the urban areas, while other
ministries have been building up their capacities in
short training courses. The Ministry of Industries has
36 centres with a total capacity of about 5,000
apprentices per year; the Ministry of Reconstruction and
New Settlement can train 16,000 workers per year, and
this capacity is to be increased to 32,000 per year.
The Armed Forces have their own training programme which
in 1979 trained more than 49,000 workers.

Besides all this, there were other training
activities in the private sector. This training takes
place usually in small workshops with one chief and a
number of assistants and apprentices. According to the
Ministry of Education, there were at least 150 of these
workshops which could train a total of about 150,000
workers in a year.

5. New trends

The problems of educated unemployment have been
discussed by the highest authorities of the country and

by the people's advisory councils. The discussion has
led to further ideas on the use of schools and training
for alleviating the problems of youth. One of these
ideas is the proposition that if the youth are kept
busy, they will be out of mischief.

Towards this end, labour market studies have been
carried out to find out what training in which sorts of
specialisation is indeed worth while for youth. The
Deputy Prime Minister for Finance and Economic Matters
has announced the pursuit of these studies, for solving
not only the problems of youth but also other employment
problems as well. Such studies, for example, could be a
good basis for determining how many should be trained in
which specialisations and by what means the training
should be conducted. Additionally, these studies might
be useful in regulating admission to the university.

IV. CONCLUSION

What lessons can we draw from this study? There
are many. First, the phenomenon of educated
unemployment can be ascribed to many causes, and almost
as many remedies can be prescribed. For instance,
demographers might say that the germ of the illness was
the post-war "baby bulge" in the 1950s which was in
school in the 1960s and in the labour market in the
1970s, and about which little could be done, except
perhaps to prevent a repeat of the bulge. The economist
would say that the origin is to be found in
mismanagement of an underdeveloped economy and that the
task ahead is to put the economy in order by correcting
and not repeating past mistakes. And educational
authorities believe, or at least argue, that the main
cause is mis-education and that the way to alleviate the
problem is to give more vocational instruction in
schools. Parts II and III of this country study focused
on two different approaches and their several remedies.
The supposed remedies were tried in Egypt but were
unable to contain the problem.

Second, the labour market policies used did not
have clear-cut effects in alleviating educated
unemployment. The desirable effects of some policies
were very fleeting, while the undesirable ones were long
lasting as the policies merely put off a large problem
to become a much larger one later.

Third, the remedy of increasing the vocational
content of instruction in schools as a means of coping
with educated unemployment had uncertain results,
because this remedy did not carry conviction or have
popular support. The purpose of teaching practical
subjects in schools was defeated because social rewards

and prospective wages were clearly not supportive of vocational training in schools. Besides, the remedy tends to overlook other flexible and highly effective means of practical training, i.e. out-of-school training, vocational training in industry and the short courses in special training centres, for example.

Fourth, because of the uncertainty of results, the educational remedy adopted by Egypt may have negative effects that may outweigh the expected positive ones. For instance the remedy is an expensive one, not only in financial terms but also in human terms of shifting the career prospects of people away from where the rewards are.

Fifth, the elements may seem simple, yet the configuration of the whole problem is extremely complex. The labour market policies cannot be detached from their political underpinnings or be understood in a political and economic vacuum. The policies had a specific purpose in a given situation; in this, they seem to have served their purpose well of trading off open internal strife for a perhaps less disastrous after-effect.

Nor can the educational policy be understood apart from its historical origins and the prevailing ideology about education, training and employment: that of making instruction in schools more practical with a view to linking education and work, especially when unemployment worsens. In Egypt, as elsewhere, reversing the forces of history and ideology requires an equally formidable force because the overriding conditions of underdevelopment reduce the range of options and leave little room for manoeuvre. To be sure, altering the wage structure would be heavily resisted, while guaranteed employment for the educated labour force might be used again, perhaps in a different form, when political expediency is compelling.

The problem becomes even more complicated if world recession continues. The outflow of migrant workers will be less, while return migrants may become more numerous. This may increase the pool of politically articulate people who will be demanding jobs and putting a further strain on the economy.

Notes

1 This proportion increased to 13.2 per cent in 1976, during which year the primary enrolment rate was 72 per cent.

2 IBRD: Some Issues in Population and Human Resource Development in Egypt (Washington, report 3175 EGT, 12 May 1981; restricted), p. 11.

3 B. Hansen and S. Radwan: Employment Opportunities and Equity in Egypt (Geneva, ILO, 1982), p. 207. This publication is also referred to as the ILO Mission Report.

4 For a review of sampling defects of the Labour Force Surveys, see I.H. El-Issawy: Employment Inadequacy in Egypt, Paper prepared for the ILO Comprehensive Employment Strategy Mission to Egypt (Cairo, Aug. 1980), p. 46. However, it is important to note certain inconsistencies in the 1960 and 1976 census data. For instance, the totals for unemployed labour classified by rural/urban sectors do not tally when classification is by age. The same inconsistency is found in employment data.

5 As far as can be discovered, there was no change in the definitions of labour force and employment used in the 1960 and 1976 censuses.

6 "Educated labour" refers to persons who have completed at least secondary schooling.

7 The term "school-leavers" is not synonymous with drop-outs. In the European sense, as used here, it refers to students who have completed their studies and passed the examination for the school-leaving certificate.

8 Primary schools of the modern type were established in Egypt in the nineteenth century, and parallel elementary schools were added in 1925. The latter were free and, in principle, compulsory unless the child was enrolled in the primary schools.

9 The term "graduate" is used in the specifically European sense of university graduates, rather than in the more general American sense.

10 Hansen and Radwan, op. cit., p. 207.

[11] Both educated and non-educated conscripts had only nominal pay during the military conscription period, except those who had already been in employment before conscription and who received salaries comparable to those of their civilian jobs after one year of military service.

[12] IBRD Report, op. cit., p. 8.

[13] ibid.

[14] ibid., pp. 141f.

[15] R. Mabro: The Egyptian Economy, 1952-72 (Oxford, Clarendon Press, 1974), pp. 131f.

[16] Hansen and Radwan, op. cit., p. 65.

[17] ibid., pp. 227f.

[18] This wage rigidity is not due to unionisation because the latter is very limited in Egypt (ILO Mission Report, p. 80).

[19] Note that the first group are all adults, because persons with secondary schooling or higher fall in the age bracket 15 years and over, who by definition are considered adults in Egypt.

[20] Calculated from Tables 11 and 12 of this chapter and from Tables 3, 7 and 8 of the 1976 Population Census.

[21] According to an economic thesis, if wages were flexible enough to move downwards, the labour market would have cleared and unemployment would have been negligible.

[22] J.S. Szyliowicz: Education and Modernisation in the Middle East (Ithaca, Cornell University Press, 1973), pp. 102-151.

BIBLIOGRAPHY

I. Reports

Al-Hilali, Ahmad Naguib. Report on the reform of education. Cairo, Government Press, 1950.

Al-Kabbani, Ismail Mahmoud. Report on the origin and
development   of   elementary   education.   Cairo,
Government Press, 1946.

Al-Sanhowry, Abd el Raxzak Ahmed. The new systems of
education. Cairo, Government Press, 1948.

Clatanoff, W. Jr. et al. Manpower projections for planning education and training. Cairo, Ministry of
Manpower and Technical Training, 1979.

"Education for comprehensive development and productive
work: An application with a view to the characteristics and trends of the Egyptian community", Paper
presented by the Delegation of Egypt to the 38th
Session of the International Conference on Education,
Geneva, 10-20 November 1981, prepared by the National
Centre for Educational Research (Cairo, 1981).

Helmy, M.K. "The speech of the Minister of Education on
its policy at the People's Assembly". Cairo, 1975.

Ibrahim, Abd el-Aziz Al Sayed. Higher education: Its
problems and principles of its planning. Cairo
University Press, 1963.

IBRD.   A.R.E. economic management in transition.
Washington, 1978.

Luca, N. Education: A working paper. Cairo, Al Maaref
Press, 1973.

Maher, A. Report on university education. Cairo, Al
Nahda Al Misriya Press, 1973.

Mann, F.O. Report on certain aspects of Egyptian education. Cairo, Government Press, 1932.

Mustafa, A.F.; Ramadan, M. University education in
Egypt and its development, A report forwarded to the
International Conference for Statistics, Computer
Science and Social Research, Cairo, 25-29 Mar. 1979.

New channels for development in the Arab States, A report
of a conference of Ministers of Education and Ministers
of Planning in the Arab States, sponsored by UNESCO
with the collaboration of ALECSO, Abu Dhabi, 7-16 Nov.
1977.

Report on comprehensive evaluation of the basic education. Cairo, National Centre for Educational Research
and UNICEF, 1980.

Sadek, H.   Problems of university education. Alexandria
University Press, 1976.

Soliman, M.S.H. Towards a new policy of admission to the
Egyptian universities, A paper presented to the 2nd
Scientific   Conference   of Egyptian   postgraduates
abroad, London, 8-13 Apr. 1980.

II. Statistics

CAPMAS   (Central Agency for Public Mobilisation   and
Statistics).   A study of employment by sample in
A.R.E. Cairo, Aug. 1977.

---. Basic statistics for A.R.E., 1952-1972.   Cairo,
1974.

---. Development of technical education graduates in
Egypt during 1972/73 - 1976/77. Cairo, Apr. 1980.

---. Dimensions of labour force in A.R.E. Cairo, 1975.

---. Education and development. Cairo, 1975.

---. Employment, wages and work hours (October 1973).
Cairo, July 1978.

---. Evolution of civil labour force in A.R.E. 1977-
1990. Cairo, 1979.

---.   General population and housing census,   1976.
Cairo, 1978.

---. Population and   development.   Cairo,   1978.

---. Population trends in Egypt until the year 2000.
Cairo, June 1973.

---. Statistical abstracts of A.R.E, 1951/52 - 1971/72.
Cairo, June 1973.

---.   Statistical   atlas   for   A.R.E.   Cairo,   1979.

---.   Statistical   yearbook   for A.R.E.   Cairo,   1980.

---.   The Egyptian child in 25 years. Cairo, Apr. 1979.

---.   The labour force sample survey, May 1975.   Cairo,
Aug. 1977.

Population and Family Planning Board.   Population
Studies, quarterly review (Cairo), 6th year, No. 50,
July/Sep. 1979.

RAPID (Resources for the Awareness of Population Impact
on Development, The Future Group): The effects of
population   factors   on   social   and   economic
development. Cairo, 1981.

III. Research working papers

El-Issawy, I.H.   Employment inadequacy in Egypt.   Paper
for the ILO Comprehensive Employment Strategy Mission
to Arab Republic of Egypt, 1980. Cairo, 1980.

Harby, M.K.; Ibrahim, M.   Description and evaluation of
the educational system in Egypt.   Cairo, Institute of
National Planning, Apr. 1981.

Institute of National Planning.   Research project on
employment and unemployment among the educated. Cairo,
1962; mimeographed.

Mohsen, M.N.   A report on the development of technical
education in Egypt.   Cairo, Ministry of Education,
Office of the Under-Secretary of State for Technical
Education, Nov. 1981.

National Specialised Councils.   A study of employment at
the government sector. Cairo, 1969; stencilled.

---. A study of employment at the public sector. Cairo,
1979; stencilled.

---. A study of employment at the private sector.
Cairo, 1979; stencilled.

IV. General References

Al-Ayubi, N.N.   Policy of education in Egypt.   Cairo,
Al-Ahram Political Studies Centre, 1978.

Al-Eyoun, Mahmoud Abu. Al Azhar.   Cairo, Al Azhar, 1949,
translated into English by Mustafa Habib.

Al-Kabbani, Ismail. Educational policy in Egypt. Cairo,
Lagnat el Targama wal Talef wal Nahr, 1944.

———. Studies in educational systems. Cairo, al-Nahda
al-Misriya, 1951.

———. A hundred years of education in Egypt. Washington,
DC, Egyptian Ministry of Education, Washington
Cultural Bureau, 1948.

Bhagwati, A. "Main features of the employment problem
in developing countries", in International Monetary
Fund Staff Papers, 20(1), Mar. 1973.

Blaug, M. Education and the employment problem in developing countries. Geneva, ILO, 3rd impression, 1978.

Chapelle, R.J. Reform and development of higher education in the United Arab Republic, Report of UNESCO
advisory mission on higher education in Egypt 1968/69,
Paris, UNESCO, 1969.

Clatanoff, W. et al. The manpower estimates to serve
education planning and training, Paper submitted to
the Conference of Egyptian Economists, Mar. 1980 (in
Arabic).

Dantwala, M.L. "Definition of unemployment and problems
of its measurement in developing countries", in OECD:
The challenge of unemployment to development and the
role of training and research institutes in
development. Paris, 1970.

El-Ghannam, M.A. Education in the Arab region viewed
from the 1970 Marrakesh Conference. Paris, UNESCO,
1971.

El-Koussy, A.H. "Education in Egypt" in Yearbook of
Education, 1952. London, Institute of Education, 1952.

———. "The future of education in Egypt" in The 50th
yearbook of the Egyptian education association for
scientific culture. Cairo, 1980.

———; Balba, S.I.; Sanyal, B.; Harby, M.K.; Noonan, R.
University education and the labour market in the Arab
Republic of Egypt. Oxford, Pergamon Press, 1982.

El-Issawy, I.H. Employment inadequacy in Egypt. Paper prepared for the ILO comprehensive employment strategy mission to the Arab Republic of Egypt, Cairo, 1980.

Ezzat, Abd al-Karim Ahmed. History of education in Egypt, 1848-1862. Cairo, Ministry of Education, 1945.

Faculty of Education, Ain Shams University. A working paper on the development of Egyptian education. Cairo, 1980.

Farid, Zeinab. Educating and training rural women for economic participation. Cairo, Anglo-Egyptian Bookshop, 1980.

Feldstin, M. "The private and social costs of unemployment", in American Economic Review, May 1978.

Final report, Arab States Conference on Elementary Education. Cairo, 1952.

Final report, Arab States Conference on Free and Compulsory Education, Dec. 1954-Jan. 1955. Cairo, 1955.

Galal, Salah, (ed.). Egypt between now and the year 2000, Report of First Conference of Egyptian Scientists, 28-30 Dec. 1974. Cairo, Al-Ahram Press, 1974.

Goldstein, M. "The trade-off between inflation and unemployment: A survey of the econometric evidence in selected countries", in International Monetary Fund Staff Papers, 19(3), Nov. 1972.

Hammad, S.I. French and British influences in Egyptian education, unpublished Master's Thesis, University of London Institute of Education, 1948.

Handoussa, H. Public sector employment and productivity in the Egyptian economy, Paper prepared for the ILO comprehensive employment strategy mission to the Arab Republic of Egypt, Cairo, 1980.

Hansen, B.; Marzouk, G. Development and economic policy in the UAR (Egypt). Amsterdam, North Holland Publishing Company, 1976.

Hansen, B. Long-term trends in Egyptian labour market from labour surplus to labour shortage, Paper prepared for the ILO comprehensive employment strategy mission to the Arab Republic of Egypt, Cairo, 1980.

Harby, M.K.; Azzaw, El Sayed. Education in Egypt in the
    20th century. Cairo, Education Documentation Centre
    of U.A.R., 1960.

Harby, M.K. Education in Egypt. Paris, UNESCO, 1965.

Harby, M.K. et al. Technical education in the Arab
    States. Paris, UNESCO, 1965.

Hussein,, M.; and Khalil, Y. Basic education. Cairo,
    Al-Ghareeb Library, 1978.

Hussein, Taha. The future of culture in Egypt. Cairo,
    Dar el Maared, 1937.

Hyde, George D.M. Education in modern Egypt. London,
    Routledge and Kegan Paul, 1978.

IBRD. Arab Republic of Egypt - Economic management in a
    period of transition, Vol. VI. Washington, 1978.

———. Arab Republic of Egypt - Domestic resource mobili-
    sation and growth prospects for the 1980s. Washington
    1980.

Institute of National Planning (Egypt). Planning the
    labour force in Egypt. Cairo, 1974.

Institute of National Planning. Research project on
    employment and unemployment among the educated.
    Cairo, 1963.

Johnson, J.G. "Review article: Disguised unemployment
    in a general theoretical context", in Economic develop-
    ment and Cultural Change, Vol. 26, No. 2, Jan. 1978.

Korayem, K. "The estimation of the disposable income
    distribution in the urban and rural sectors in Egypt",
    in Cairo Papers. (Cairo, The American University of
    Cairo), 1981.

Mazumdar, D. "The urban informal sector", in World Devel-
    opment, Vol. 4, No. 8, Aug. 1976.

Ministry of Education (Egypt). A guide to basic educa-
    tion in the compulsory stage 1981-82. Cairo, 1981.

Ministry of Foreign Affairs, Institute of Diplomatic
    Studies. Trends and issues about the construction of
    modern Egypt. Cairo, 1980.

Mohie-Eldin, A. "The development of the share of agricultural wage labour in the national income of Egypt", in G. Abdel Khalek and R. Tignor (eds.): The political economy of income distribution in Egypt. New York, Holmes and Neier Publishers, Inc., 1981.

The National Bank of Egypt. Economic Report, Cairo, Vol. 32, No. 1, 1959 (in Arabic).

National Centre for Educational Research. Education in Egypt. Cairo, 1978.

National Specialised Councils. Economic studies about the seven issues announced by the President. Cairo, 1982.

---. Policy of education in Egypt - Principles, studies and recommendations. Cairo, 1981.

Nofal, M.N. Education and economic development. Cairo, Anglo-Egyptian Library, 1979.

Pigou, A.C. The theory of unemployment. London, Frank Cass and Co., 3rd impression, 1968.

Radwan, A.A. Old and new forces in Egyptian education. New York, Columbia University Teachers' College, 1951.

Salama, G. History of foreign education in Egypt. Cairo, Al-Shaab Press, 1963.

Selim, Imam. Planning for development. Cairo, Institute of National Planning, 1974.

Solow, R.M. "On theories of unemployment", in American Economic Review, Vol. 70(1), Mar. 1980.

Strand, D. and K. "Hidden unemployment 1953-62: quantitative analysis by age and sex", in American Economic Review, Vol. 56(1), Mar. 1966.

Turnham, D. The employment problem in less developed countries. Paris, OECD Development Centre, 1971.

UNESCO and International Association of Universities. Access to higher education. Paris, 1965.

4 THE PHILIPPINES

I. OVERVIEW

In this study the Philippines is seen as presenting the following features: mild educated unemployment in a market economy, whose growth has been medium to fast but has later been slowing down; high enrolment rates; and a school system comprising an extensive private sector, particularly from high school to higher education. Without much government intervention this sector has been heavily influenced by market forces and ought therefore, according to conventional theory, to be more flexible and responsive to labour market conditions than a totally state-controlled school system.

Unlike most poor countries the Philippines has only about 10 per cent of its labour force in the government service. According to the ILO Employment Mission, these civil servants, whose entry to established posts is by competitive examination, represented only about 25 per cent of the educated labour force.

How all these elements interact in the labour market and how they determine the employment and unemployment situation in the country are discussed in two parts. The first outlines a general background of economic trends, unemployment conditions and the absorption of college graduates into the labour force. This is followed by what would appear to be the lessons to be learned from the country's responses to unemployment and from the impact of these responses. The second part describes a labour market model which tries to explain why the impact took the form it did.

1. Background

Trends in the economy

A brief economic boom immediately after 1945 was not sustained, and food deficits became a major problem. The country's earnings from primary products such as minerals, timber, sugar, coconuts and fibres were used to import food, and what was left from the food bill was siphoned off as capital for manufacturing

industries in the cities. Manufacturing was inward
looking, i.e. largely import-substituting, and its
products were intended mainly for domestic consumption
rather than for export. High tariff walls propped up
inefficient industries, while an over-valued currency
and artifically low interest rates on capital for the
so-called infant industries made those industries
heavily capital-intensive. All these circumstances
reduced the capacity of the country to absorb labour in
gainful employment.

Manufacturing grew by taking advantage of
short-term gains up to the limits of artificially cheap
capital and of what could be supported by domestic
markets. As the limits of the latter were nearly
reached, growth rates could not be sustained.

That frontier was soon reached because the rural
sector was virtually neglected, rural institutions and
land tenure were obsolete, not to say feudal, and
agriculture was technologically stagnant. Food prices
were kept low in favour of the politically articulate
city dwellers but to the disadvantage of farmers and
producers. Consequently, except in a few areas, the
productivity of farms was generally low and the
purchasing power of farmers and the rural population was
at a standstill, even declining (Corpuz, 1982, p. 30).

Farming communities were economically depressed
areas. Whatever surplus the peasants produced was
creamed off by middlemen and landowners, while
government expenditure programmes for physical
infrastructure were concentrated in the big towns and
cities. Thus it was quite natural for people to respond
to this urban bias of development by moving towards the
cities, especially towards Manila. With the spread of
education migration continued unabated, depleting the
rural areas of educated people while causing congestion,
open unemployment and related social problems in cities.

The slow development of the countryside also had
many other effects. Depressed areas became hotbeds of
sedition and the seat of anti-government movements,
threatening law and order and prompting the declaration
of martial law and heavy military spending which might
have been used for rural development in the first
place. Sporadic clashes between government and
anti-government forces induced more people to move to
towns and cities, thereby putting serious strain on
urban social amenities. Efforts to alleviate this
strain begot further waves of migration and costly
remedial effort which should have been done in the
countryside to begin with. The magnitude of the problem
can perhaps be conveyed by citing the urban growth of
Manila which in 1960 had only a population of 2.12

million. The population had increased to 3.16 million
in 1970 (Abad, 1972, p. 19), and rose to 6.4 million in
1980.

At the time of the ILO Employment Mission in 1973,
the Philippines was already in the process of changing
its development path. Many policies were modified, and
most of the changes were later endorsed by the Mission.
Rural development was given emphasis, and a drive was
launched for industrial development. Exports were to
have an increasing labour content, moving from raw
primary products to semi-processed and processed goods.
Trade was to be liberalised and made more competitive,
not only by an appropriate choice of technology but also
by proper changes in tariffs and taxation, capital
lending, currency exchange rates and in export
promotion.

A massive drive for production was undertaken.
Self-sufficiency in food was the first objective, and
this objective was achieved, thanks to the new rice
technology and favourable changes in farm-gate prices.
Labour-intensive items like footwear, garments,
handicraft products and the like were produced by
cottage industries for overseas markets. Likewise,
there were incessant efforts to find and exploit new
mineral resources for processing and export. All this
required considerable quantities of capital which had to
be secured mostly by foreign borrowing either as
development loans, or as equities of foreign companies
or both.

There was also a concerted campaign to develop the
country's tourist industry. Air transport was improved,
resorts and tourist attractions were developed and
hotels were built. Advertising was also undertaken to
attract tourists to the country, and in due course
foreign visitors flocked in.

But when the OPEC shocks came, all this effort was
thrown into disarray. Most of the foreign exchange
earnings of the country went to cover the fuel bill.
Costs of production soared, while the prices of
Philippine exports dropped when countries which used to
buy those goods went into economic recession. These
countries became increasingly protective of their own
markets and imported less and less. Production
decreased and, correspondingly, foreign exchange
earnings dwindled to a point at which even the servicing
of foreign loans became extremely difficult. Following
the oil shocks, economic growth rates were much below
target, so economic plans had to be revised
accordingly.

Many projects for industrial development,
principally in heavy industries such as integrated steel

mills, petro-chemical complexes, pulp and paper mills,
copper and aluminium smelters, cement and fertiliser
factories, and automotive engine assembly plants, have
been running much behind schedule. A number of them
have been scaled down or replanned and some may have to
be abandoned, at least temporarily. All this has had
deleterious effects on linkages, i.e. the industries
dependent on these projects, as well as on employment,
especially of the educated labour force.

Trends in unemployment

Aggregate unemployment was 8.5 per cent in May
1961, 6.1 per cent in October 1965 and 7.8 per cent in
May 1968, indicating a narrow band of variation despite
the timing of data collection. (May was just a few
weeks after the end of classes and would show a high
count of jobseekers, while October was well into the
school year when the number of jobseekers would not be
at its peak.) More recent estimates, however, revealed
lower figures, ranging between 3.9 per cent and 5.2 per
cent from 1974 to 1978 and suggesting that indeed
unemployment had decreased to levels at which the
economy could be supposed to be running at full
employment.

These rosy figures were no more than estimates from
head counts of persons who had worked during the
'reference week'. The estimation never considered how
much time was spent at work or how much income was
earned from that work, and hence, the figures never
accounted for underemployment and its full arithmetic
equivalent in unemployment. However, indirect estimates
by the ILO Mission showed that far from the 4 to 8 per
cent range, unemployment could be placed at 25 to 34 per
cent of the labour force in 1971.[1]

At the time, unemployment rates were found to rise
with the level of schooling, i.e. from primary grades 1
to 4 to the first three years after high school. From
there the rates for those who had completed at least
four years of college dropped to figures lower than
those of aggregates or totals, suggesting that the
educated labour force was already experiencing serious
problems of finding employment, even though graduates
tended to have the better chances.

Another way of gauging unemployment is through the
ratio of the number employed to the population. This
ratio indicates to what extent valuable human resources
are being utilised. As shown in Table 18, the
utilisation rates were rather low, especially among
school drop-outs, the lowest being among those who
dropped out of college. The base figures of "college 1

Table 18:   Utilisation rates of human resources

Educational level	1965[a]	1969[b]	1974[b]	1975[a,c]
High school 1 to 3	58.9	61.3	56.1	–
High school 4	63.1	78.0	74.9	–
College 1 to 3	35.5	38.3	38.4	–
College 4 to 5	73.6	60.6	40.5	78.2
Total	62.4	65.0	66.3	–

[a] Actual

[b] Estimate

[c] Sanyal et al., op. cit.

Sources: ILO Mission Report, 1974, p. 310;   Sanyal et
            al., p. 136.

to 3 years" in 1965, including their projections for
1969 and 1974, never reached 39 per cent, suggesting
that the non-utilisation rate was 61 per cent, or that
about 6 out of every 10 educated persons in this
category were not working. Of course, many of these
(prospective) workers were attending school rather than
work. But even for those who had completed college,
i.e. 4 or more years after high school, the figures seem
to suggest an increasing number who were not working,
that is, from 1 out of 4 in 1965 to 6 out of 10
mentioned above.

The actual figures in 1975 seem not very different
from those of the preceding years. A manpower inventory
(to the last man!) showed that the country had 1,206,286
university graduates but that only 1,023,548 were in the
labour force, out of which 943,039 were working. These
figures imply a utilisation rate of 78.2 per cent.[2]
Hence, the non-utilisation rate was about 22 per cent,
indicating that more than one out of every 5 graduates
were not working (Sanyal et al., pp. 136f).

Whether the situation has improved or deteriorated
since then is difficult to ascertain, because more
recent information is not available. But there is every
reason to believe that the situation has been no better,
especially after the 1974 oil shock, after the falling
prices and decreasing production of traditional exports
of the country, and the increasing supply of educated
labour turned out by the school system of the
Philippines in the intervening years.

Pattern of labour absorption

Before considering how the country reacted to the
situation described above, it would be instructive to
examine in some detail how particular groups of educated
labour were absorbed into or employed in the labour
market. The data are from a cohort of graduates in 14
areas of specialisation and from institutions scattered
across the breadth of the country. The year was 1969,
just a few years before the oil shock when so-called
educated unemployment was still mild or at least less
severe. The purpose is to show the pattern of labour
absorption during that situation of the labour market.

Educated labour absorption proceeds as follows.
Starting from zero at graduation the absorption is rapid
until the second year, but slows down in the third year
before reaching a plateau in the fourth and fifth
years. In some cases the upper limit of 100 per cent
absorption, i.e. with all the graduates in the sample
employed, was achieved in the second year. But in most
cases the process dragged on to the fifth year without

ever getting to a point near the limit of 100 per cent employment. This means that many graduates had been unable to find employment or were not working even 5 years after graduation.

Again, the absorption rates within five years after graduation varied from one school to another, as they did by area of specialisation and by region. As the data show, graduates of the University of the Philippines (U.P.) had fast and high absorption rates in all areas of specialisation. The absorption rates of graduates from other schools varied widely. For instance, among civil engineers the range was from 60 to 81 per cent in Manila and 90 per cent in the provinces. Among primary school teachers the range was from 35 per cent in a school in Manila to 93 per cent in another school in Cotabato, Mindanao, or from 73 per cent (U.P.) to 84 per cent (another school) in Manila.

It would seem that these rates show a pattern. They indicate a labour market condition and they reveal to some extent the capability of schools within a region to respond to that market condition. For example, while the U.P. School of Education may have been producing school teachers for a saturated market in Manila, another school in Mindanao has not been able to graduate enough for its surrounding communities.

Lastly, there is the element of substitutability which was mentioned by the ILO Mission but was left barely explored. Further analysis of the data presented by the Mission showed that while average incomes in "own field" were slightly better than in "all fields", the absorption rates in the latter were in most cases much better than in the former. Thus when average incomes were adjusted for absorption rates the result tended to show that the adjusted average incomes were much better in "all fields" than in "own fields", implying that on the whole employment of a few in high-income jobs outweighed that of many in low-income jobs. This is illustrated, for example, by the absorption rates and incomes of graduates in what might be called the "soft" subjects which, incidentally, are the least expensive subjects to study, and whose enrolment and graduates form the bulk of the educated population of the country. This is even better illustrated by data from Metropolitan Manila, a more or less saturated labour market where unemployment information is perhaps better than in other parts of the country. As shown in Table 19, the adjusted average incomes were much better when the graduates worked in fields other than their own.

It may be noted, too, that substitutability was not total. Otherwise, absorption rates and incomes would not vary much between areas of specialisation. The

Table 19: Unweighted average absorption rates and monthly incomes of college graduates, 1969

Absorption rates (%)

	Years 1	2	3	4	5	All fields	Own fields
All regions	64.47	82.05	86.73	90.47	93.19	80.01	69.67
Region 4	70.33	85.50	88.17	92.50	92.00	79.83	65.63
Other regions	70.86	81.59	86.31	90.17	92.63	79.90	71.21
Manila	63.89	82.11	87.19	90.56	94.26	80.26	67.89

Monthly average incomes (Pesos)

	All fields	Own field	Adjusted all fields	Adjusted own field
All regions	276.18	284.28	220.95	198.06
Region 4	262.33	276.33	209.42	181.36
Other regions	249.04	256.21	198.98	182.45
Manila	326.64	333.11	262.16	226.15

	Absorption rates		Monthly income		Adjusted income	
	All	Own	All	Own	All	Own
	%		Pesos		Pesos	
Selected fields of specilisation, Manila						
Primary education	72.00	63.29	238.57	240.29	171.77	152.08
Commerce	86.67	52.67	300.00	313.67	260.01	165.21
Business administration	85.50	60.00	340.00	405.00	290.70	243.00
Liberal arts	90.50	81.00	310.00	305.50	280.55	247.45
Agriculture, Region 4						
Univ. of Phil.	64.00	85.00	P279.00	P291.00	P178.56	P247.35
School code 2310	92.00	81.00	236.00	232.00	217.12	187.92

Source: Calculations are based on figures from ILO Mission Report, Table 157, pp. 636-9.

variations in fact did seem to show that graduates in some subjects had better access to well-paid employment opportunities than graduates in other subjects. What seems to be a plausible explanation is that certain labels indicating areas of specialisation, tend to shorten the range of substitutability and restrict access to good jobs.

Another aspect of substitutability, perhaps an influence of quality, can be inferred from data from two well-known schools of agriculture, one of which is a private school and the other is a state school. The latter is renowned for its instruction and research facilities, and its graduates seem to command a much higher price in their own field of specialisation than in other fields. In this particular case, substitutability led to lower incomes. However, the opposite was true of the graduates from the private school. Average incomes of graduates from this school were higher when employment was in all fields. These results suggest that substitutability can be either a boon or a bane to the graduates, depending upon the marketability of their skills.

2.   Lessons from policy responses

Education systems are not particularly noted for their responsiveness to changing situations. Certainly, the Philippine education system is no exception. It is not that the system never responded at all to the worsening employment problems of the educated labour force, but rather that its responses were self-defeating. At best the result has been uncertain, as will be seen below.

Reducing the supply of graduates

This was an obvious solution, but it would only nudge the educated unemployment problems to the lower levels of schooling. Besides, the measures to achieve this solution were politically difficult to implement. The first of these measures was to discourage the opening of new schools in the reputedly overcrowded areas of specialisation such as primary education (teacher-training), commerce and the liberal arts. The next measure was to curtail enrolment in these subjects in the already established schools. And the third measure was the institution of a national college entrance examination (NCEE). The first two merely shifted the composition of enrolment away from the "over-enrolled" subjects and did not reduce total college enrolment at all.

But the effect of the third, the NCEE, was rather mixed. The reason for this unforeseen effect was that the cut-off "pass" score for the examination could not be raised so easily as had been thought. Starting at the 25th percentile in 1973, the cut-off had not risen beyond the 35th percentile by 1983, an increase of only 10 percentiles in 10 years!

However, the examination did draw the line between those who should not and those who in principle might be allowed to continue their studies in college. In addition, the examination also singled out the high schools whose school-leavers were not good enough for college, thereby casting a spell on the existence of not only the self-help village high schools but also their variants such as the village development high schools (Richards and Leonor, p. 158).

But the most significant effect of the examination was the identification, perhaps the creation, of a category - about one-third of the total output of the high schools - who were neither acceptable for college studies nor prepared for immediate employment. This effect triggered off the release of a large number of unemployed high school-leavers to the labour market, when they could have been kept in schools and neatly hidden from unemployment statistics.

Curricular reforms

The immediate reaction was the development of what might be called the technicians' curricula for, but not exclusively for, those who did not pass the NCEE. Several examples of these curricula exist in agriculture, mechanical and electrical trades, fishery and even in the art of healing. These curricula make the already vocationally specific training even more skill-specific.

There were also curricular changes which accompanied the upgrading of vocational high schools to technical colleges. The change started with two-year technical curricula leading to a certificate in teaching practical arts or pre-vocational subjects in elementary schools. Then two curriculum years were added on, leading to full-fledged four-year bachelor's degree programmes. The emphasis was on practical subjects and pedagogy. As the new colleges expanded, curricula became more diversified, but the diversity was merely a further subdivision or fragmentation of the already occupationally specific subjects, the emphasis of which was on applied, practical training to meet supposed labour market demand. When these colleges became state universities, curricular offerings became even more

diverse and specific. Liberal arts subjects were
introduced but the vocational bias in the curricula was
still very pronounced.

The effects of these reforms have not been well
documented, but there is evidence that the vocational
high school graduates practised their vocation only as
the last resort. Most of them continued their studies,
preparing themselves for teaching others to practise
their vocation rather than directly engaging in the
vocation itself (Castillo, 1973, pp. 311-336). Those
who did not study further were found to be earning much
less than general high school-leavers (Williamson and De
Voretz, 1969), and those who did study further and who
completed their college degree in a vocational field
were reported to be earning much less on average than
college graduates in other subjects (cf. Mission Report,
pp. 629-650).

Why this result ensued has been the subject of
speculation on the part of school authorities. But
their diagnosis almost always laid the blame on
inappropriate curricula, i.e. not practical enough,
poorly trained teachers and badly equipped schools.
Remedies for these shortcomings, assisted by World Bank
loans, may have improved the situation, but whether
these remedies can go very far is, of course, a
different story.

The vocational emphasis in the curricula was
present not only in high schools and higher education
but also in the primary (elementary) schools, through
pre-vocational studies. The purpose was to inculcate
desirable work habits in pupils, particularly the
favourable attitudes towards work. However, the
emphasis was not only in practical arts subjects but in
all subjects of the curriculum. This emphasis was made
even more insistent by a national drive with the slogan,
"WORK IS THE CORE OF OUR CURRICULUM".

Whether this emphasis had any measurable impact
would be extremely difficult to tell, but there is
reason to believe that, had the national drive been
successfully carried out, its impact would have been
negative. Firstly, the working environment was not
supportive of the emphasis, that is, the work condition
to which the pupils were exposed was not rewarding
enough. Secondly, the method used to influence work
attitudes, as shown by the attitudes revealed by pupils,
was not good enough (Leonor, 1981).

The general trend of these curricular changes has
been towards making education "more practical",
skill-specific or job-oriented. This was true for both
state and private schools. The latter made their
general courses more specific as shown by degree

programmes such as Bachelor of Science (B.Sc.) in Economics, major in marketing; B.Sc. with major in courses preparing for employment as medical secretaries, and B.Sc. in Commerce, major in agri-business. Skill labels have become so distinctly narrow that they create categories or boxes from which the graduates can hardly extricate themselves, especially when employment opportunities change. All this has made college degree programmes almost as job-oriented as those offered in vocational high schools.

Non-formal education

The response under this heading was nationwide. It was co-ordinated by the National Manpower and Youth Council (NMYC), an inter-ministerial Council chaired by the Minister of Labour and Employment. Training was grafted onto existing programmes and facilities of the various ministries represented in the Council, making the spread extensive and the scope comprehensive (Diaz, 1972).

The training had many interesting features. It took the form of short courses and therefore could be made much more flexible than diploma or degree programmes. It had a built-in responsiveness to the immediate training needs of those who wanted to take advantage of new employment opportunities. It was modular, i.e. in small complete units which could be taken progressively at any time on demand. This safeguarded relevance, that is to say, only courses that were in demand would be taught, while the rest could be put away.

The scope of the subjects covered by the programme was extensive. It embraced agricultural skills - both farm and non-farm; industrial skills such as those required in manufacturing, building construction, repair and maintenance of machinery and physical plant of factories and offices; service skills in hotels and the tourist trade; skills for cottage industries; training skills and even supervisory and managerial skills for executives. This list is not exhaustive, but it does indicate comprehensive coverage as well as the sort of clientele to which the NMYC has addressed itself. This clientele was the great majority of the educated labour force, from high school-leavers and out-of-school youth to college graduates.

The effect of the NMYC programme in actually alleviating educated unemployment is difficult to assess precisely, because there is no quantitative evidence available. Early evaluation studies of rural training programmes only indicated the "teething problems" of

their implementation rather than the utilisation of
skills acquired from training (Diaz, op. cit.).
However, right from the start it can be said that the
beneficiaries, i.e. the educated labour force mentioned
above, must have markedly increased their chances of
getting employed, especially in times of skill scarcity,
e.g. when the outflow of skilled manpower to the Middle
East was at its peak. At that time the sure sign of
scarcity was the high rate of turnover of workers in the
country, including even the instructional staff of the
NMYC itself (ILO, PHI/74/010). Efforts to replace
departing staff naturally created a chain of vacancies
which when filled could also reduce the pool of
unemployed workers.

Training for employment overseas

Training for employment overseas was a major
preoccupation of many educational establishments in the
1960s and 1970s, when the demand for medical workers in
North America was almost a bottomless pit. Medical
workers of all kinds, ranging from nursing aides,
laboratory technicians, to doctors, were produced in
large numbers by the school system. Had they not been
allowed to leave the country, inventories of medical
professionals would have increased tremendously to the
point of underemployment, perhaps even open
unemployment. The reason is that not many villages
could afford their service, nor were the medical workers
trained for village work or for the medical needs of the
urban poor. Now that the demand for medical workers
abroad has subsided, training in this line of work has
correspondingly dwindled.

An increasing demand for skilled workers overseas,
from about 12,500 in 1975 to about 141,700 in 1980 (see
Table 20), has given rise to recruitment, training and
skill certification for employment overseas.

Whether training for this purpose was something to
be encouraged or discouraged was a debatable question,
because in principle such training ought to be used for
the country's needs. That, at least, was the belief at
the time when developing countries were always thought
of as experiencing serious skill shortages. But this
thinking has changed, indeed had to change, as the
numbers of skilled and educated jobseekers have
increased. Besides, adequate control of skill outflow
is extremely difficult to impose, even in a country
surrounded by seas and oceans, especially when
remittances from overseas workers have created visions
of an El Dorado.

Table 20:   Overseas contract workers by major
             occupational group, 1975-80
             (excluding seamen)

Year	Departures			Blue collar as % of total
	White collar occupations	Blue collar occupations	Total	
1975	9 800	2 700	12 500	22
1976	11 200	8 000	19 200	42
1977	12 500	24 100	35 700	65
1978	21 200	29 800	51 000	59
1979	36 200	57 300	93 500	61
1980	53 000	88 700	141 700	63
Total	143 900	210 600	354 500	59

Source: World Bank Report No. 3750b-PH, Philippine
          vocational training project, Aug. 26, 1982,
          p. 4.

In any case, economic booms in America and Europe created shifts in skill demand. This prosperity changed the work preferences of American and Europeans away from certain tasks which many workers from less developed economies are prepared to perform. Thus, among other nationals, Filipino seamen figure in the manning tables of merchant ships of many countries in Europe and North America. Filipinos are also on the staff of hotels in the English-speaking world, banks and accounting firms in the Pacific area, construction and engineering firms in the Middle East, and even of schools and colleges in Africa (Abella, 1976). All this alleviated educated unemployment at home, besides bringing in remittances (about $664 million in 1980) which in recent years have been a tremendous help in augmenting the country's foreign currency reserves.

II. A MARKET MODEL

1. Introduction

Philippine educational experience after the Second World War has been notable for the essentially private character of post-primary schools and for fast growth of enrolment at all levels. In about two decades, universal basic education, meaning grades 1 to 4, was achieved. Growth of college education was equally phenomenal. The number and capacity of colleges and schools increased quite easily to accommodate the rising enrolment. By the 1970s, the college enrolment rate ranked third or fourth in the world.

The growth of the demand for schooling reflects the people's recognition of literacy and "numeracy" as a basic need and the people's response to new opportunities that have been created by economic and political change. Since 1945 public services have been expanded, financial institutions have been established and industrialisation has been stimulated. These changes created not only entrepreneurial opportunities for self-employment but also white-collar jobs in private firms and public offices. These opportunities required well-educated workers, and the realisation of this fact gave rise to an unprecedented demand for schooling. Demand which state schools could not cater to was met by private initiative.

Private schools have been relatively free to respond to student demand. Restrictions were few and state control has been mainly administrative and supervisory, mostly in keeping records and maintaining certain standards of instruction and curricula.

State support for education has concentrated very much on making provision for elementary education. This, and limited resources, deprived other educational activities and programmes of administrative and financial support. Consequently, the State has not been able to establish effective units for curriculum planning and development, a fact that may help to explain the rather passive state supervision of private schools and the small share of state-supported higher education, which until the early 1970s had only 5 per cent of total college enrolment. State participation at this level has since been increasing, mainly in an attempt to sustain quality in instruction, to redress inequality of educational opportunities and to alleviate the unemployment of college graduates.

The State's role in post-elementary education is largely a complementary one. Provincial governments support public high schools, while the national Government operates about 40 colleges and universities. Support of state universities, though limited in extent relative to total education, is of primary importance because it permits the teaching of courses that private colleges do not provide. However, funds for newly established state colleges and universities seem destined to have a more doubtful impact because many of these institutions appear to be mere copies of many private schools.

It is to be noted that the rapid expansion of the school system took place in a period when the country's per capita income was low and the initial stock of people with advanced degrees was small. Over the years about three-quarters of all college teachers have only had their first university degree. Besides, library and laboratory facilities were in acutely short supply. As a result, most colleges offered degree programmes in inexpensive fields such as teacher-training, commerce and the liberal arts. These limiting factors determined the quality and variety of schooling that could be supplied on the scale desired by the people. Thus on the whole, quality had to give way to quantity.

The educational system that evolved was market-determined. Private schools behaved like firms, and the students like customers. Both faced financial constraints which influenced the structure of demand for various types of schooling.

The interaction between students and schools in the labour market under these conditions is analysed below. A model of how this market interaction works in a less developed economy is set up (see chapter appendix) to help to explain certain observed phenomena such as mismatching of skills, unemployment among some types of

educated labour and the rather low rate of returns on
schooling.

With a focus on higher education, this section
presents a theoretical framework of what might be called
an "education market". This presentation is followed by
an empirical analysis of education and labour market
policy and by a conclusion.

2.   Theoretical considerations

The nature and choice of education capital

The decision to pursue a certain type of education
is treated here as an investment decision. Studies on
motives for acquiring education strongly support this
proposition. More than 80 per cent of students cite
financial and other job-related benefits as the major
reason for studying (Sanyal et al., 1981). However, the
theory of choice may be applied to education only at the
cost of great simplification, because education is not
directly observable. Education can be defined more
meaningfully in a philosophical sense than in the sense
of a physical commodity. As a capital good perceived at
a point in time, education is the whole range of
knowledge, skills and attitudes acquired by an
individual. It consists of all scientific, linguistic
and artistic information absorbed, together with the
discipline to reason, analyse information and make
correct choices in relation to certain norms, and the
ability to search for new information and create new
knowledge.

Owing to its complex nature, education is difficult
to apprehend and assess. For this reason, it has been
measured roughly in years of schooling or in such crude
categories as levels of attainment, e.g. elementary,
high school, first degree, advanced degree, etc. This
conventional classification is useful in countries where
the quality of schools is fairly homogeneous at each
level and in each specialisation. In places where this
is not so, the rough categories for gauging educational
attainment are of questionable relevance.

A special feature of formal school is its fairly
rigid annual progression from kindergarten up to the
university. The early part of this process consists of
general education, which starts from primary school and
continues to the second year of college. After this
curriculum year, specialisation begins. In
sub-professional or vocational-technical training,
however, specialisation takes place at an earlier
stage. Whether in professional or sub-professional

education, the intensity of specialistion increases with
the number of years spent in school.

Because of this sequential nature, an important
benefit of attaining a certain level of schooling is the
access it gives to the next level. In this sense,
completion of grade 1 permits the pupils to move to
grade 2, while completion of high school is valuable
because it allows students to pursue one of a number of
alternatives for post-secondary education.

Another feature of formal schooling is its general
education content, which confers flexibility in
adjusting to changes in skill requirements. (But any
reduction of this content by introducing vocational
subjects would certainly decrease that flexibility.)
Students with a good general education can easily change
their fields of specialisation towards the later stages
of schooling or even after joining the labour force, and
these changes can be accomplished in a fairly short
time. A shift of specialisation in college may be
completed in just one year, but a shift in major
subjects at the post-graduate level may take as much as
the full length of the programme, i.e. at least two
years for the master's degree and four years for the
doctor's degree.

Ability and cost of education

People are born with different and unequal genetic
attributes. In addition, people are born into families
with different historical and cultural backgrounds which
in turn instil dissimilar values and attitudes. In the
individual these characteristics influence the kind of
schooling that he or she wants or finally acquires.

Because of these differences, individuals will not
be indifferent to education options that give equal
monetary returns; they tend to choose options that are
suited to their personal attributes. Conversely, an
increase in the relative monetary returns attaching to
an option will not attract everyone to it. One can
expect instead an upward-sloping supply curve of
students because a certain amount of monetary return has
to make up for personal cost. Students whose abilities,
attitudes or both are unsuited to a given option may shy
away from it. At some point, the supply line may turn
vertical as personal cost becomes prohibitive in terms
of utter lack of talent and interest in the given
option. For this reason, the elasticity of supply is
likely to decrease with intensity of specialisation and
to be low in fields that require special abilities.

There are, however, levels and areas of education
where supply is fairly elastic. In the Philippines, for

example, it is easy to enter at the lowest level of general education. Thus most first degree programmes consisting of courses that are of interest to everyone should have fairly elastic supply. This is, in fact, a feature of subjects such as teacher education, business, psychology, liberal arts and even engineering, which have experienced a shifting supply of students when monetary returns change.

The monetary cost of education varies with the level and field of specialisation. In general, cost increases with level, but some economies of scale are possible in higher education. For this reason, relatively large colleges and universities have been established in major population centres. However, some fields of specialisation necessitate expensive facilities and highly qualified teachers, all of which imply a high capital investment per student.

In addition, geograhical access to schools varies with the level of education. Primary schools are provided in all towns and large villages, while high schools are increasingly accessible, often now existing even in large villages. By contrast, colleges and universities are mostly found in cities. This dispersal of schools partly determines the private cost of education. In general, students from remote provinces have to bear greater cost than city residents.

From the above, we note that the geographic location of schools and the differing abilities and aptitudes of students are the basic factors that determine the cost structure of education. These factors also affect the supply of students to each programme.

Supply of skills in labour markets

The supply of skills varies because of differences in cost and ability requirements. Certain skills necessitate only average general abilities but other skills, such as those of brain surgeons, concert violinists and financial managers, demand rare and special gifts. Obviously, the horizontal part of the supply curve will be shorter, the higher and the more specific the talent required. The positive part of that curve reflects the increasing marginal cost of learning and working with a skill. In the labour market, the supply curve of each skill corresponds to the supply of graduates with this skill, as shown in Figure 2.

In the model (see chapter appendix) we assume fluidity among workers in the labour market. Workers can move between jobs with varying degrees of ease, depending on the ability and the difficulty of the

Figure 2:   Labour market for graduates and
            skilled workers, I

GR, Gross Return

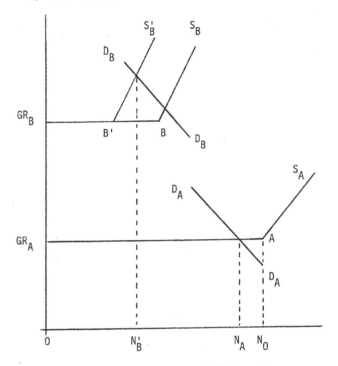

Number of graduates and skilled workers

training required. The latter may range from training
of a few weeks to years of graduate study or artistic
discipline, but many jobs have fairly easy or short
training requirements. Similarly, many graduates can
move among a number of white-collar occupations such as
teaching, office work, sales, management, clerical work,
etc. without much additional formal training. The same
holds good for most blue-collar jobs.

Those with a high level of education can also move
downward, if they wish. An excess of highly qualified
labour tends to oust the less qualified and the latter
in turn push the least qualified to the next lower level
jobs. The result is that unemployment of the skilled or
qualified labour will be concealed in employment in
low-skill jobs. This type of hidden unemployment is not
easy to identify and quantify because there are other
reasons why individuals may take on jobs other than
those for which training was undertaken. The switch
might be to correct a wrong initial choice of field,
because many students decide on their schooling or
training when possessing less-than-perfect information
about their own talents and inclinations, and about the
labour market. The shift may also be in response to
changes in market opportunities. These are desirable
adjustments in the labour market. So the resulting
"mismatch" of original skills with job requirements
should not be considered as disequilibrium
underemployment.

This fluidity of the market is restricted by
constraints on individual choice. The market can shift
labour downward to lower-cost skills because those who
can afford to acquire expensive skills can also acquire
inexpensive ones. The opposite does not apply,
however. Even if there are shortages in high-cost
skills, the financial constraints will not allow the
unemployed in the lower-skill market to move up.

In Figure 2, consider the market for low-cost skill
A with its demand and supply curves $D_A D_A$ and
$GR_A A S_A$. Equilibrium employment is N_A with
unemployment of N_0-N_A. In the market for high-cost
skill B with its demand and supply curves, $D_B D_B$ and
$GR_B B'S'_B$, there is full employment at N'_B. The
supply is smaller than the total of qualified people for
B, $GR_B B S_B$ because of financial constraint. The
overall labour market reaches an equilibrium with excess
supply in A and a shortage in B, and an unequal rate of
return on the investment in the two skills.

The situation may be described as a labour-abundant
economy in which there is a surplus of labour in the
agricultural and other informal sectors at a subsistence
wage GR_A. Unemployment will tend to be distributed

among low-cost skills but not among skills which only few can afford.

The responsibility of the schools in unemployment

The responsibility of the schools in unemployment depends on how well they interact with students and employers in the labour-education market. Unlike other components of this market, schools are not motivated purely by economic gain, for many of these institutions are founded on lofty objectives such as Christian education, equal educational opportunities, etc. Although these objectives may be pursued independently of perceived market demand, they are not usually at variance with it. For instance, religious education is given in the form of additional courses and, more commonly, through the social environment in school. The lofty objectives need not, therefore, make schools oblivious to market demand, or unresponsive to it.

However, the demand for various categories of skills is not clearly and easily gauged. Information about this demand tends to spread slowly, unevenly and sometimes inaccurately. Before any disequilibrium can be noticed, it must be large enough to constitute an unequivocal phenomenon, and this in turn implies a time-lag before it is perceived. Any consequential curricular change requires much time for training teachers in new skills. Hence, schools cannot be expected to respond quickly and infallibly to market demand.

The quality problem

Without fixed standards the quality of schools is dependent on what students demand it should be. It is likely, therefore, that the quality of schools varies widely according to the ability and financial capacity of their clientele. To some extent this variation conveys "false signals" to employers, so much so that they often judge prospective workers not only on the basis of schooling but also on that of the institution where the schooling was obtained. In a sense, this casts doubt on paper certificates as indicators of quality and leads to greater costs of hiring and job-search.

3.   The role of the Government in education

Educational planning has just begun in the Philippines. The 1978-82 Five-Year National Development

Plan called for the formation of a planning group that
would be expected to develop a manpower plan. The plan
in question would try to match supply with demand for
various types of educated labour, with a view to
alleviating educated unemployment and avoiding apparent
mismatches between skills and job requirements.

The State's role in higher education is mainly
supportive of the private sector. This role involves
direct participation in higher education itself and is
conceived as leading rather than competing. In many
cases state schools complement the effort of private
schools and sometimes the former fill gaps which the
latter are unable to close.

This supportive role is evident in the expansion of
state colleges and universities from an enrolment share
of only 5 per cent in the 1950s to 15 per cent
recently. The expansion was effectuated in areas and
specialisations which are financially prohibitive for
private schools. For instance, many science degree and
graduate programmes of acceptable standard are offered
only in a few state universities. In addition, the
National Manpower and Youth Council has established
about 10 vocational-technical training centres in Manila
and in the provinces. This move once more rightly
filled a gap in training.

Further, through education, the State has also
played an active role in coping with the following
social and economic problems: widespread unemployment of
college graduates, uneven quality of instruction and
inequality of educational opportunity. For the first
two, the State instituted a national college entrance
examination (NCEE) in 1974, mass-produced elementary
school textbooks and established the training centres
mentioned above. The NCEE was intended to sift out
well-prepared students seeking high education, with the
aim of reducing college enrolment and eventually the
supply of graduates. At the far end of this sequence
was the hope that educated unemployment could be
alleviated by jugulating the supply.

The last problem mentioned above, that of
inequality of educational opportunity, was also of great
concern to the State. In the past two-and-a-half
decades the Gini ratio as an indicator of income
inequality has been rather high, fluctuating around
0.50. Because quality in education has been constrained
by family income, income inequality leads to inequality
in education. The programmes addressed to this problem
that have been instituted in the last few years include
land reform, expansion of state colleges and
universities, and increased allocations for loans and
scholarships.

The impact of State educational programmes has however been limited. Part of the reason was that state institutions enrolled only about 15 per cent of the total number of college students, while a leading state university, the University of the Philippines, catered mainly for well-to-do city dwellers (Tan and Uy, 1976). Another reason is that less than 10 per cent of college students received any scholarship or loan support (Sanyal et al., 1981).

Turning to the demand side, many policies for industrial promotion led to the cheapening of capital in relation to labour. The result was misallocation of capital and unemployment of the abundant labour available. Several studies criticised these policies for dampening the growth of employment (Sicat and Power, 1971; ILO, 1974; Bautista and Power, 1979). There were of course employment generating programmes, e.g. the incentive programmes for small-scale industries, but they represented only a minor part of the schemes for industrial promotion.

We may conclude then that state intervention in the labour market through a complex scheme of incentives and disincentives was not very successful, and it did not change the essentially market-oriented nature of the educational system. The State's role in higher education has been mainly complementary to a relatively free, market-determined private school system.

4. Empirical evidence

It has been argued above that because of financial constraints the education market could not move to an efficient equilibrium. Most of the college-going population would tend to acquire inexpensive education and training, because only a minority could afford to pursue the expensive, even if highly rewarding, sort of schooling or training. Similarly, schools that were dependent on student fees would tend to operate inexpensive curricular programmes. Consequently, the market would supply a large number of inexpensively trained graduates. Returns on investment in inexpensive programmes would then tend to be lower than those of costly programmes. Further, unemployment would be more likely to occur among graduates of the former than of the latter.

Unemployment of educated labour may take different forms. One is open unemployment; another is unutilised skills due to over-qualification in a job or due to a mismatch of one's skills with the skills required by the job. On the other hand, very imperfect or incomplete certification of education may lead to longer job-search

and hiring and, therefore, to an increase in the
unemployment rate. This is reflected in the rate of
unemployment of new graduates and directly in the length
of their search for jobs.

The school system

Private colleges and universities grew fast but at
fluctuating rates; they offered few, and similar, areas
of specialisation. Growth was fastest during the first
few years after the Second World War when these
institutions quadrupled from 100 in 1945 to 400 in
1950-51. Apparently this expansion was not always
economic, so that some colleges had to close down. The
number fell gradually to 339 in 1960-61, but it
increased to 566 schools in 1967-68, and by 1978-79, the
total had reached 792. These institutions and their
students were concentrated in Manila.

This expansion of higher education has broadened
the range of subjects taught. Over the decade colleges
offering engineering courses rose from 44 to 191;
agriculture, from 2 to 93; and medical science courses,
from 14 to 186.[3] But in law and foreign service the
number of institutions remained practically the same, 62
in 1967-68 and 61 in 1978-79. Business schools,
however, decreased from 424 in 1969-71 to 376 in
1978-79. There was a drop in the number of liberal arts
colleges from 480 to 401, but teacher-training schools
increased, albeit slowly, from 402 to 433 in the same
period. Despite these variations, however, the
concentration of schools (and enrolment) was in
commerce, liberal arts and teacher-training.

In the following investigation of the cost
structure of colleges and universities, it is assumed
that tuition fees represent this cost in private schools.

In 1968-69 the average annual fees in private
schools in such courses as business, teacher-training
and the liberal arts ranged from P315 to P465 ($53 to
$78 at P6/$1 exchange rate). Scientific and technical
courses necessitating laboratory and engineering
equipment required higher fees. But these fees were
still within the reach of a large proportion of
college-bound students, except in medicine, where the
fees were about three times as high as in other
courses. Over time, tuition fees rose with inflation
but their structure did not change significantly.

As regards the variations in cost among fields of
specialisation, as represented by fees charged by
private schools, Table 21 shows that the fees were
highest in medical and legal education and lowest in
commerce, liberal arts and teacher-training. The fees

in engineering schools were only slightly higher than in
other schools.

The cost also varied by type of institution. The
fees which represented the cost in private schools were
very much lower than the average per student cost in the
University of the Philippines, one of the state
universities. The differences in these "costs" were
very wide in science-based disciplines such as medicine
and engineering. In 1968-69 the per student costs in
medicine were P4,273 in U.P., P1,474 in sectarian
schools and P1,207 in non-sectarian schools. The
corresponding figures in engineering were P1,859, P483
and P470. It is noteworthy that the per student cost in
other state universities was less than a third of the
cost in U.P., an indication of the extent of cost
differences between state schools.

In Table 22, it is apparent that the concentration
of college students was in the inexpensive fields.
About 74 to 78 per cent of the students were in the
liberal arts, teacher-education and business.
Interestingly, however, there were substantial shifts
towards other fields. For example, enrolment in
engineering, a modestly priced course, showed a fairly
high growth, but enrolment in medicine did not rise as
fast as in other fields, despite a keen demand for
medical doctors.

It will be seen from Table 23 that in 1968-1969
more than 70 per cent of instructors in private colleges
in the provinces held the bachelor's degree only. (Even
in some state universities many instructors had only
this qualification.) However, the percentage of all
private school faculty members with advanced degrees
rose from 25 per cent in 1969-70 to 28 per cent in
1972-73.

This perhaps was not a real improvement because
well-qualified staff members were lost to well paid
positions in non-teaching institutions. The very
competent ones were drawn to executive positions in
business or to administrative jobs in government
agencies. Some of these ex-faculty members continued to
teach as part-time lecturers and increased the number of
instructors in the staff list of private schools. This
observation is prompted by the presence of a large
proportion of temporary or part-time lecturers, most of
whom had better qualifications than the few regular and
full-time faculty members.

Unemployment trends

Despite the slow growth of non-agricultural
employment and a high population growth of about three

Table 21: Average annual tuition fees in universities and colleges by field of study and type of school, (in Philippine pesos)

Fields	1968-1969 Sectarian (private schools)	Non-Sectarian (private schools)	U.P. Dept. cost	1972-73 All private schools
Business	315	401	569	509
Teacher training	335	421	908	595
Liberal arts	465	421	514	
Engineering	483	470	1 859	
Law	541	612	842	
Nursing	468	552	752	
Medical technology	588	562	–	
Medicine	1 474	1 207	4 273	1 792

Region and type of school	1973	1974	1975	1976	1977
1. Metro Manila					
1.1 Private schools	428.48	460.08	553.71	592.81	611.48
1.2 University of the Philippines (U.P.)	2 267.83	1 810.08	3 539.48	3 668.62	3 814.31
1.3 Metro Manila – other state colleges and universities	638.09	678.63	988.13	1 047.23	999.04
2. Non-Metro Manila					
2.1 Private schools	286.47	325.70	386.41	452.73	491.45
2.2 Non-Metro Manila – state colleges and universities	831.74	979.54	1 267.30	899.18	1 521.54

Sources: (a) Bikas C. Sanyal, Waldo S. Perfecto and Adriano Arcelo: _Higher education and labor market in the Philippines_ (Paris, UNESCO, 1981), Table 3.6;   (b) 1968-69 Progress Report on the "Study of the tuition fees for the last 5 years in private institutions" (Manila, Division of Research and Evaluation, Ministry of Education and Culture), May 1969.

Table 22: Growth and distribution of enrolment in private colleges by field of study, 1967-72

Major field of study	1967-68	%	1968-69	%	1969-70	%	1970-71	%	1971-72	%
Agriculture	3 279	0.6	3 340	0.6	3 445	0.6	3 349	0.6	4 059	0.7
Engineering and technology (including nautical science)	60 404	11.2	60 533	10.7	62 423	10.9	64 600	11.1	76 019	12.6
Teacher training	190 653	35.4	165 602	29.3	146 631	25.5	108 309	18.5	84 391	14.0
Commerce & business adm.	139 490	25.9	167 188	29.6	187 634	32.7	217 218	37.1	245 062	40.7
Law & foreign service	13 428	2.5	15 195	2.7	15 624	2.7	15 037	2.6	15 075	2.5
Music & fine arts	1 584	0.3	6 657	1.2	6 506	1.1	7 657	1.3	7 013	1.2

Medical sciences	22 512	4.2	23 488	4.2	24 947	4.3	31 345	5.4	32 547	5.4
Food and nutrition	3 771	0.7	4 337	0.7	4 568	0.8	4 463	0.8	4 981	0.8
Liberal arts	92 612	17.2	103 149	18.3	106 939	18.6	113 225	19.4	122 378	20.3
Chemistry, physical & biological sciences	2 498	0.5	3 882	0.6	2 095	0.4	2 351	0.4	2 797	0.5
Others	8 979	1.7	11 664	2.1	13 208	2.3	16 600	2.8	7 551	1.3
Total	539 210	100.0	565 035	100.0	574 020	100.0	584 154	100.0	601 873	100.0

Source: NEDA: Philippine Statistical Yearbook, Manila, 1978, pp. 284-285.

Table 23: Educational attainment of faculty of the
University of the Philippines and private
schools, 1968-69 (in percentages)

	B.A./B.Sc.	M.A./M.Sc.	Ph.D.
University of the Philippines	46.4	36.1	17.5
Private schools			
In Metro Manila	53.2	40.2	6.0
Provinces	73.6	24.4	2.0

Note: Figures for private schools are unweighted
averages of data from 33 and 35 schools in
Manila and the provinces, respectively.

Source: Edita A. Tan and Evelyn Miao: "The structure
and performance of Philippine educational
institutions", Discussion Paper No. 71-12, July
12, 1971, Institute of Economic Development and
Research, School of Economics, University of
the Philippines, Diliman, Quezon City.

per cent per year the unemployment rate decreased substantially in the period from 1956 to 1975.[4] Open unemployment fell by more than one-half, from 10.0 per cent to 4.2 per cent of the labour force, as shown in Table 24.   Likewise, the full-time unemployment equivalent of underemployment of those working below 40 hours per week but desiring to work additional hours also fell by half from its level in 1956. However, this downward trend was reversed after 1975.

The amelioration of the unemployment situation may be explained by a number of factors. One is the increased enrolment rate of the school-age population from 47 per cent in 1960 to 68 per cent in 1975. This is partly reflected in the reduction of the labour force participation rate from 57 per cent in 1956 to 50 per cent in 1975. Another factor is the change in the occupational composition of employment and in the organisation of work which led to an increase in the number of wage and salary workers. The latter tended to work more regularly and full time than the self-employed and unpaid family workers.

To be noted is the high proportion of inexperienced labour among the unemployed – about one-half in most years. Their unemployment rate was greater than that of the experienced group: 5.5 per cent versus 4.5 per cent in 1956, 4.0 per cent versus 2.1 per cent in 1965, and 2.7 per cent versus 2.5 per cent in 1971. These differences decreased in the 1970s. Children aged 10–14 had a very low unemployment rate because most of them were in school; thus, unemployment among the young must have been concentrated among the 15–24 year-olds.

The incidence of unemployment varied substantially among various categories of labour and among industrial sectors, as shown in Table 25. In 1956, the open unemployment rate among occupations ranged from 3.1 for farmers to 15.8 per cent for non-farm manual workers; and among industrial sectors, from 3.1 per cent in agriculture to 15.7 per cent in construction. Over time, the range and variation narrowed, as shown by the fall in the standard deviation of unemployment rates from 3.06 in 1956 to 1.63 in 1975 among industries, and from 3.26 to 1.51 among occupational classes during the same period. These changes might be related to adjustments in labour market conditions, such as the movement of workers away from occupations or industries where the risk of being unemployed was relatively high and towards sectors where this risk was low.

The probability of finding a job in any part of the labour market depended on the initial level of unemployment and on the number of new job openings. Sectors like construction, transport and government

Table 24: Number and per cent distribution of unemployed labour, by nature of unemployment, 1956-75

	1956	1961	1965	1971	1975
Labour force	8 561	9 713	10 764	12 895	15 160
Employed	7 702	9 095	10 101	12 228	14 517
Unemployed	859	618	663	667	643
Experienced	389	327	228	325	375
Inexperienced	470	219	435	342	268
Underemployed	384	396	362	259	299
Unpaid family workers	1 842	2 096	2 212	2 634	3 295
Unemployment rate (%)					
Open unemployment	10.0	6.4	6.2	5.2	4.2
Experienced	4.5	3.4	2.1	2.5	2.5
Inexperienced	5.5	3.0	4.0	2.7	1.8
Underemployed	4.5	4.1	3.4	2.0	2.0
Total	14.5	10.5	9.6	7.2	6.6
Unpaid family workers	21.5	21.5	20.5	20.4	21.7

Source: NCSO: Labor Force Survey.

service were growing fast; they attracted labour from other sectors, including new entrants to the labour force. In construction, for instance, the labour force increased so fast that the rate of unemployment though decreasing, remained relatively high at 9.3 per cent.

Open unemployment of college graduates, as shown in Table 26, was about equal to that of the total labour force. Their underemployment rate in terms of hours worked, however, was lower than the aggregate because they were employed in white-collar jobs that were stable and had regular work hours. For instance, in Table 25, the full-time equivalent of underemployment among the professional, administrative and clerical occupations in 1975 was low, because more than 90 per cent of the incumbents were in wage earning and salaried jobs. This made the effective unemployment rate of college graduates much lower than that of the aggregate.

One feature of employment among college graduates in the Philippines was the wide variation in occupation. They were employed as professionals or technical workers, as administrative personnel or secretaries. As such the rates of unemployment of the graduates also varied widely. Unemployment among professional workers was lowest, while that of clerical workers was high among occupations. The difference reflects relative scarcity and perhaps also the relative quality of the graduates. Really well-qualified graduates tended to search out the professional posts. With additional indicators of quality such as grades and name of school, these graduates were readily considered for professional jobs and were thus first selected. Because their supply was relatively small, these graduates had little difficulty in finding jobs. The average graduate, on the other hand, had greater uncertainty about his or her qualifications and tended to apply for a much broader range of jobs. He also faced additional screening devices, with the result that the hiring process and job-search were usually somewhat lengthy. The supply of such graduates was also larger than the demand, and consequently, open unemployment was high.

Evidence for this structure of unemployment is found in the 1976 and 1978 surveys conducted by the Fund for Assistance to Private Education (FAPE). They showed that the absorption rate from the time of graduation varied by field of specialisation and by specific school type or school where the degree was obtained. The average waiting time for the first job was quite long. In the 1978 survey of employed graduates, about 23 per cent were not employed after one year from graduation and 9.2 per cent after two years. These figures may be

Table 25: Open unemployment rate of experienced labour force, by sector and occupation, 1956-71

	1956	1961	1965	1971	1975
Total	4.8	3.5	2.2	2.8	2.5
1. Agriculture	3.1	2.8	1.4	1.4	1.4
2. Construction	15.7	12.8	7.3	9.3	9.3
3. Manufacturing	5.3	4.6	3.3	3.4	4.0
4. Commerce	5.1	3.7	2.2	3.3	2.2
5. Transport	8.1	2.8	4.0	4.0	4.4
6. Government service	10.2	2.7	3.0	3.6	2.7
7. Domestics	5.2	1.3	2.2	2.1	3.0
8. Personal	10.0	3.3	3.4	5.8	5.6
9. Other ind.	13.3	14.7	5.1	16.8	4.8
Standard deviation	3.055				1.63
Coefficient of variation	1.57				1.53

	Open unemployment					1975	
	1956	1961	1965	1971	1975	Under-employed	Total full-time equivalent unemployed
Total	4.8	3.5	2.2	2.8	2.5	7.6	10.1
1. Professional	6.9	1.3	1.8	2.6	0.7	1.7	2.4
2. Proprietors, administrators	4.6	2.0	1.1	1.7	0.0	2.0	2.0
3. Clerical workers	11.0	12.8	4.6	4.7	5.9	1.0	6.9
4. Salesmen	4.8	4.6	2.9	3.3	2.2	7.6	9.8
5. Farmers	3.1	2.8	1.4	1.4	1.4	10.3	11.7
6. Transport workers	5.2	2.1	2.9	2.8	3.9	2.3	6.2
7. Craftsmen	6.6.	5.3	3.8	4.9	4.7	10.9	15.6
8. Manual workers	15.8	16.1	8.4	8.7	9.4	3.7	13.1
9. Service workers	6.6	2.1	2.7	3.4	3.6	3.1	6.7
Standard deviation	3.26				1.51		

Note: The equivalent in unemployment computed for those who worked less than 40 hours per week.

Source: NCSO: Labor Force Survey, May Series, 1956-1971, Aug. 1975.

Table 26:   Reported unemployment by educational
             attainment, 1961, 1965, 1977[1]

	May 1961	October 1965	4th Quarter 1977
Total	8.6	6.1	4.5
Elementary 1-5	6.2	4.0	2.9
6-7	9.8	8.3	3.4
High School 1-3	16.2	9.5	6.8
4	18.5	11.3	6.8
College 1-3	20.0	14.1	7.6
4 or more	7.9	5.8	5.2
Not reported	3.1	2.8	

[1] The questionnaire was changed in 1976 so that the measurement of unemployment is not exactly comparable to previous years.

Source: NCSO: Labor Force Survey for each year.

compared with those of the graduates in specific years:
1963-64, 17.3 and 12.7 per cent; 1967-68, 15.5 and 8.3
per cent, as shown in Tables 27 and 28.

However, all those who were not "absorbed" could
not be considered as unemployed in the sense used in
labour statistics. In anticipation of good jobs some
graduates voluntarily did not accept the first ones
offered during the first months of job-search. Instead,
they waited. They cited various reasons for waiting,
some of which were voluntary while others were
involuntary. As waiting time lengthened, the proportion
that might be considered involuntarily unemployed, i.e.
those graduates who cited "no job opportunity" and
"ineligibility", decreased. Thus, the comparable
measure of the unemployment rate during each search
period was probably between the non-absorption rate and
the involuntary unemployment rate. After one year the
rate would be between the non-absorption rate of 22.8
per cent and the involuntary unemployment of 8.7 per
cent. After two years, the corresponding figures would
be between 9.2 and 4.0 per cent.[5]

The 1978 survey also supplies certain information
that permits inferences to be drawn from the labour
market "performance" of the graduates. It will be noted
(in Table 29) that graduates of state universities seem
to have the highest and fastest absorption rates, while
graduates of proprietary institutions have the lowest
rates. It is interesting to observe that graduates of
agricultural colleges were absorbed rather slowly but
that in the end they tended to catch up with the rest.
Further, graduates from Protestant and foundation
(non-profit, non-sectarian) schools tended to have
moderate absorption rates. The job success of graduates
from good private schools could compare well with
graduates from state universities. It would seem then
that the fast absorption rates were dependent not only
on the quality of schools but even more so on that of
the graduates themselves. But a firm relationship
between these variables cannot be established in the
absence of precise information.

Returns on college education

There have been some attempts to estimate the rate
of returns on various levels of education. The results
of the estimates indicate that the average returns on
college education were low. They were not uniformly
low, however. Basing itself on the FAPE Survey of
graduates who completed their studies in 1964 and 1965,
the ILO in 1974 estimated the rate of returns on various

Table 27: Percentage distribution of college graduates, by waiting time from graduation to first job in 1970, 1978

Waiting time	1963-64 Graduates	1967-68 Graduates	All graduates Surveyed in 1978
0	16.5	29.1)	55.2
Less than 6 months	55.3	39.7)	21.9
6 months to less than 1 year	11.3	15.7	13.6
1 year to less than 2 years	4.6	7.2)	
2 to 3 years	7.8	4.0)	9.2
3 or more years	4.9	4.3)	
Total of those responding	100.0	100.0	100.0
No response	28.1	20.4	-

Note: A preliminary report by FAPE's Higher Education and Labor Market Survey (HELMS) of 1978-79 graduates showed that the average rate of unemployment of the graduates was 21.4 per cent. The figure was from a draft table of the FAPE researchers.

Sources: (1963-64 and 1967-68), Higher Education Research Council: Higher education in the Philippines, 1970-71: A survey report. Manila, Ministry of Education, 1972; (1978), Table 19, "Higher education and labor market", Fund for Assistance to Private Education (FAPE) Review, Vol. X, Nos. 3 and 4, Jan./Apr. 1980.

college programmes to be roughly between -5 and +18 per cent. This surprisingly favourable result is, however, difficult to explain. It may be claimed that it was due to wide variations in relative scarcity and perhaps also in quality of graduates. The data to hand do not permit rigorous testing of this claim. For one thing, quality is difficult to measure; relative scarcity is equally elusive. It is however a hypothesis which cannot be ruled out.

College enrolment and graduates

Changes in enrolment and in the supply of graduates are analysed below as responses of students to conditions in labour markets.

College enrolment grew at a rapid but uneven rate during the post-war period. Enrolment in 1945-46 was 47,690; this number quadrupled in five years. A period of fluctuation ensued, moderate growth in later years, as shown in Table 30. By 1975-76, however, the enrolment reached a little over one million or 21 times the level in 1945-46. Over these years the average annual growth rate was 10.7 per cent.

The fluctuation in enrolment seems to reflect student response to market conditions. Increases in supply alternately overshot and undershot increases in demand. Apparently, the rapid growth in supply around 1950 outstripped the growth of demand for educated labour; hence, the sharp drop in enrolment in 1953-54. After overshooting the employment opportunities in 1956-60, the supply of new college graduates in the next 10 years increased as shown in Table 31. The market might have tightened somewhat after this period, giving encouraging signals for students to enrol. Thus we find that in the next five years, the total of graduates exceeded the additional employment openings.

This seems to imply that adjustment to demand was imperfect and came with a long time-lag. Imperfect information and delayed transmission of market signals led to over- and under-shooting of market demand. There was also a response-lag, due to the length of schooling, after the signals were recognised.

On the whole, however, we find (in Table 32) that the number of graduates produced closely matched the employment created from 1956 to 1977, after adjusting for their non-participation in the labour force. Labour force participation of college graduates was about 80 per cent. If this factor were applied to the total number of graduates from 1956 to 1977, the number

Table 28: Number and per cent distribution of employed graduate respondents, by reasons for delay in job and by waiting period, 1978

Reasons for delay	Low salary offer		Working condition		Advancement opportunity		Job too far		Voluntary (2)+(4)+(6)+(8)	No job opportunities	
Waiting period	(1)	(2) %	(3)	(4) %	(5)	(6) %	(7)	(8) %	(9) %	(10)	(11) %
Less than 1 month	0	0.0	1	50.0	1	50.0	0	0.0	100.0	0	0.0
1-2 months	167	29.2	63	11.0	120	20.9	73	12.8	73.9	145	25.3
3-4 months	80	24.3	37	12.2	60	18.2	47	14.3	69.0	120	31.0
5-6 months	67	21.7	30	9.7	55	17.8	54	17.5	66.7	96	31.1
7-12 months	77	16.0	58	12.1	82	17.0	71	14.8	59.9	189	39.3
More than 1-2 years	63	21.1	23	7.7	44	14.7	50	16.7	60.2	114	38.1
More than 2 years	43	21.3	15	7.4	27	13.4	29	14.3	56.4	87	43.0
0-6 months	314	25.5	131	10.7	236	19.2	174	14.1	69.6	361	29.3

Reasons for delay Waiting period	Eligibility (12)	(13) %	Unemployment (11)+(13) (14) %	Marriage (15)	(16) %	Underage (17)	(18) %	Total (19)	(20) %	Unemployment rate (20)+(14) (21) %
Less than 1 month	0	0.0	0.0	0	0.00	0	0.00	2	0.1	0.0
1-2 months	3	0.5	25.8	0	0.00	1	0.17	572	25.9	6.7
3-4 months	3	0.9	31.9	0	0.00	0	0.00	329	15.7	5.0
5-6 months	5	1.6	32.7	1	0.32	1	0.32	309	14.0	4.6
7-12 months	4	0.8	40.1	0	0.00	0	0.00	481	21.8	8.7
More than 1-2 years	3	1.0	39.1	1	0.33	1	0.33	299	13.5	5.3
More than 2 years	1	0.5	43.5	0	0.00	0	0.00	202	9.1	4.0
0-6 months	11	0.9	30.2	0	0.00	2	0.20	2 211	100.0	

Source: FAPE Review, Jan./Apr. 1981, Vol. X, Nos. 3 and 4, Table 19.

Table 29:   Absorption rate by school type (in percentages)

Waiting Period	School type					Private schools			
	U.P.	Other state colleges	Teacher training institutions	Agricultural colleges	Arts & trades	Catholic	Proprietary	Protestant	Foundation
After 6 months	79.8	80.0	78.6	72.2	76.6	64.81	61.8	72.0	62.4
After one year	93.7	94.4	88.4	85.4	89.4	81.71	80.3	85.5	85.3
After two years	97.9	97.7	94.9	96.3	93.6	91.61	91.1	93.2	97.8

Source: FAPE Review, Jan./Apr. 1980, Vol. X, Nos. 3 and 4.

Table 30: Growth of enrolment in higher education by sector, 1945-46 to 1975-76, selected years

School year	Public[a]		Private		Total
	No.	%	No.	%	
1945-46	2 812	5.90	44 878	94.10	47 690
1950-51	12 449	6.57	176 996	93.43	189 445
1953-54	14 967	8.74	156 208	91.26	171 175
1955-56	31 283	15.23	174 099	84.77	205 382
1960-61	39 095	13.01	261 477	86.99	300 572
1965-66	48 713	9.41	469 038	90.59	517 751
1970-71	53 109	8.33	584 171	91.67	637 280
1971-72	57 130	8.67	601 835	91.33	658 965
1972-73	130 105[b]	15.72	697 724[b]	84.28	827 829[b]
1973-74	145 097[b]	16.11	755 728[b]	83.89	900 825[b]
1974-75	154 326[b]	20.09	613 807[b]	79.91	768 133[b]
1975-76	183 502[b]	18.33	817 500[b]	81.67	1 001 002[b]

[a] Technical and normal schools, including state colleges and universities

[b] Projections only.

Sources: NEDA: 1977 Philippine Statistical Yearbook, pp. 559-561.

Table 31: <u>Growth and distribution of college graduates by area of specialisation (in percentages)</u>

	Commerce & business	Liberal arts & sciences	Teacher training	Engineering	Medical sciences	Law & foreign service	Music & fine arts	Food & nutrition	Nautical science	Agriculture	Chemistry	Total No.	Total %
1951-55	14.1	12.4	56.7	4.5	6.7	3.6	0.3	0.5	0.6	0.4	0.2	208 582	100.0
1956-60	30.8	17.2	20.2	8.3	12.3	6.7	0.6	1.4	0.9	0.8	0.6	176 095	100.0
1961-65	25.3	9.4	40.2	7.6	8.3	3.6	0.5	2.2	0.7	1.1	1.1	252 950	100.0
1966-70	22.4	10.9	50.9	5.8	4.9	1.6	0.6	1.1	0.7	0.7	0.5	431 194	100.0
1971-75	46.2	16.6	20.0	5.9	6.1	2.2	0.8	1.0	0.6	0.5	0.3	418 536	100.0

1964–65	18.7	9.9	55.2	5.6	5.6	1.6	0.2	1.2	0.6	0.6	0.7	81 295	100.0
1965–66	17.0	10.0	54.3	6.7	6.3	1.7	0.2	1.6	0.6	0.6	0.8	86 190	100.0
1966–67	17.6	11.0	55.7	5.5	5.2	1.6	0.6	1.1	0.5	0.8	0.3	84 023	100.0
1967–68	29.1	9.3	47.7	5.3	3.6	1.5	0.7	0.9	0.8	0.6	0.4	83 127	100.0
1968–69	28.7	14.3	42.6	5.6	3.9	1.7	0.7	0.9	0.7	0.6	0.2	96 642	100.0
1969–70	31.3	14.2	37.4	4.6	5.8	2.4	0.6	1.0	0.5	1.8	0.4	93 116	100.0
1970–71	38.6	15.0	26.6	7.8	5.7	1.8	0.7	1.1	0.6	1.7	0.3	91 371	100.0

Note: Row totals of percentages do not add up to 100.0 due to rounding of figures.

Source: Ministry of Education and Culture.

Table 32:   Increments in supply of college graduates and in employment, 1951-55 to 1975-77

	1956	1961	1965	1971	1975	1977
No. employed (in 000)	256	278	502	1 013	1 171	1 309
Change in employment		22	224	511	158	138
Attrition: 2% retirement		26	20	31	20	5
1% mortality, others		13	10	16	10	3
Change in total demand		61	254	558	188	146
Graduates		176	187	497	331	
Adjust for 80LFPR[a]		140	150	398	265	

a 80 per cent labour force participation rate.

Sources: 1980 Philippine Statistical Yearbook; NCSO: Labor Force Survey.

available for employment would be 1,188,000 (1,485,000 x 0.80). When this figure is further adjusted for emigration of about 300,000, it will be found that the country did not really produce many more college graduates than the estimated 1.4 million available jobs. This finding is consistent with the observed low unemployment rate of less than 2 per cent in professional and related occupations that required college-educated workers. However, this inference has to be qualified for possible underemployment of graduates due to mismatching and the unemployment of those who did not complete their college studies. All in all, it would seem that the main problem of the graduates was in finding where the suitable jobs were.

Student response was also shown in choice of field. There were fairly significant changes in the proportion of students who were in each field. Yet the three inexpensive but generally useful fields, i.e. business, liberal arts and teacher-training, continued to attract about 70 per cent of total enrolment. Engineering, law and medical sciences enrolled less than 10 per cent. Among these three, engineering enrolled more and more students, presumably because it could be offered at low cost. In the medical sciences, enrolment in the relatively inexpensive nursing programme increased more rapidly than in medicine. This growth was stimulated by foreign demand. All this seems to support the contention that enrolment in a programme is determined both by cost and by the demand for graduates of that programme.

5.   Concluding remarks

The foregoing is an analysis of the unemployment problem among the educated in the context of an imperfect labour surplus condition. This condition influences the decision of three economic units that interact in the labour-education market, viz. manpower, schools and employers. In a labour surplus situation, unemployment tends to be distributed to various groups or categories of labour and is unlikely to be confined to the unskilled agricultural workers in which the surplus is concentrated. The unemployment rate together with the wage rate affects decisions on education and jobs, because students try to choose the sort of education that will give them the highest wage for a given probability of unemployment or the lowest unemployment probability for a given wage rate. This choice, however, is constrained by their financial resources and available information about the labour market and about their personal abilities.

The study has highlighted the implication of these
constraints on decisions made by students and
consequently on the response of schools. Limited
financial resources due to low incomes and the
unavailability of loans for education restrict choices
to low-cost programmes. Schools that are wholly
dependent on student fees, in turn, cater for the
maximum number of students by offering low-cost
courses. The educational system thus allocates
resources to these programmes irrespective of their
relative returns or the relevant rate of unemployment.
At the same time, imprecise information leads to
erroneous estimation of expected benefits and prospects
of employment. These imperfections slow down market
adjustment.

The availability of inexpensive college education
has permitted the rapid growth of college-educated
labour, the overall result of which was the so-called
educated unemployment. The reported open unemployment
rate for college graduates was high relative to the
total, especially in comparison with that of elementary
school-leavers. But after adjusting the other rates for
underemployment in terms of desired work hours and
employment as unpaid family workers, it was found that
the comparable rate for college graduates was low.
College graduates worked in white-collar occupations at
regular hours on a full-time basis so that
underemployment due to short hours was low, while that
for manual workers was high.

Mismatches among college graduates were also high.
Almost one-half of employed graduates worked in
non-professional callings and in jobs that normally
required below-college qualifications. It has been
argued that the mismatches were more apparent than real
and that the opportunity cost of unutilised college
education and academic specialisation may not be large.
Some graduates who were employed in jobs requiring less
than college education might not be underemployed at
all, if that education was adequate for the job. It is
not clear, therefore, whether underemployment due to
mismatching was really high. In the face of imperfect
knowledge and financial constraints, the apparent
mismatch was perhaps a measure of flexibility on the
part of both labour and employers in job placement
decisions. This may after all be considered as a
positive thing because it minimises the cost of
potential structural unemployment.

The responsibility of the schools in the
unemployment problem lies not so much in catering for
student demand for low-cost programmes but in the lack

of creativity shown in producing educational programmes that meet the skill requirements of the economy.

There is strong reason to believe that the uneven quality of schools made college diplomas poor indicators of educational proficiency. Thus employers have to incur high costs in obtaining reliable information about the qualifications and skills of applicants. This process lengthens recruitment, implies prolonged job-search and explains in part the high unemployment rate among new graduates.

The relative abundance of college graduates accounted for the generally low rate of return on educational investment. The rates are not uniformly low, but vary with relative scarcity and with success in employment performance.

Moreover, Government policy did not seem to help much in improving the functioning of the labour market. Its policy in the development of the post-elementary education system has been almost one of laissez faire. However, the Government has been expanding its role in higher education since the mid-1970s and this trend is expected to continue. A programme for improving elementary education is "on stream", and the new target for quality improvement is secondary education. This was envisaged in the 1978-82 National Development Plan which called for the institution of an educational planning office. According to the Plan, the planning office would be given the task of solving efficiency and equity problems, especially in higher education. This task would not be easy, given the size and complexity of the system, including the freedom that the latter has been used to.

Finally, this study analysed the root cause of the problem to be the reliance on market forces in a situation of poverty and the virtual lack of loans to finance education. This did not permit the students to make the socially optimum education decisions, the results of which are the observed level and structure of unemployment, occupation and earnings.

CHAPTER APPENDIX

CONSTRAINED OPTIMISATION MODEL
AND THE SUPPLY OF GRADUATES

In the model below, we assume that families maximise the net worth of the education of each of their children over mutually exclusive options, j, j=1, 2, ... E, subject to two constraints, namely, cost and ability. ("Net worth" is used as synonymous with returns on education.)

$$\text{Max} \quad (NW_j)$$

$$NW_j^i = \sum_{t=1}^{j} \frac{R_t^{ij} - C_t^{ij}}{(1 + r)^t} - \sum_{t=1}^{e} \frac{R_t^{ie} - C_t^{ie}}{(1 + r)^t}$$

s.t.

$$C_t^j \leq B_t^i, \quad C_t^e \leq B_t^i$$

for each year of schooling, t=1, 2, ..., j corresponding to age 7, 8, ... j+6. For those desiring college,

$$A^i \geq \bar{A}^j, \quad A^1 \geq \bar{A}^e$$

R is expected benefit, C is total cost for each year t in pursuit of education, j or e by child i. The budget B_t for each child of age $\underline{a}$ is a function of family income Y_f.

$$B_t^i \equiv B_a^i = b_a(Y_f^i)$$

$\bar{A}$ is the minimum ability required for education e, j. These constraints determine the set of alternatives that are relevant to each child of a given background and ability.

Consider a population of children with its distribution by family income and distance to schools. Classify the children according to their school budget at each school age and map this distribution as to the cost of schooling at each level, Grades 1, 2, ..., that corresponds to each age. Children of age a can go to school so long as $C^j \leq B_a$. From this mapping, distinguish the children who can from those who cannot pursue each education option that corresponds to age a. Then impose an ability constraint. This reduces the number of children who can choose certain options.

In practical terms, this scenario means that the richer and brighter a child is, the larger is his or her opportunity set. But a poor dull child in a distant location may face a much smaller set than that of a bright counterpart. On the other hand, superior quality of home environment and of school to which rich children are sent can, up to certain limit, sometimes offset inferior inherent ability and break the (learnt) ability constraint of higher education.

In the scenario above, market adjustments relative to rates of return on education are made within defined sets of alternatives. A decreasing proportion of the population is expected to respond to positive returns on higher education or in particular, on the expensive college degree programmes. For this reason, disequilibrium in rates of return between costly and inexpensive programmes may occur and persist. This is illustrated in Figure 3.

Without financial constraints, the potential supply curves of graduates of programmes requiring different abilities may be represented in Figure 3 as GR_AAS_A, GR_BBS_B and GR_CCS_C. The curves are, respectively, the supply curves of graduates from programmes with increasing ability requirements. GR is the gross return that just covers the cost of going from a low programme to the next higher programme, say, from A to B, then from B to C. More precisely,

$$GR_B = \sum_{t=1}^{T} \frac{R_{Bt}}{(1 + r)^t} - \sum_{t=1}^{T} \frac{R_{At} - C_{At}}{(1 + r)^t} = \sum_{t=1}^{T} \frac{C_{Bt}}{(1 + r)^t}$$

$$GR_C = \sum_{t=1}^{T} \frac{R_{Ct}}{(1 + r)^t} - \sum_{t=1}^{T} \frac{R_{At} - C_{At}}{(1 + r)^t} = \sum_{t=1}^{T} \frac{C_{Ct}}{(1 + r)^t}$$

$$GR_A = \sum_{t=1}^{T} \frac{R_{At}}{(1 + r)^t} - \sum_{t=1}^{T} \frac{R_{Ot}}{(1 + r)^t} = \sum_{t=1}^{T} \frac{C_{At}}{(1 + r)^t}$$

R is the expected monetary benefit and C is cost of tuition, books and supplies at time t.

Assume that the demand curve for B is D_B. Equilibrium will be at Q_1 and gross return at GR'_B.

Figure 3:   Labour market for graduates and skilled
            workers, II

GR, Gross Return

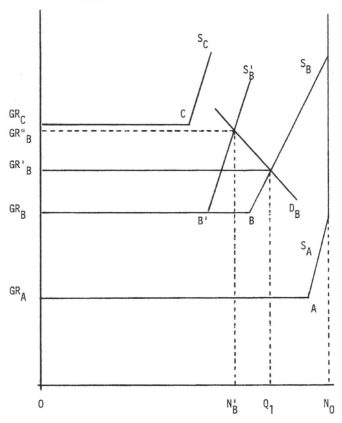

Number of graduates and skilled workers

Individuals with talent for programme B, i.e. $GR_B B$ will reap some rent to this ability by income $GR'_B - GR_B$. Consider a case where there are financial constraints that reduce and shift the supply curve to $GR_B B'S'_B$. With the same demand curve, D_B, equilibrium is now at N'_B and returns on the programme are now GR''_B. The additional returns on the investment in the programme are due to the financial constraint that makes its graduates scarce. The supply of A is given by the initial population N_0. Assume the wage of A is GR_A. Those who will remain in programme A will be $N_0 - N'_B$. The observed wage differential is increased from $GR'_B - GR_A$ to $GR''_B - GR_A$. One part of this average differential is rent to ability; the other is rent to affluence.

We underscore the implications of the budget constraints on decision. Irrespective of what may be the relative non-negative gross returns on schooling at different levels, school attendance at each level will be mainly a function of such variables as family income, distance to school, and level and type of programme. Here we note how the ability requirement and the cost of schooling determine the position and slope of the supply curve of graduates.

Notes

[1] These estimates are based on an inadequate-income concept of underemployment. In 1971, 70 per cent of the urban labour force, excluding professionals and civil servants, were earning 68 per cent of the wage in the organised sector. The gap of 32 per cent times 70 per cent plus 11 per cent open unemployment gives a total of 33.4 per cent unemployment. A similar estimate of total unemployment in the rural sector was about 32 per cent. See Mission Report, pp. 7f.

[2] The figures also imply an employment rate of about 92 per cent, or an unemployment rate of 8 per cent.

[3] About one-third of all medical science students in 1978-79 were in nursing. Enrolment increased from about 7,000 in 1960 to almost 29,000 in 1978-79, mainly in response to demand for nursing personnel overseas.

[4] Trend analysis of labour force characteristics is for the period up to 1975, when the population base and reference period used in the surveys were changed.

[5] Some 38.1 per cent of the 22.8 per cent of the graduates who were not employed reported "no job opportunities". Hence, involuntary unemployment would be (0.381 x 0.228 = 0.0869), 8.7 per cent. Further, the 4.0 per cent is the product of 0.092 and 0.430.

BIBLIOGRAPHY

Abad, G.S., S.J. "Urban unemployment in the Philippines", in Papers and proceedings of the workshop on manpower and human resources. Los Banos, Laguna, Philippines, Continuing Education Centre, UPLB, 13-15 Oct. 1972.

Abella, M. "Export of Filipino manpower: A question of competitive advantage", in Philippine Labour Review, Vol. I, No. 2, Aug. 1976, pp. 89-94.

Bautista, R.; and Power, J. Industrial promotion policy in the Philippines. Manila, Philippine Institute for Development Studies, 1979.

Blaug, M. "Educated unemployment in Asia: A contrast between India and the Philippines", in Philippine Economic Journal, Vol. XI, No. 1, First Semester, 1972.

Castillo, G.T. "Education for agriculture", in P. Foster and J.R. Sheffield (eds.): Education for rural development. London, Evans Brothers, Ltd., 1973.

Corpuz, O. "Sociological environment of the management of rural development", in Roger Cuyno et al. (eds.): Management of rural development in the 80s: Philippine reflections. Los Banos, Laguna: Centre for Management of Rural Development (MARD), University of the Philippines, 1982, pp. 29-36.

Diaz, R. "The role of vocational and accelerated training programmes", Papers and proceedings of the workshop on manpower and human resources, Part III: Policy. Los Banos, Laguna, Continuing Education Centre, 13-15 Oct. 1972.

FAPE. "Higher education and the labour market", Fund for Assistance to Private Education (FAPE) Review, Vol. X, Nos. 3 and 4, Jan./Apr. 1980.

Felipe, M. "Earnings of University of the Philippines graduates", Unpublished undergraduate paper for the U.P. School of Economics, 1978.

Higher Education Research Council. Higher education in the Philippines, 1970-71. A survey report. Manila, Ministry of Education, 1972.

Hooley, R. An assessment of macroeconomic policy framework for employment generation in the Philippines, a report submitted to the USAID/Philippines, Apr. 1981.

IBRD. Philippine vocational training project, Report
No. 3750b-PH. 26 Aug. 1982.

ILO. Philippines National programme for development and
training of manpower for employment; Project findings
and recommendations. Geneva, 1980, PHI/74/010,
restricted.

---. Sharing in development: A programme of employment
equity and growth for the Philippines. Geneva, 1974.

Leonor, M.D. "Human capital and migration", in Journal
of Agricultural Economics and Development, Vol. III,
No. 1, Jan. 1973, pp. 73-79.

---. "Diplomas for development? Focus on graduate
unemployment in the Philippines", in Studies in
Education and Development, University of the
Philippines at Los Banos, Discussion Paper No. 3, s.
1973.

---. "The uses of the National College Entrance Examination (NCEE) in research and evaluation", in Technical
papers for the seminar workshop on the relevance of
the NCEE programme for career guidance. Manila, FAPE,
1974.

---. "Non-formal education and rural development in
Seameo countries", in Journal of Agricultural
Economics and Development, Vol. V, No. 1, Jan. 1975,
pp. 36-50.

---. "How attitudes towards work develop: Evidence from
Project Soutele, Philippines, 1975", Geneva, ILO,
1981, typescript.

---. "Setting targets for education as a basic need", in
Richards and Leonor (eds.): Target setting for basic
needs. Geneva, ILO, 1982.

Miao, E. "The stucture and performance of the proprie-
tary institutions of higher education in the
Philippines", Ph.D. dissertation, University of
Wisconsin, Madison, 1971.

Ministry of Education and Culture. "Progress report on
the study of tuition fees in private institutions",
Division of Research and Evaluation, Manila, 1969.

Richards, P.; Leonor, M.D.   Education and income distribution in Asia. London, Croom Helm, 1981.

Sanyal, B.; Perfecto, W.; Arcelo, A.   Higher education
and the labour market in the Philippines. Paris,
UNESCO, 1981.

Sicat, G.; Power, J. Industry and trade in some developing countries. Oxford University Press, 1971.

Tan, E.; Miao, E.   "The structure and performance of
Philippine education institutions", IEDR Discussion
Paper No. 71, 12 July, 1971, U.P. School of Economics,
Diliman, Quezon City.

---; Uy, B.B.   "Determinants of performance - the
University of the Philippines entrance examination",
in Population, resources and education in the
Philippine future. 1977.

---; Nayavitit, W.   "Distribution flow of education in
Thailand", IEDR Discussion Paper No. 80-08, November
1980, U.P. School of Economics, Diliman, Quezon City.

Tidalgo, R.L.   Wage and wage structure in the
Philippines, 1956 to 1969. Quezon City, School of
Economics, 1981.

Williamson, J.; DeVoretz, D.J.   "Education as an asset in
the Philippine economy", in M. Concepción (ed.):
Philippine population in the seventies. Manila, U.P.
Population Institute, 1969.

5 INDONESIA

I. INTRODUCTION

Unemployment is a relatively new concept to Indonesia, following on the international concern reflected in the ILO Reports of the 1970s. While the problem of surplus labour in Java was noted as far back as the middle of the last century,[1] measures to deal with it until very recently emphasised population movement rather than job creation. The first clearly employment-oriented programme was the major public works project begun in the early 1970s to provide off-farm employment for the rural poor in Java. There has been no equivalent programme for the urban unemployed. Educated unemployment is an even newer concern; indeed, for many years, overemployment of the educated, "job inflation", and multiple job holding has been considered an equally great, if not greater, problem.[2]

In the 35 years of its nationhood, Indonesia has gone through several distinct phases, each of which has had its own impact on education and on employment. In the first ten-year period (1945-1955) there were enormous efforts to develop the educational system with few resources, either human or capital. This was a period of intense private sector contribution to education at all levels, and also a period when the lack of trained manpower necessitated the intake of many into posts which had heretofore been reserved for those with high educational qualifications. The expectations of parents and students from education were inflated as those with even modest levels of education were pressed into service to replace the departing colonial officials. This was the beginning of the "job-inflation" where the services of a handful of highly educated persons were rationed out among many agencies of government as well as among the private sector.

The period which extended roughly from the mid-1950s through the mid-1960s was one of increasing economic chaos, galloping inflation and the cessation of international aid. Salaries eroded and the phenomenon of multiple jobs increased accordingly, but now with

more emphasis on the individual's need for additional
salary than on the needs of the economy for scarce
skills. The quality of education became more dilute as
greater numbers pressed on existing facilities. Towards
the end of this period, enrolments began actually to
decline as the burden of financing the system was thrown
more and more heavily on the parents of those seeking
schooling.[3]

With the accession of the New Order Government in
1966, attention was turned first towards monetary
control, then to rehabilitation of old and creation of
new economic infrastructure, where little had been done
since the colonial period. It was only with the sudden
increase in government income from oil, beginning around
1973, that a period of expansion in education began,
first with the primary level, and subsequently at
secondary and higher levels. The private sector
continued to play a large part in educational provision,
particularly at secondary and higher levels, and aid
programmes were reinstated. This period also saw the
first of a series of national studies on labour force
and employment.[4] In line with its new emphasis on
distributing the oil windfall more equitably, the
Government developed its first major labour-intensive
public works programmes and, formally at least, included
labour intensity as one of the goals of industrial
development and foreign investment. Along with this,
the traditional methods of dealing with surplus labour
in Java by moving poor households to the Outer Islands
continued.[5]

Indonesia now appears to be on the threshhold of
yet another phase. The massive increases in oil income
which were a major feature of government activity in the
last half of the 1970s are expected to level off, and
the favourable balance-of-payments situation of the past
seven or eight years may be giving way to somewhat more
austere conditions. The recent redistributional
policies of the Government are only just beginning to
have a noticeable impact on the labour force. Only
preliminary figures from the 1980 Population Census on
labour force have been published as yet, while the 1976
and 1978 Labour Force Surveys tend to reflect the impact
of various policies of the 1950s and 1960s. It may be
five or ten years more before national data can show
clearly the impact of these more recent policies.

The 1980 Census has been widely publicised as
showing average annual growth rates of population of
2.34 per cent, giving rise to early estimates of annual
labour force growth during the next few years of well
over 2 million a year. But while this population
growth rate was the average for the period, by the end

of the period the growth rate had decreased to something like 1.9-2.0 per cent per year.[6] Even so, annual increases in the labour force may still be expected to be of the order of 2 million during much of the next decade.

The dimensions of the problem of unemployment in Indonesia form the first part of this paper, followed by a discussion of recent trends in employment and unemployment in so far as they can be identified. Some preliminary results of a study of the employment experience of a large sample of recent school-leavers lead into a discussion of the education system and its relation to educated unemployment. The second main section looks at economic policies and their impact on employment; this is followed by an examination of wage structure and effective demand for educated labour. The final section raises economic and educational issues and concludes with some alternatives for the reduction of educated unemployment and underemployment.

This paper, therefore, tries to bring together a picture of the current labour force and educational system, outcomes of two quite distinct periods of recent history, at a time when the impact of a third period is not yet fully felt, and also at a time when a fourth period may be expected to emerge. The efforts of government, academics and researchers have so far been taken up with dealing with short-term developments in a series of five-year plans, each of which has grown out of an earlier one. The coming phase will certainly provide the incentive, and must be given the opportunity, to look at these problems from a longer-term perspective.

II. THE DIMENSIONS OF UNEMPLOYMENT

The labour force of Indonesia in 1980

The 1980 National Census of Population of Indonesia reported open unemployment at 1.7 per cent of the labour force, scarcely a rate to cause alarm when compared to rates of 3-5 per cent in neighbouring countries, or 10-15 per cent or more in industrialised countries.[7] But, as has often been pointed out, a country can have almost any rate of unemployment it chooses, depending on how it measures employment and labour force participation.

In both the 1978 Labour Force Survey and the 1980 Census the "employed" were defined as those who worked at least one hour in the week preceding enumeration, for pay or profit, or in a household enterprise without pay. Farmers (including landless labourers as well as

landholders) waiting for harvest or planting were
considered employed even if they did not work the one
hour; tradesmen and professionals who maintained a
practice were also considered employed. This
definition of "employed" naturally cast the net very
wide and resulted in low rates of unemployment.

Labour force participation rates

Censuses and labour force surveys in Indonesia
measure labour force participation from age 10, although
the legal minimum working age is 14.[8] The extent to
which children aged 10-14 are available or ready for
work depends on the economic status of the household and
on the availability of schools. It is not surprising,
therefore, to see that participation rates of this age
group are only about 4 per cent in urban areas. In
rural areas where "participation" may quite possibly
rise and fall with household need for casual work
opportunity, the rates are higher, particularly for
males (Table 33).

With the exception of the youngest age group in
urban areas, female participation rates are everywhere
lower than male. But, as will be seen below, the
unemployment rate of females is heavily dependent upon
how participation rates are defined. As Arndt and
Sundrum have pointed out, "A woman who works in the
field as an unpaid family worker helping to produce a
crop of rice which could be sold on the market for
'profit' even if it is in fact consumed by the
subsistence household, is classified as a member of the
labour force, but not if she merely hand-pounds or cooks
the rice".[9]

At the age of 15 and above, where participation in
the labour force is to be expected, less than 40 per
cent of the 15-19 age group were reported to be in the
labour force in 1980. In urban areas the proportion
was less than one-quarter, a low rate which is perhaps
accounted for .by the location of secondary schools
almost exclusively in these areas. In rural areas,
however, the low participation rates for males aged
15-19 (55 per cent) cannot be attributed to high
educational provision. The low rates may be due to the
non-participation of "discouraged" workers whose
inactivity may have something to do with the definitions
of employment used in the census, particularly as unpaid
family labour, or to the respondents' understanding of
the question.

Participation rates by educational level indicate
that those with vocational education maintain
consistently and substantially higher rates of

Table 33: Labour force participation rates, 1980 (in percentages)

| | Age groups | | | | | |
	10–14	15–19	20–24	25–29	30 +	Total
Indonesia	11.1	39.2	54.4	63.9	63.3	49.9
Urban	4.0	24.7	47.0	59.8	58.3	41.9
Rural areas	13.2	44.5	57.2	65.3	64.8	52.3
Males	12.6	47.6	79.3	92.2	88.3	68.2
Urban	3.3	27.2	67.5	89.6	85.4	60.0
Rural	15.2	54.8	84.2	93.2	89.1	70.6
Females	9.5	31.1	33.2	36.1	39.4	32.2
Urban	4.7	22.3	26.9	28.1	30.2	24.0
Rural	10.9	34.4	35.4	38.6	41.7	34.6

Source: Population of Indonesia, Results of the Sub-Sample of the 1980 Population Census, Series S1, (Jakarta, Central Bureau of Statistics, 1982).

participation than do those from the general academic
schools (Table 34). It is perhaps not surprising to
see that 30-40 per cent of males with lower secondary
education are not in the labour force, considering the
almost universal desire to return to school, but the
rate of only 72 per cent for males with upper secondary
education shows the degree to which this group also
holds out for further education.

Unemployment rates

The pattern of unemployment rates by age, sex, and
urban/rural distribution is given in Table 35 for
1980. The pattern is one which it has by now become
common to expect: higher rates for urban than for rural
areas, and the highest rates among the young, almost all
of whom are first-time jobseekers. The very low rates
in rural areas do not, of course, indicate full
employment, given the definition of employment used in
the census. Where as many as 20 per cent of the
employees in agriculture are landless labourers,
employment of a few hours a week is insufficient to
provide a living wage.[10] The extent of
underemployment and unemployment in rural areas is
probably seriously underestimated in both the labour
force surveys and the census. In urban areas, the
disguised unemployment common to rural areas (where some
kind of traditional village welfare still operates,
though certainly not to the extent that it has in the
past) is less possible, and open unemployment more
visible. But even in urban areas, by the age of 30
unemployment rates drop to less than 2 per cent.

The same rate of unemployment can, of course, arise
as a result of small numbers of persons being unemployed
over long periods of time, or of large numbers of
persons being unemployed for short periods. The 1980
Census does not give any information on the length of
unemployment, although the 1978 Labour Force Survey
indicated that in urban areas about one-third of the
unemployed had been looking for work for less than three
months and "hard core" unemployment of more than a
year's duration accounted for only about one-quarter of
the total (Table 36).

Underemployment

The census and labour force surveys do not provide
breakdowns on labour utilisation by level of education,
but two large sample surveys during the 1970s attempted

Table 34:   Labour force participation rates by
             educational level, 1980
             (population aged 10+)

	Urban	Rural	Total
Males	%	%	%
No school	71.7	81.4	80.4
Some primary	49.7	64.0	61.6
Completed primary	61.5	73.5	70.3
Lower secondary			
Academic	52.4	60.5	56.4
Vocational	64.8	73.5	69.8
Upper secondary			
Academic	70.3	76.9	72.3
Vocational	80.5	85.6	83.3
Tertiary	89.1	89.9	89.4
Females			
No school	31.9	40.4	39.2
Some primary	20.8	30.0	28.1
Completed primary	18.9	31.4	27.9
Lower secondary			
Academic	14.4	23.1	18.0
Vocational	23.8	30.4	27.3
Upper secondary			
Academic	29.7	36.4	31.6
Vocational	52.5	62.7	57.4
Tertiary	64.3	54.4	61.6

Source: As in Table 33.

Table 35: Unemployment rates, by sex, age and urban/rural location, 1980 (first-time jobseekers in parenthesis) (in percentages)

	Age groups					
	10-14	15-19	20-24	25-29	30+	Total
Indonesia	3.7 (2.7)	4.0 (3.0)	3.6 (2.5)	1.6 (0.8)	0.8 (0.2)	1.7 (1.0)
Urban areas	6.9 (6.3)	8.0 (7.1)	7.5 (6.2)	2.8 (1.7)	1.7 (0.3)	3.1 (2.3)
Rural areas	3.5 (2.4)	3.2 (2.1)	2.4 (2.1)	1.2 (0.5)	0.8 (0.2)	1.4 (0.7)
Males	3.0 (2.2)	3.7 (2.8)	3.4 (2.4)	1.4 (0.6)	0.3 (0.1)	1.5 (0.8)
Urban	6.3 (5.9)	8.4 (7.5)	7.6 (6.2)	2.6 (1.3)	1.8 (0.3)	2.9 (2.0)
Rural	2.9 (2.0)	2.9 (2.0)	2.0 (1.2)	1.0 (0.3)	0.5 (0.1)	1.1 (0.5)
Females	4.7 (3.3)	4.5 (3.2)	4.0 (2.6)	2.1 (1.2)	1.3 (0.8)	2.4 (1.3)
Urban	7.3 (6.5)	7.5 (6.6)	7.2 (6.2)	3.5 (2.9)	1.7 (0.5)	3.5 (2.9)
Rural	4.4 (2.9)	3.8 (2.3)	3.2 (1.7)	1.8 (0.8)	1.4 (0.4)	2.2 (1.0)

Source: As for Table 33.

Table 36: Unemployed workers, by period of time seeking work

	Less than 3 months	4-12 months	More than 1 year	Total %	Number
Urban males	34.5	45.3	20.2	100	393 778
Urban females	30.8	41.8	27.4	100	99 390
Rural males	61.5	33.3	5.2	100	585 167
Rural females	51.5	34.7	13.8	100	238 401

Source: Keadaan Angkatan Kerja di Indonesia 1978, (Jakarta, Central Bureau of Statistics) Feb. 1981, Report No. VP-KK 0062-8101.

to assess underemployment in terms of hours worked and
in terms of income earned.   Both found that the
educated worked fewer hours than the less educated and
that the educated had negligible rates of
underemployment in terms of insufficient income,[11]
probably because the educated were more likely to be
visibly unemployed while waiting for suitable work than
they were to be employed in part-time or low paying
positions.

Unemployment and education

     In his study of unemployment and education, Blaug
points out that the educated have high rates of
unemployment, not because they are educated, but because
they are young and inexperienced.[12]   Table 37
confirms that general finding for Indonesia, where
unemployment rates rise regularly with educational
level, and rates are generally higher for those with
academic education than for those with vocational.   But
it is also important to keep in mind that high rates may
be associated with very small numbers: thus the 4.6 per
cent rate for females with tertiary education refers to
less than 4,000 persons, while 0.7 per cent for rural
males with no education refers to more than 50,000
persons.
     Data on the unemployed by age and educational
attainment are not yet available from the 1980 Census.
Table 38, with 1978 Labour Force Survey data, indicates
that not only do rates increase with educational level,
but they do so for the older age groups as well as the
younger, though not to the same degree.   Even among
those aged 30 or more, higher educational levels are
associated with higher rates of unemployment.   One
reason is the late age of completion of tertiary
studies.   Not only is age 20 or 21 common for
completion of secondary studies, but students completing
tertiary education in the past have commonly been in
their late twenties or even in their thirties.   Up to
very recently, the university system allowed almost
unlimited time to complete a course and it is quite
possible that a fair number of first-time jobseekers may
be found even among the 30+ group.   Another reason is
that entry to the labour force is, especially for the
better educated, a fairly leisurely process.   On the
other hand, it must be kept in mind that the very small
size of sample of the labour force surveys may affect
some of these results.
     In the 1980 Census, 1.6 million young men in the
15-24 age group were neither working, nor looking for

Table 37: Unemployment rates by educational level, 1980 (in percentages)

	Urban		Rural		Total	
	Male	Female	Male	Female	Male	Female
No school	1.0	0.7	0.7	1.8	0.7	1.7
Some primary	2.2	2.9	0.9	2.1	1.1	2.2
Completed primary	2.9	4.5	1.3	2.4	1.7	2.8
Lower secondary	3.6	6.1	2.2	4.4	2.8	5.2
Academic	3.7	6.8	2.4	4.7	3.0	5.7
Vocational	3.1	3.3	1.7	3.5	2.2	3.4
Upper secondary	4.8	7.9	2.7	5.3	3.8	6.7
Academic	4.4	10.2	3.2	10.0	4.0	10.1
Vocational	5.2	6.4	2.3	4.0	3.7	5.1
Tertiary	1.4	5.4	1.0	2.3	1.3	4.6
Average	2.9	3.5	1.1	2.1	1.5	2.4

Source: As for Table 33.

Table 38: Unemployment by age and level of education, 1978 (in percentages)

	Age Groups					
	10-15	15-19	20-24	25-29	30 +	Total
Indonesia	3.3	8.0	7.6	2.1	0.4	2.5
No school	0.5	3.9	3.7	1.3	0.2	0.6
Some primary	4.2	6.1	3.9	1.2	0.4	2.0
Completed primary	3.2	9.6	6.1	1.9	0.5	3.4
Lower secondary						
Academic	0	16.6	16.4	5.0	1.5	7.5
Vocational	0	22.5	12.3	1.6	0.5	5.8
Upper secondary						
Academic	0	66.1	26.9	6.3	2.0	9.5
Vocational	0	39.5	27.5	5.3	1.5	11.0
Tertiary	0	0	27.0	11.6	1.1	4.5

Source: Keadaan Angkatan Kerja di Indonesia 1978 (Jakarta, Central Bureau of Statistics), Report VP KK-0062.8101, Feb. 1981.

work, nor attending school.   An additional 600,000
inactive males gave as their reason for their inactivity
"home housework".   The high rates of young able males
who are thus outside the labour force have been noted by
several authorities who attribute their inactivity to
their being "discouraged workers".[13]   These responses
do not explain why such large numbers of young able
males should consider themselves outside the workforce,
but this problem was investigated in more detail in a
recent study of school-leavers.

The 1976-1978 tracer study

Governmental and parental concern over the high
rates of unemployment among recent school-leavers and
over the "relevance" of the school system to the
national development programme led the Department of
Education to conduct a three-year longitudinal study of
the employment experience of some 10,000 students
completing the final year of primary and secondary
school cycles between 1976 and 1978 in eight widely
varying regions of Indonesia.[14]   The study set itself
to investigate whether the vocational schools were
indeed acting as terminal schools, whether they were
justified in terms of the kinds of employment found by
their graduates, how this compared to employment
obtained by students from the general academic schools,
and what role, if any, the schools played in assisting
their graduates to find employment.   The second main
area of investigation was the process by which new
entrants made their way into the labour force, what
kinds of efforts they made and, for those who obtained
jobs, how occupation and remuneration related to the
level, type and quality of the school attended.

Entry into the labour force
and duration of unemployment

The point at which a young person ceases to be
economically inactive and becomes "unemployed" is vague
and ill-defined.   Does a first-timer become unemployed
when he first feels or decides that he would like a job,
or when he first makes an effort to find one?   Is a
single effort over a period of a year sufficient to make
him "unemployed", particularly if at the same time he
still harbours hopes of continued study?   These
questions were not adequately answered by the tracer
study but some data were collected which throw a little
light on this grey area.
Among those who were employed a year after leaving
school, two-thirds to three-quarters had found work

within three months of beginning the job search, and
only about 10 per cent had taken more than eight months
to find work (Table 39).   In contrast, two-thirds of
those who had not found work within a year after leaving
school had been looking for work for longer than eight
months.

The study also found that only a very few of those
still looking for work at the end of one year after
leaving school had begun their search immediately after
leaving school; almost all had had a "resting" period,
ranging from a few weeks to several months, before they
reported themselves as actively seeking work.   For most
school-leavers there is clearly an elastic but fairly
lengthy period when the hope of continuing to the next
level of education takes precedence over the less
attractive and certainly less familiar alternative of
employment.   It was found, furthermore, that this
queueing for return to school was worth while in that
about one-third did manage to re-enter after a year's
wait, though often not in the school of their first
choice.   While there are, undoubtedly, many discouraged
job seekers among Indonesia's unemployed, the tracer
study indicates that many of the young inactive are not
so much "discouraged" workers as "hopeful" candidates
for re-entry to the educational system, particularly in
urban areas.

The job search

Students in the tracer study felt that the main
factor in finding a job was having good "connections",
and the principal (and for many the only) means of
search was informing one's friends and family that one
was in the market for a job.   Of those who were still
unemployed a year after leaving school, 15 per cent had
done nothing specific to look for work, half had made
one or two efforts, usually verbal, and only 35 per cent
had made more than three efforts to find work.   This
low level of activity seems to be related to a common
and pervasive feeling among young first-timers, more
exaggerated among those from general than among those
from vocational schools, that they had little or nothing
in the way of skills to offer employers.

One important obstacle in the job search was the
school-leaver's identification of the kind of job or
jobs for which he might be qualified.   Both the
employed and the unemployed school-leaver felt narrowly
bound to the specialisation of the school attended; as
just noted, this specialisation was not necessarily one
chosen for its own sake.   The extent to which this

Table 39:   Duration of unemployment of the employed and unemployed (in percentages)

School Level	Less than 3 months	4-7 months	8 months or more	Total
Employed				
Primary/Lower secondary				
Males	74	14	12	100
Females	81	5	14	100
Average	76	12	13	100
Upper secondary				
Males	57	22	12	100
Females	67	22	5	100
Average	65	23	10	100
Unemployed				
Primary	9	2	88	100 (44)
Lower secondary	15	15	70	100 (127)
Upper secondary	18	20	63	100 (757)
Average	16	18	65	100 (928)

Source: C.M. Widodo and Konta Damanik, The employment experience of school leavers (Jakarta, Indonesia Department of Education and Culture, Office of Educational and Cultural Research and Development, 1979), p. 69, mimeo.

variety of specialised schools limits the confidence of
their graduates needs to be more seriously considered.

Reliance on casual information for job search is
understandable, given the nature of newspaper
advertisement or the role of employment agencies. In a
small study of the role of newspapers in employment
recruitment, it was found that less than 3 per cent of
all jobs advertised were posts for which inexperienced
school-leavers or graduates would be considered.[15]
Vacancies registered with the employment agencies
operated by the Department of Manpower were also
overwhelmingly for experienced workers, while private
employment agencies dealt only with top management and
the highly skilled. Recruitment through newspaper
advertisements is moreover limited to the largest of the
national dailies and little use is made of this channel
in any but the capital city and half a dozen of the
largest cities. Many students in the tracer study were
quite unaware that the Department of Manpower maintained
employment registries.

Those who were looking for jobs were somewhat more
mobile than those who had already found them and
unemployment rates were much higher among those who had
never moved than among those who did move. One-fifth
of the active males moved residence in the year after
leaving school; of these, nearly two-thirds were
unemployed. About half the movers went to the five
large cities of Java, two-thirds of them to Jakarta and
the remaining one-third to the other four major cities.

Clark analysed the movement of school-leavers into
and out of jobs.[16] Many first-time jobs are
temporary and the proportion of school-leavers who have
worked at least once since leaving school is somewhat
higher than the proportion at work two years after
leaving school. It was not uncommon to have two or
three such short-term jobs before moving into relatively
permanent employment, but it appears that this kind of
experience is not a stepping stone to more satisfactory
employment. Those who waited did, in general, get
better jobs than those who entered the labour force
immediately after leaving school. Girls tended to find
work more quickly than boys, but at lower rates of pay.

Aspirations

One of the more interesting points which arose out
of the tracer study was the attempt to identify and
measure attitudes towards work. A list of 36
occupations was given to both the employed and the
unemployed school-leavers during an interview conducted
one year after they left school. The school-leavers

were asked first whether they felt physically and educationally competent to do the jobs that were actually held by peers who had already found employment. For every student who felt competent to do any job there were four who felt incapable. The only exception to this was the civil service where ten said they would be competent to one who would not.

Students were also asked whether they would prefer work in offices or in factories; the preferences were overwhelmingly in favour of offices, even when factory work paid better; the graduates of technical schools were more willing to work in factories than those from general academic schools who almost totally rejected factory work.[17]

The unemployed were asked what they thought a prospective employer required from them. Their expectations were first a skill, then, in order, honesty, ability to learn quickly, obedience and hard work. For themselves, the things they looked for in a job were first of all security – a pensionable post took precedence over every other consideration – followed by interesting work, and only thirdly good pay.

The tracer study also conducted a small "jury sample" of teachers, headmasters, and educational administrators, using a ranked list of 36 occupations. On the whole, the "jury" assessment of posts was higher than that of students: teachers and headmasters had more ambitious (as well as more limited) ideas of the types of jobs their graduates could do than did the graduates themselves, while educational administrators (mainly ministry officials) held that graduates should be able to do a much wider range of jobs. Only in the case of the teacher-training school did administrators, headmasters, teachers and students agree as to the kind of job – primary school teaching – their graduates could do.

The first response interviewers got to the query "What kind of job are you looking for" was, with very few exceptions, "something suitable to my education". Few students were able to go beyond this; if pressed, most nominated civil service. Even graduates from the technical schools felt limited to the actual machines they had worked with. A typical case concerned graduates from a school which had obtained old sugar machines from a nearby sugar mill for practical work. These students felt that their employment possibilities were limited to working with the (now obsolete) sugar mill machinery and, of those still unemployed a year later, none had searched beyond the local sugar mill for employment.[18]

Using the same list of graded occupations, interviewers asked school-leavers whether they would take each job if it were offered, at rates of pay about 20 per cent lower than that being received by their peers already in employment. Only about 20 per cent of the unemployed reported that they would. All were then asked the same questions again, but at rates of pay actually being received in these occupations by their peers. At these rates, only 40 per cent of the unemployed would have accepted work if offered.

Thus, of those still unemployed a year after leaving school, only about 20 per cent said they would be willing to accept work at any rate of pay, another 40 per cent would take current wages, and a final 40 per cent were holding out for rates above those being currently paid. Again, the civil service was an exception: more than 40 per cent would accept government employment at any rate of pay, and only 20 per cent would reject it at current rates.

The schools and unemployment

Table 40 shows the performance of school-leavers in the tracer study sample. Unemployment rates for state school-leavers were somewhat higher than for private schools. This may reflect the dual nature of private schools: the high quality schools have greater freedom in establishing community relationships than do state schools, so that their graduates more readily find jobs; the poorer quality private schools cater for lower income households and their graduates may not have that advantage.

While results are far from conclusive because of the small sample, it would appear that the "employment success" rate of a school (the number of its graduates economically active who had obtained jobs by the end of one year) varies inversely with supply, that is, the scarcer a certain type of school is in the region, the more likely are the graduates to find a job. But there are still many difficulties in interpreting these results, not the least of which is mobility.

Movement into employment

If one thinks of the transfer from school to employment as a movement along a continuum, three rough stages can be identified. First are those who move straight into the labour force on leaving school and rather quickly into employment. We saw in Table 39 that two-thirds of those who were employed within a year of leaving school had found jobs within three months of

Table 40: Employment, unemployment and schooling rates, one and two years after upper secondary school (in percentages)

	One year			Two years		
	Male	Female	Total	Male	Female	Total
Working	22.8	30.4	26.1	32.8	42.6	36.9
Wanting work	33.7	31.2	32.6	20.1	14.0	17.5
Schooling	38.6	35.7	37.4	44.7	38.5	42.1
Inactive	4.9	2.7	3.9	2.4	4.9	3.5
	100.0	100.0	100.0	100.0	100.0	100.0
Wanting work as percentage of economically active	59.7	52.2	55.7	37.9	24.7	32.1

	General academic	Vocational			Teacher training
		Commercial	Technical	Domestic science	
Working	17	34	42	15	84
Wanting work	14	28	27	21	2
Schooling	65	33	28	57	13
Inactive	4	5	3	7	1
	100	100	100	100	100

Source: Tracer Study.

beginning their search. This is a not unimpressive
performance, and the concern over unemployment should
not obscure the fact that large numbers of young
school-leavers do find jobs without much difficulty. The
second group are those who enter the labour force soon
after leaving school but move into employment only
through a slowly moving queue. Clark's analysis of the
tracer study data showed that only about five per cent
of those looking for work in any one month would have
found work by the following month.[19]   At the far end
of the continuum are the third group, who do not (or do
not yet) consider themselves unemployed, but are waiting
in the hope of returning to school or university.
One-third of these will succeed, and many others will go
on to courses of one kind or another, postponing entry
into the labour force. The remainder will at some
point almost surely join the queue, but at what point
remains a subject for further study. It is probable
that, in retrospect, such young people may think of
their entire period since leaving school as a period of
"unemployment" when interviewed in census and labour
force surveys, even though for some part of that period
they neither looked for work nor were prepared to take
jobs.

Trends in educated unemployment

    Tables 41 and 42 bring together major recent
sources of data on unemployment by age and educational
level.   At first glance they appear to show a
substantial decline in unemployment over time.   They
also seem to show a more substantial decrease for young
females than for young males over time.   The trends are
not so regular when broken down by educational level;
the irregular patterns alert us to the dangers of
comparisons   among   data   sources   marked   by   wide
variations.   Not only are definitions of labour force
participation,   employment   and   unemployment   not
particularly suitable to developing countries, but they
also vary among the censuses and surveys, as do
reference periods and imputation procedures.[20]
    As noted in the section on underutilisation above,
it is generally considered that the educated are more
likely to be visibly unemployed than to be underemployed
by reason of short hours of work or low pay, so that it
is not likely that unemployment rates for the more
educated would be much higher than reported.   It is
possible, however, that if the reasons for the high
inactivity rates among the young educated were better
understood, this might affect both levels and trends of

Table 41: Unemployment rates by age and sex, urban and rural residence, various sources, 1971-80 (in percentages)

		Ages 10-14		Ages 25 +		Total	
		Male	Female	Male	Female	Male	Female
1971 Census	U	20.6	21.8	7.6	13.5	10.8	17.1
	R	10.9	13.6	5.4	9.4	6.9	10.7
1976 Supas	U	14.2	13.2	1.8	1.8	5.4	5.9
	R	3.1	2.5	0.3	0.9	1.2	1.5
1976 Sakernas	U	21.1	12.6	2.0	1.3	6.9	5.1
	R	5.4	3.1	0.5	0.3	1.9	1.1
1978 Sakernas	U	20.0	9.2	2.7	1.1	7.0	3.8
	R	6.2	4.4	0.5	0.3	2.0	1.4
1980 Census	U	7.8	7.4	1.3	1.7	2.9	3.5
	R	2.5	3.6	0.6	1.4	1.1	2.1

Table 42: Unemployment rates by educational attainments and sex, various sources, 1971-80 (in percentages)

	Male					Female				
	Census 1976[a]	Supas 1976	Sakernas 1976	Sakernas 1978	Census 1980[b]	Census 1971[a]	Supas 1976	Sakernas 1976	Sakernas 1978	Census 1980[b]
No education	6.0	0.4	0.7	0.7	0.7	9.7	1.1	0.4	0.5	1.7
Some primary	6.9	1.3	1.9	2.3	1.1	12.6	1.6	1.0	1.4	2.2
Completed primary	8.3	2.8	3.4	3.5	1.7	15.5	3.5	3.1	3.0	2.8
Lower secondary	12.0	5.5	7.0	6.3	2.8	-	8.3	9.1	8.7	5.2
Academic	12.5	na	7.2	7.0	3.0	22.5	na	10.5	9.3	5.7
Vocational	10.8	na	6.5	5.5	2.2	13.0	na	5.7	7.2	3.4
Upper secondary	13.7	8.3	8.7	9.3	3.8	18.1	13.8	12.7	13.9	6.7
Academic	14.3	na	9.7	8.3	4.0	23.8	na	16.5	15.3	10.1
Vocational	12.9	na	7.9	10.2	3.7	14.6	na	11.1	13.3	5.1
Higher	11.2	3.4	4.4	4.3	1.3	22.6	2.6	8.6	5.9	3.9

[a] E series.
[b] Series S1.

young educated unemployment, conceivably as much as doubling their unemployment rates.

Published data from censuses and surveys do not afford any information on underutilisation by educational level over time. It is expected that it would be an important factor among the young less educated. Trends over time for length of unemployment by educational level are also not yet available.

The problem of educated unemployment as it is known in the West, or among some developing countries, is thus less of a worry in Indonesia than the concern for improving the employment and incomes of the educated labour force, or the concern over the productivity of the less educated.

III. THE EDUCATION SYSTEM AND UNEMPLOYMENT

The education system

Introduction

While the sense of concern over educated unemployment in Indonesia is still very new, the concern with employment problems has been a principal feature of the educational system in Indonesia since Independence, and indeed since the colonial period. Indonesia inherited from its colonial past a school system geared to the satisfaction of quite specific manpower needs for the colonial bureaucracy - and virtually limited to those needs. When the 350 years of colonial rule ended in Indonesia in 1945, literacy stood at about 7 per cent, there were virtually no qualified secondary or university teachers of Indonesian nationality, and a mere handful of persons with post-secondary training in a population of more than 60 million. In 1938 there were fewer than 10,000 Indonesians in secondary education, and only about 150 in all kinds of post-secondary training. The language of instruction in all schools except the three-year village schools and the five-year second-class Indonesian schools was Dutch; in primary schools it was a local, not a national, language.[21]

The 1945 Constitution adopted at Independence declared education to be the right of all Indonesian citizens. In spite of the internal strife and occupation suffered during the first five years (1945-50), education was considered so important that primary enrolments shot up to nearly 5 million, and the nation's first two universities were established. In these early years educational policy was directed towards the forging of national unity, the development

of a national language, universal literacy,
encouragement of religious education and of higher
education. Primary education was to be free, and
universal primary education was to be reached within ten
years. Special attention was to be given to technical,
commercial, agricultural, industrial, shipping and
fishing schools. The establishment of such special
schools to produce graduates to meet narrowly specific
manpower needs was a continuation of the colonial policy.

The pattern of growth

Primary and secondary schools continued to show
strong growth during the 1950s principally through
private provision and support. But the goal of
universal primary education remained distant. The late
1950s and early 1960s, a period of rampant inflation and
economic chaos, was marked by slower growth in
enrolments; and during the first few years of the New
Order (1966-72) enrolments slowed even further, as all
available resources were directed towards monetary
control and economic rehabilitation - which specifically
excluded school building - and rationalisation of the
civil service - which specifically excluded recruitment
of new teachers.

Universities had been established in each of the
provinces during the 1950s and early 1960s. Buildings
were borrowed from secondary schools, lecturers
recruited from practising professionals, a few aid
programmes and resident foreigners, with "flying
professors" visiting from the relatively
well-established universities in Java for a few days
each month. Classes were conducted in the evening
hours, while libraries, laboratories and even textbooks
were luxuries of the future. Private initiative was
active here too, and numerous private institutions
opened under much the same circumstances, often with no
more than 100 students or so, and one or two faculties.

When receipts from oil began to rise around 1973,
the Government took note of falling enrolments at
primary schools and undertook a massive primary school
building campaign which averaged 10-15,000 buildings a
year. Over the past ten years, primary education
enrolments have increased at about 10 per cent a year,
and universal primary education is now targeted
officially for 1984. Between 1971 and 1980, lower
secondary enrolments grew at an average annual rate of
24 per cent, and upper secondary enrolments at 16 per
cent. Tertiary education too continued to grow
rapidly. Figure 4 illustrates the pattern of growth at
all three levels.

Figure 4.   Growth of Indonesian education, 1900-80

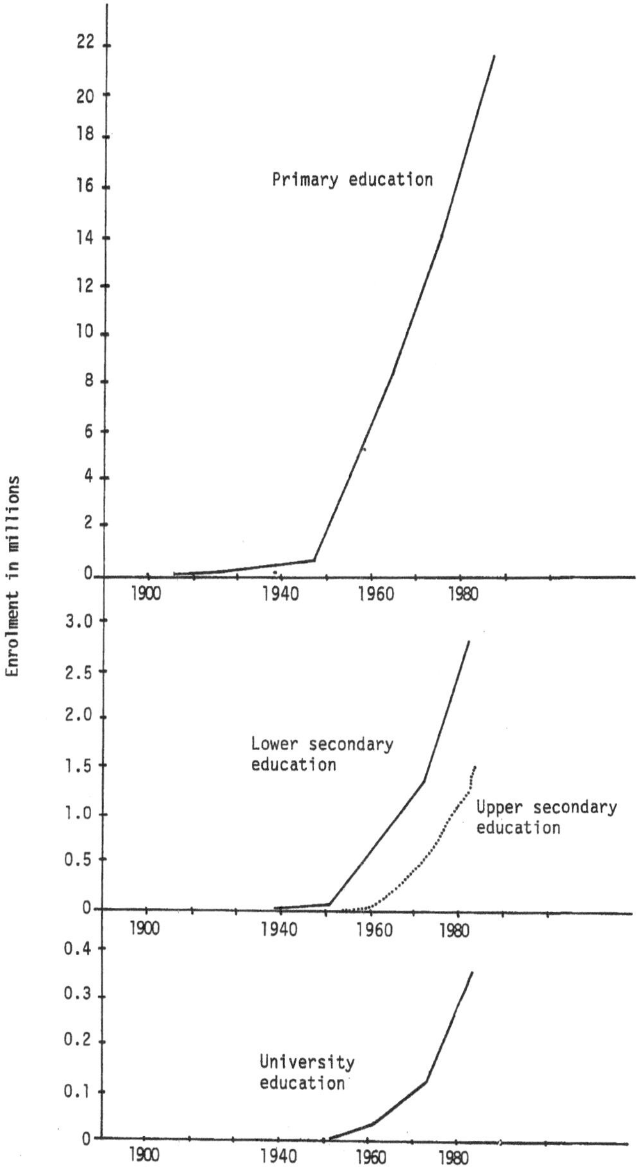

The manner in which new schools are established has
an important bearing on the pattern of expansion.
Initiative may come either from the State or from the
community.[22] For state secondary schools, initiative
lies in the Department of Education which allocates
schools to the regions. The receiving region may
request, but it does not have the power to decide, how
many or what kind of state schools it will receive. It
is thus possible for several secondary schools of
different types to be set up in one region or city and
none whatsoever in another. However, primary schools
in the past were set up by provincial governments or
local communities.

In addition, schools may be established by private
organisations, a right that is guaranteed in the
Constitution, but so far the Government has had little
part in directing private organisations as to where or
what kind of schools to establish. Private schools
which have strong financial backing and maintain high
quality levels may either respond to local pressure for
a particular type of school, or they may have policies
of their own which determine what kind of school they
establish. But the majority of private schools do not
have such sound financial backing; they are small, many
are of low quality and they appear to respond more to
the volume of private demand than to demand for a
particular type of school.[23]

Private schools around 1980 accounted for only
about 10 per cent of primary enrolments, but for just
over half of secondary enrolments. (Because private
schools are on average smaller than state schools, they
account for 70 per cent of total secondary schools.) At
upper secondary level, enrolments in private schools
over the past ten years grew at an average rate nearly
twice that of state schools, with highest rates in the
teacher-training and technical schools. Growth was
both through creation of new private schools (there
were, for example, 104 new private teacher-training
schools as compared to six new state teacher-training
schools established during that period) and by expansion
(average size increased by 50 per cent in private, and
by 20 per cent in state schools). Altogether there
were three times as many new schools created by private
initiative at the secondary level during the past ten
years as by state initiative.

This diverse pattern of state and private
initiative has determined the present composition and
the very uneven regional distribution of education in
Indonesia. In the absence of any long-range plan this
development of the education system has been determined
by private demand; this in turn has meant that teacher

preparation has had to follow expansion, rather than precede it. The absence of a long-term plan has also meant that technical assistance from developed countries seems to have influenced to a substantial degree the priorities of educational development in Indonesia.

Growth of expenditure

The characteristic which most marked the first 25 years of Indonesian educational development was its "raising itself by its own bootstraps", the manner in which parents and local communities assisted the Government in its efforts to raise the educational level of the nation under conditions of severely limited resources. After 1973, when the national budget began to increase rapidly with income from oil, both the amounts and the proportions used for education began to expand rapidly as well. By 1980, education accounted for almost twice the proportion of the development budget that it had in 1975 (Table 43); year to year increases have also been substantial, with education receiving by far the greatest proportional increase of any sector between 1980/81 and 1981/82. The routine budget allocation for education is also the largest for any department of government with the exception of home affairs (which is responsible for primary teachers' salaries). The magnitude of such increases has naturally made some important changes and improvements in education, but there are also many problems which are less amenable to the "Midas touch", particularly when urgent decisions about use of funds must be made without any long-term framework of development.

Educational issues affecting employment

In the following sections we will look at a number of features of the education system which have important impacts on employment and unemployment, concluding with an estimate of the flow from schools into the labour force.

Compulsory primary education
and the drop-out problem

Universal primary education, as noted above, has been targeted for 1984, and efforts to establish compulsory primary education are under way in selected regions. In 1980/81, however, the completion rate for the 1973 cohort of primary school entrants was 52 per cent, only 4 percentage points higher than it had been in 1972.

Table 43:   Share of education in the development budget

	Education[a] (Rp b)	Per cent	Total (Rp b)	Share of education in total development (per cent)
1975/6	112	–	1 268	8.8
1976/7	142	27	1 920	7.4
1977/8	220	55	2 168	10.1
1978/9	269	22	2 455	10.9
1979/80	356	32	3 448	10.3
1980/81	575	61	5 027	11.4
1981/82	787	37	6 399	12.3
1982/83	1 302	65	8 605	15.1

[a] The "Education" item in the budget refers not only to the costs involved in establishing and maintaining schools, but also to all "educational" and upgrading and training activities of government departments for civil servants. The Education Department receives about 65-70 per cent of this budget on average.

Source: Nota Keuangan, various years.

High rates of drop-out give rise to a number of
employment-related problems including the early loss of
literacy and numeracy, the entry into the labour force
of children at young ages and consequent longer periods
of unemployment; the low productivity and low income
levels attained by those with less than primary
education; the costly nature of subsequent training
programmes and their duplication with services available
in primary schools; and possibly the retardation of
national integration when the level of education does
not guarantee command of the national language (regional
languages may be used as a medium of instruction up to
grade 4).

The general/vocational balance
of secondary schools

That the education system must somehow assist in
preparing young people for employment has always been
taken for granted in Indonesia. But difficult
questions arise from this proposition: Should such
pre-employment training necessarily be provided in
schools operated by the Department of Education? Should
the training be provided in separate schools? And how
are the desirable proportions between employment
preparation and general education to be decided and
implemented?
With regard to the first question, training centres
of various kinds have been set up by other government
departments and by industry, but apparently no studies
of the costs and benefits of this type of training
compared to that provided by the Department of Education
have ever been made. The possibility of integrating
these centres with secondary schools to provide both
academic and pre-vocational training has been discussed,
and pilot projects set up. But such integration could,
as Beeby pointed out, succumb to the tendency of the
academic streams to swamp the vocational.[24] Further,
the cost of providing an effective range of
pre-vocational studies in general schools has usually
been considered to be prohibitive. Whether, in fact,
it would be more expensive than the present system of
separate schools is a matter for future research. With
regard to the third point, the current Five-Year Plan
actually sets out the "desirable" proportions of
vocational to general enrolments (3 per cent at lower
and 52 per cent at upper secondary), but there is no
indication of the rationale for these proportions, nor
are the means of achieving them outlined.[25]
Recognising that the employment obtained by the
lower secondary vocational schools graduates varied

little from that of primary school graduates, the
Government phased out the lower secondary commercial
schools and cut down the number of technical schools in
favour of an "integrated" lower secondary general school
in 1980.

At upper secondary level the 52 per cent "target"
for vocational schools appears to be receding. In 1974
nearly 60 per cent of upper secondary enrolments were in
vocational schools, but by 1980/81 the advance of
general academic education left vocational schools with
only about 40 per cent of the total. Three-quarters of
vocational school graduates entered the labour force
almost immediately, in contrast to only about 40 per
cent for the general academic.

Non-formal education and other
forms of delivery

Beginning with the Second Five-Year Plan (1973/74),
and largely as a result of initiatives from aid donor
agencies, "non-formal" education became a popular
panacea for some of Indonesia's most pressing
educational problems. There are, as a result, a wide
variety of programmes directed towards adult
illiterates, primary school drop-outs, and unemployed
primary school graduates. What has not been clarified
is the relation of the programmes for drop-outs to the
attainment of universal or compulsory primary education.

Curriculum

In 1975 a new curriculum was introduced in the
primary and general academic secondary schools. Its
distinguishing feature was its increased emphasis on
pre-vocational activities, which now take up about 15
per cent of total time at primary and lower secondary
and 7 per cent at the general upper secondary level. It
is also far more diverse than formerly, with 37 lesson
periods and 13 examinable subjects. Subjects are
divided into three main groups: general, academic and
skill development. At primary level, 30 per cent of
total lesson hours are devoted to general subjects, of
which inculcation of the national ideology is given
pride of place and time; 55 per cent of time is for
academic subjects, and 15 per cent for skill
development. At lower secondary level the proportions
are 24, 61 and 15 per cent, and at upper secondary 21,
72 and 7 respectively. There were, however, very few
teachers (or teacher trainers) in skill development
subjects and schools generally have to use other subject
teachers to deal with this part of the curriculum. The

amounts and timing of routine grants to schools for expendables for these subjects also cause difficulty, and pre-vocational courses are generally dependent upon parental contributions for materials.

Other quality factors: time, teachers and equipment

The primary school graduates entering the labour force over the past ten years or so have had hardly more than 60 per cent of the lesson time of their peers in neighbouring countries. The major reason for shortened hours of instruction was lack of space and overcrowding. Besides, there were problems of teacher quality. Around 1970 nearly 50 per cent of all primary teachers were unqualified or underqualified; however, recent sample studies indicate that by 1980 almost all primary teachers had at least 12 years of education.[26]   The recent expansion of teacher training schools was not, however, matched by an increased number of teacher trainers, so that improvement in the quality of teacher training has not kept pace with expansion.   Moreover, teaching quality, particularly in the technical and vocational courses, is also affected by lack of practical experience in industry or commerce.

Standard national examinations were abolished a decade ago and at present all schools set their own entry and leaving examinations. As there are no national standards or examinations for skilled and semi-skilled trades, the schools have nothing to measure their training against. Partly as a result of this, prospective employers tend to recruit from specific schools known to maintain high quality, rather than from any specific school type.

University reform

In an effort to make higher education more relevant to national development needs, the Directorate General of Higher Education has undertaken a series of long-term studies.[27] As a result of this effort practical work is receiving more attention through the establishment of undergraduate and post-graduate diplomas.   Steps are also being taken to increase efficiency by decreasing the amount of time taken to complete the programmes. Further, universities are expected to fulfil three functions: teaching, research and community service. As part of the last function, final-year students spend a period of about three months working as volunteers in local government offices or programmes for which they receive living costs and credits toward graduation.

This programme known as the Kuliah Kerja Nyata or KKN,
emphasises community service rather than career
preparation, and the nature of the service is left to
the graduate or to his faculty. The programme is
voluntary in some faculties and compulsory in others.
Some 7,600 students were involved in 1980/81. Students
who have been successful in the KKN find that it has
been a contributing factor in finding employment.

Another volunteer programme for university
graduates (BUTSI) is now operated through the Department
of Manpower who recruit and place graduates as
volunteers throughout the country, mainly in rural and
isolated areas. In 1980/81 there were 2,500 persons
serving in village administration, agricultural
extension, health and family planning and
transmigration. For those who serve two years, an
additional training period is offered after which they
may be employed as fieldworkers in the public works or
transmigration programmes.

Stock and flow of educated manpower

The quite clear differences in rates of absorption
into employment of those with general and those with
vocational education, as well as among those with
different levels of education, have been noted above. It
may be noted further that while the definition of
general academic education is the same in the Department
of Education and in census and labour force survey data,
vocational education in the census and labour force
series includes religious schools as well as all schools
operated by government departments other than the
Department of Education. Even so, the labour force
survey data on vocational graduates among the population
appear to be much too high.

The data in Table 44 show an increase of nearly
half a million vocational graduates between 1976 and
1978, during which time these schools produced only some
15-20,000 graduates. Between 1972 and 1980, Department
of Education schools produced about 4.5 million
graduates from the academic lower secondary and about
775,000 from vocational schools. At the upper
secondary, over the same period, the general academic
schools produced about 1 million and the vocational
schools about 1.4 million. In terms of flow, the lower
vocational schools produced annually about 80,000 around
1972, then rose to a peak of 120,000 in 1975 and dropped
back to about 30,000 by 1980; the academic schools at
this level doubled from 325,000 a year in 1972 to over
800,000 a year in 1980. At upper secondary level,
annual production of vocational graduates increased from

Table 44: Population by educational attainment,
           1971-80, (in thousands)

	Census 1971	Labour Force Surveys		Census 1980
		1976	1978	
Lower secondary	3 528.6	5 101.3	5 255.2	6 299.8
Academic	2 589.3	4 133.4	3 805.3	5 150.0
Vocational	939.3	967.9	1 449.9	1 149.8
Upper secondary	1 645.2	2 732.3	2 855.1	4 401.2
Academic	912.7	1 410.8	1 278.8	2 166.8
Vocational	732.5	1 321.5	1 576.3	2 344.4
Tertiary	271.4	346.8	279.1	545.3

100,000 in 1972 to 215,000 by 1980, while academic
school production rose from 70,000 in 1972 to over
200,000 a year in 1980. The proportions of the
population by educational level thus show a much closer
fit between the censuses and the Department of Education
statistics than do the labour force surveys.[28] It is,
however, important to remember these variations in
measurement and definition in interpreting data on
average wages by educational level and type in the
discussion below.

However, at the tertiary level, the 1980 census
count (Tables 44 and 45) agrees very closely with other
independent estimates of graduate production.[29] The
fact that enrolments and graduates have always been
heavily biased towards the non-exact subjects, with
science and mathematics lagging far behind, also affects
wage distribution. In 1980, for example, only 9 of the
26 provincial universities had faculties of science or
mathematics; of these 6 were in Java and 3 in
Sumatra. From very small bases, the highest growth
rates of the past few years have been in graduates from
agriculture and science faculties. Tables 46 and 47
show enrolment distribution by subject in degree and
non-degree programmes and Table 48 an estimate of
graduates produced between 1950 and 1980 by subject
discipline.

Self-employment status of the educated

In Indonesia one-quarter of all employed are
own-account workers, and another 21 per cent unpaid
family workers. Self-employment is not, however,
particularly important among the young or the
educated. Only 10 per cent of those under 24 years of
age were self-employed, as contrasted with 30 per cent
of those over 30. In the 1980 Census among those with
lower secondary education, about 20 per cent were
self-employed, at upper level 9 per cent, and at
university level only 7 per cent. A similar pattern
was found in the tracer study. In any case,
self-employment for the educated is probably a fruitful
possibility only for those with considerable experience
and mature age. Even professionals generally spend a
few years as employees before striking out on their own.

Occupational structure of
the educated labour force

The tiny administrative sector (Table 49) absorbs a
high proportion of the secondary and tertiary educated,
while the professional occupations are dominated by

Table 45: Educational distribution of the population and of the labour force 1971-80 (in percentages)

		Census 1971		Labour force surveys 1976		1978		Census 1980	
		Pop.	LF	Pop.	LF	Pop.	LF	Pop.	LF
No school	(M+F)	40.4	42.6	28.1	30.9	28.6	31.6	27.3	29.0
	(F)	41.3	60.0	36.4	46.0	37.6	47.1	35.7	43.4
Some primary	(M+F)	33.2	28.5	39.1	35.3	40.8	36.8	40.6	37.1
	(F)	29.1	44.6	37.3	32.8	37.8	32.3	37.9	33.0
Completed primary	(M+F)	19.6	21.8	23.4	24.4	21.6	22.0	21.2	21.9
	(F)	15.4	13.3	19.7	15.6	18.4	14.9	18.4	16.0
Lower secondary Academic	(M+F)	3.2	2.7	4.6	3.7	4.1	3.6	4.9	4.0
	(F)	2.3	1.4	3.6	1.8	0.3	1.9	3.9	2.2
Vocational	(M+F)	1.2	1.2	1.0	1.1	1.5	1.5	1.1	1.2
	(F)	0.7	0.8	0.8	0.7	1.1		0.8	0.7
Upper secondary Academic	(M+F)	1.1	1.2	1.6	1.7	1.4	1.6	2.1	2.5
	(F)	0.6	0.5	1.0	0.8	0.8	0.9	1.3	1.3
Vocational	(M+F)	0.9	1.2	1.5	2.1	1.7	2.4	2.2	3.3
	(F)	0.6	0.9	1.0	1.8	1.2	0.7	1.6	2.8
Tertiary	(M+F)	0.3	0.5	0.4	0.6	0.3	0.5	0.5	0.9
	(F)	0.1	0.2	0.2	0.2	0.1	0.3	0.3	0.5

Table 46: Enrolment in tertiary education, around 1978

| | State universities and institutes | Teacher training colleges | Private universities, institutes and TTCs | Total | | Private as % of total |
	1978		1977	No.	%	
Education[a]	19 443	9 645	17 993	47 081	18	38
Social sciences	15 441	12 000	8 223	35 634	14	23
Economics	23 514	–	9 657	33 171	13	29
Law	22 834	–	8 483	31 317	12	27
Engineering	17 196	6 731	5 082	29 009	11	18
Agriculture	18 960	–	6 746	25 706	10	26

Medicine and health	13 103	–	8 360	21 463	8	39
Humanities and literature	5 573	8 176	567	14 316	6	4
Science	6 735	5 755	408	12 898	5	3
All other	1 077	2 310	1 230	4 617	2	27
Total	143 846	44 617	66 749	255 212	100	26

[a] TTCs have been distributed by subject specialisation; education in state universities refers to pedagogy rather than subject specialisation; no breakdowns by subject are available for private TTCs.

Sources: Data Perguruan Tinggi Negeri 1978 Buku B1, Jumlah Mahasiswa Pada Program Gelar, (Jakarta, Dept. Pendidakan dan Kebudayaan, Proyek Pembinaan dan Pengendalian Proyek-proyek Direktorat Jenderal Pendidikan Tinggi, 1980); and Statistik Perguruan Tinggi Swasta 1977, (Jakarta, Badan Penelitian dan Pengembangan Pendidikan dan Kebudayaan dan Direktorat Jenderal Pendidikan Tinggi, Departemen Pendidikan dan Kebudayaan, Dec. 1978).

Table 47: Enrolment in tertiary non-degree programmes
           (state institutions only)

	Enrolment
Administration	3 136
Librarianship	43
Technical studies	23 854
Medical technology	135
Agricultural extension	128
Foreign languages	27
Tourism	35
Teaching disciplines	1 694
Total	29 052

Source: As for Table 46.

Table 48:   Estimate of Sarjana (5-year) graduates
1950-80 by field of study (state
universities and teacher-training
institutes only)

	Graduates
Science	5 274
Engineering	14 374
Medical and related	21 947
Agriculture	10 266
Economics	11 408
Law	14 534
Teacher training	4 300
All other	17 839
Total	99 942

Source: Estimated by extrapolations from Data Perguruan
Tinggi Negeri 1979/80 - Buku V. Lulusan Sarjana
Muda, Sarjana dan Profesi Non-Gelar (Jakarta,
Directorate General of Higher Education, 1981).

Table 49: Educational and occupational distribution of employed workers, 1980 (in percentages)

	Profess-ional	Admin./Manag.	Clerical	Sales	Services	Farmers	Production Workers	Total
No school	3.3	5.3	2.6	28.9	28.9	36.3	19.5	29.2
Some primary	6.1	11.1	12.0	5.0	36.3	41.3	38.5	37.3
Completed primary	8.0	9.7	20.5	25.0	24.2	19.3	29.0	21.9
Lower secondary								
Academic	5.7	7.4	14.4	5.5	4.8	1.7	5.9	4.1
Vocational	5.8	2.1	4.0	1.1	1.3	0.4	2.0	1.2
Upper secondary								
Academic	9.5	6.5	22.0	2.7	2.3	0.4	2.1	2.4
Vocational	50.1	12.8	16.6	1.4	1.8	0.04	2.6	3.0
Tertiary	5.7	24.7	7.9	0.2	0.4	0.02	0.3	0.9
Unknown	5.8	20.4	–	30.2	–	0.54	0.1	–
Total	100.0	100.0	100.0	100.0	100.0	100.0	100.0	100.0
Number	1 542 380	75 520	1 908 283	6 606 207	2 373 729	27 983 520	9 609 777	51 191 512

	No school	Some primary	Completed primary	Lower secondary		Upper secondary		Higher	Total
				Acad.	Voc.	Acad.	Voc.		
Professional	0.4	0.5	1.1	4.3	14.7	12.1	46.4	35.9	3.0
Administra- tive/mana- gerial	0.02	0.04	0.06	0.3	0.3	1.6	0.6	5.3	0.1
Clerical	0.3	1.2	3.5	13.6	12.6	34.6	19.0	38.6	3.7
Sales	12.8	12.2	14.7	18.1	11.7	14.5	5.4	6.7	12.9
Services	4.6	4.5	5.1	5.6	5.3	4.5	2.8	4.7	4.6
Farmers	68.1	60.6	48.3	23.8	19.2	9.2	6.8	2.7	54.7
Production	12.5	19.4	24.7	28.2	31.1	16.1	15.3	6.0	18.8
N.e.c.	1.3	1.6	2.6	6.1	5.1	7.4	3.7	0.1	2.2
Total	100.0	100.0	100.0	100.0	100.0	100.0	100.01	100.0	100.0
Number	14 934 450	19 076 895	11 211 710	2 021 689	606 809	1 213 297	1 664 416	440 364	51 191 512

Source: As for Table 33.

vocational secondary school graduates. Teachers in particular form nearly 60 per cent of this category. The administrative, professional and clerical occupations are the only ones that do not draw at least half of their workers from the primary educated. It is rather surprising to see in Table 49 the fairly high proportions of those with secondary general education going into farming and, also somewhat surprising in view of the expressions by students in the tracer study, to see that proportionately more of the general secondary educated are reported to go into production work than the vocationally educated.

The civil service

The civil service of Indonesia in 1980 was reported to be 2.3 million, excluding the military. The 10 per cent of these who had university degrees represented 40 per cent of the total with such degrees as reported in the 1980 Census. Though this 40 per cent is not as high as other estimates in the past, there is little doubt that government is the chief employer of educated manpower. Using 1980 census participation rates and educational distribution, it is estimated that the civil service has absorbed about one-quarter of the total labour force with secondary education. Over the past ten years, the structure of the civil service has been changing markedly from one dominated by primary education or less (Grade I) to those with secondary (Grade II) or higher, as shown below:

	1971 structure	1981 structure
Grade I	58%	28%
Grade II	35%	56%
Grade III	7%	13%
Grade IV	0.8%	1.3%

It seems reasonable to assume that, while the expansion of the civil service may not be so great in future as it has been in the past, the more educated will continue to replace the less educated and that the civil service will continue in the near future to absorb a substantial proportion of the educated labour force.

Looking ahead

The data given above allow us to estimate that, of the nearly 2 million persons entering the labour force annually around 1980, something like 25,000-30,000 will have some tertiary qualifications. From the upper secondary level, about 250,000 young people enter the labour force annually, and from the lower secondary level less than 100,000. This means that with only about half a million entering the labour force with completed primary education, there remain almost a million children a year who will enter with incomplete primary education, although many of them will not consider themselves economically active for some years to come.

Those with only a year or so of primary school will be disadvantaged and their chances on the labour market lessened not only because of insecure literacy and lack of skills but also because of lack of a common language. Entry to the labour market from lower secondary level is negligible, but this level is bound to increase sharply in the very near future. While proportionately more enter the labour force from the vocational (technical, commercial and teacher-training) schools, the actual numbers entering with general secondary education are greater and are increasing even more rapidly. There will be great pressure for increased provision of places at secondary and higher levels, but this increase will not be the principal avenue to a well-educated productive workforce unless massive and effective programmes of quality improvement are undertaken.

IV. SOCIO-ECONOMIC POLICIES INFLUENCING
     EDUCATION AND EMPLOYMENT

When the New Order Government came to power in 1966, it faced inflation rates running well over 100 per cent a year; virtually no investment in infrastructure had been made for decades, and exports were at their lowest ebb. Children continued to be enrolled in schools, but at the expense of multiple sessions, shortened hours of instruction and overcrowded classrooms. The new Government gave its attention first to the containment of inflation, then to the repair and construction of infrastructure, both through renewed aid programmes and through efforts to increase exports and other sources of domestic revenue. Food self-sufficiency was a high priority goal, not least because of needed savings in foreign exchange. Export crops were promoted and import-substituting industries encouraged, as was foreign investment, which showed particular interest in oil and mineral industries. Family planning was officially adopted, and programmes of population movement out of Java to other islands were continued. A central planning agency was established and in 1969 Indonesia embarked upon the first of a

series of Five-Year Plans.   In the First Plan, the
development priorities of provincial governments were
required to be adapted to national priorities, but in
the subsequent plan periods more emphasis was put on
regional development.   Foreign aid once more began to
flow in, and the contributing nations organised and
co-ordinated their aid through the Inter-Governmental
Group on Indonesia (IGGI).

Around 1973, the character of the development
activities of the central Government began to change as
the receipts of the oil bonanza flowed in.   At around
the same time, both international and domestic attention
began to be focused on better redistributional
policies.   Thus, in the mid-1970s, there was a
discernible change in emphasis towards greater regional
participation in implementation of development
programmes (though not yet so much in decision-making);
towards more efforts to provide employment, particularly
for the rural poor;   and towards the provision of
physical infrastructure in both rural and urban areas -
not only roads and irrigation and other "economic"
infrastructure as in the early 1970s, but now extended
to schools, public housing, government offices, urban
redevelopment, health clinics and other services.

Before dealing with the main policies in each of
the sectors, two somewhat more general issues, both
subject to varied interpretations and each responsible
for some stress within and among groups in the society
and the Government, will be noted: the
decentralisation/deconcentration issue, and the
Pancasila philosophy.

Early in its nationhood Indonesia specifically
rejected a federal form of government and established a
unified state with a strong centralised bureaucracy.
Though centralised, the Government, like the nation, is
far from monolithic, and is made up of numerous ethnic
groups, languages, religions and political
affiliations.   The attainment of national unity out of
this diversity has been, and continues to be,
indispensable.   The terms "deconcentrate" and
"decentralise" refer to the delegation of authority now
held by the central government, in the first case to
regional offices of central government ministries, and
in the second to the regional governments themselves.
The second can involve delegation from the so-called
"vertical" ministries such as education, health, public
works, etc. to the regional governments via the
Department of Home Affairs which is responsible for the
civil administration of each of the provinces and the
sub-provincial administrative units, the kabupaten and
kecamatan.   In the field of education, for example,

responsibility for primary schools was formerly in the hands of the provincial governments, and for secondary and higher education, in the hands of the Department of Education.   Formally, this distinction still exists, but with the recent central government initiative in constructing primary school buildings and recruiting teachers, the distinction has become clouded and is now being reviewed as part of a larger re-evaluation of central/regional financial relations.   The provincial and local governments frequently provide quite substantial financial inputs at all levels of education as well.

In the past few years there has been increasing public discussion of an essentially Indonesian approach to economic and social policy.   This has reached only an inchoate stage so far, but it is clear that government, political leaders and academics are striving for a clearer expression of it.   This is _Pancasila_, the five guiding principles of the Indonesian state (belief in One God, humanity, national unity, social justice and the sovereignty of the people).   The parts of this discussion which bear on this paper are, in the economic sphere, attempts to bring national economic practice into line with these principles, particularly the emphasis being put on mutual assistance and co-operation in place of economic competition; and in the educational sphere, the study of _Pancasila_ morality and ethics as a subject in the school curriculum.

The economic interpretation currently under discussion is much influenced by Article 33 of the 1945 Constitution which states that all natural resources should be controlled by the State and the basic needs of the people managed by co-operatives.   Those parts of the economy which fall outside these two major categories are seen as the suitable area of private enterprise.   "In all sectors economic enterprises would be expected to operate on 'harmonious and family principles' (azas kekeluargaan dan prinsip harmoni)."[30]   The recent effort by government to distribute more equitably than formerly the proceeds of the oil windfall by concentrating on affirmative action to assist the "economically weak" groups is often cited as a concrete example of _Pancasila_.   Policies for this group, generally acknowledged to refer to indigenous (pribumi) Indonesians, include provision of credits, floor prices for agricultural products, protective tariffs on imports, the encouragement of co-operatives, and a number of programmes in which larger and more stable firms are to assist newer and less experienced ones.   The transmigration programme and the nucleus estate programme are also seen as implements in this policy.

The impact of policies on wage structure and demand for educated labour

Some of the indirect influences of recent social and economic policies may be observed in Table 50 which shows (subject to the usual caveats about comparability of sources) that those with general academic education receive higher wages on average than those with vocational education, and that the biggest differentials are between those with tertiary and those with secondary education. This is not uncommon among developing countries, as Sundrum points out:

> The large income differentials between educational categories in less developed countries were initially due to the fact that educated workers were so scarce relative to demand and because the demand was partly met by expatriates from the metropolitan countries. Thus the difference should have declined with educational expansion in the less developed countries. However, this process has been very slow; one reason is that the more educated workers are mostly employed in the public sector where their salaries are in the nature of 'administered prices' kept at a high level because of their greater political strength in influencing government decisions. Another reason is that the salaries of the most highly educated workers in less developed countries are kept close to the incomes they can earn by migrating to developed countries, whereas the less educated who do not enjoy such international mobility are tied to the average incomes of the less developed countries. Hence, there is a great spread of incomes.[31]

These conditions also exist in Indonesia as shown by the following: the tiny number of those with secondary and university education during the colonial period, and the subsequent rapid expansion to meet private demand undertaken with severely limited resources and consequent dilution of content; the necessity of replacing colonial administrators and the consequent absorption of almost all available tertiary trained manpower into government service; and, arising out of this, the somewhat exaggerated expectations for jobs and salaries by the young about to enter the labour force. In addition to the indirect effects on wages,

Table 50: Index of monthly wages per employed person by educational level (urban area of Indonesia)

	1968/69		1976		1978	
	% of employed	Index	% of employed	Index	% of employment	Index
Less than primary	38.4	100	32.0	100	38.1	100
Completed primary	34.3	139	27.8	167	25.1	112
Lower secondary						
Academic	10.7	179	11.6	244	10.5	324
Vocational	5.0	198	4.0	212	4.1	250
Upper secondary						
Academic	5.9	228	9.9	267	8.7	413
Vocational	3.1	220	9.6	256	9.6	312
Tertiary	2.6	500	5.1	666	3.9	667

public sector wage policies and economic policies
governing the private sector have had more direct impact
on demand for educated labour. We turn first to public
sector wages, then to a discussion of demand by public
and private sectors, followed by an overview of the
impact of economic policies by occupation, industry and
sex.

Public service wages

The public service wage system has, since
Independence, been turned towards social security rather
than efficiency objectives,[32] and the structure of
public service wages has had an important impact on the
semi-government (state enterprise) and private sector
wage systems as well. Civil service incomes have been
analysed by Gray into four components: (i) salary and
automatic cash allowances; (ii) automatic allowances in
kind; (iii) discretionary supplements which may include
incentive payments, project honoraria, housing and
travel; and (iv) a range of income sources without
legal sanction, not all of which are illegal. The sum
of these supplements may be far greater in value than
the sum of salary plus in-kind allowances, and is
proportionately much greater for those in the top ranges
of the civil service than for the lower levels.[33] But
the supplements are of an uncertain irregular nature and
do not show up in the salary scales or estimates of
"average wages".

In the past two or three years there have been
efforts to make the public service wage system more
efficient by reducing many of the allowances and
providing health insurance, workmen's compensation and
by controlling urban food prices. Many of the payments
in kind instituted during periods of high inflation have
now given way to cash payments. The private sector as
well as the public sector has in the past had to reward
workers through a variety of medical, food, housing,
transport and other services. Though established during
periods of inflation, such supplements were not
automatically lifted when inflation came under control.

We do not yet have any clear idea of how demand is
determined in the public service. For teachers,
medical personnel and extension services the
requirements may be determined by population of the
client group; but it is probable that in the
administrative services manpower requirements are
determined principally by structural/pyramidal
considerations. Nor have we a very clear idea of how
allocation of scarce skilled manpower between the public
and the private sector operates. It has only been in

the past few years that the public service has had to
compete with the private sector for university-trained
or other highly skilled manpower since, for the first 20
years or so of Independence, state enterprise dominated
not only the plantations but also the modern sector in
industry, banking and commerce.

Allocation of skilled manpower

Although reliable data on average wages by employer
status are not available, there is little doubt that the
modern private sector pays significantly higher wages
than the public sector or the traditional private
sector, and pays also for its regional allocation.
Recent newspaper reports suggest that a new entrant to
the labour force with technical qualifications can
obtain a starting wage in the modern private sector
three times greater than he can command in the public
sector. The complicated system of wage payments in the
civil service, particularly the supplements available to
the highest level, is still considered necessary to
compete with the recent demand from the modern private
sector.

At the medium and lower levels the public service
pays definitely more than the traditional private
sector. The role of public service as a "model
employer", the emphasis on protection of weak economic
groups, the role of the civil service in absorbing
excess labour during the late 1950s and early 1960s and,
most importantly, the ability to pay the salaries
because of the oil boom, have all contributed to set
administered salaries of the lower grades of the public
service well above the rates paid by the rest of the
public sector for primary and secondary educated
manpower. The public service is thus uniformly and
with good reason more desirable to the primary and
secondary school-leaver than traditional private sector
employment.

Recruitment to public and private sector employment
differs substantially. Private employment agencies
which recruit for modern private sector firms put more
emphasis on personal characteristics such as initiative
and interpersonal skills than on educational
qualifications (beyond a basic minimum). Except where
licensed professionals are concerned, both foreign and
domestic firms appear to be as willing to recruit a
university drop-out with the right personal attributes
as one who has a degree. The modern private sector
generally specifies faculties and institutions when
recruiting university-level staff, and particular
schools when recruiting from secondary level.

Moreover, the modern firm is more likely to recruit even its skilled production workers from general secondary schools and then provide them with firm-specific training; they find this more efficient than trying to "unlearn" undesirable skills and habits (in terms of their firm-specific needs) taught or absorbed in many vocational schools.

The public service, on the other hand, is only just beginning to classify and describe jobs, and for the great bulk of clerical and administrative jobs no very definite job description yet exists. Because productivity is very much more difficult to determine in the public service than it is in the modern private sector, more reliance is put on selection by mechanistic multiple-choice examination. Graduates of non-technical studies thus have chances as good as, or better than, those of graduates from technical studies to gain admission to the public service. Flowing back from this, students entering higher education (or even secondary education) are content with, and most even prefer, the "soft" rather than the technical subjects, and there has thus been, up to the present time, little effective demand for the extension or expansion of sciences, mathematics and other exact subjects in comparison with such subjects as law, journalism, or social and political studies.

It thus appears that there may be a kind of allocation system working, though not yet clearly understood, by which the modern private sector gets its choice of the technical graduates and of the small number of generalists that it needs; the public service by means of its examinations gets largely generalists; and the traditional private sector eventually absorbs those who are left. There are some clear signs that personal characteristics play a significant part in defining the type of manpower recruited to each level, though it certainly would not be true to say that the private sector gets all or even most of the dynamic and inventive people among the young recruits. There still remains some of the idealism of the early years of nationhood among the young, and a desire to help their country; there are also quite strong reward systems, though their existence is not always formally recognised, in the prestige and authority of the public service. The public service also is the main avenue to a career in research or to scholarships for overseas training.

Minimum wages

In 1972 the ILO Asian Regional Team for Employment Promotion (ARTEP) mission quoted Professor Galenson as saying that "a national minimum wage that would have any substantial effect on wage levels does not make sense at the present time".[34]   The difficulties of protecting workers by means of minimum wage legislation are illustrated by almost daily stories in the press about firms which pay wages well below that minimum.   One of the principal difficulties in fixing a minimum wage is the determination of the level at which it should be set.
Relevant to such determination is the fact that "money wages move independently of the cost of living [and] the cost of living can - and does - move independently of the money wage and have an autonomous impact on real wages".[35]   Using consumer expenditure patterns, Arndt and Sundrum showed that 12 per cent of urban and 32 per cent of rural Java had expenditures less than one-half the national average.[36]   When minimum wage standards are set, as they tend to be now, on subjective criteria of basic needs, a vast proportion of the population will be below the minimum.   Further, even if implementation were to be stepped up to the point where minimum wages could be monitored in industry, it does not seem possible that they could affect the millions in small-scale farm operation or household industry, for whom the "basic needs" approach is just as valid.

Regional wage variations

Regional variations are recognised in setting minimum or "guideline" wage rates for the regions for the purpose of public works contractors.   Variations within a province or even within a kabupaten, it has often been pointed out, may be as great as 100 per cent, depending on accessibility of site.
Government service does not discriminate by region, all central and all regional government employees being paid on a single scale.   One result of this is that areas of high cost of living are unpopular and positions there difficult to fill;   this has been a particularly important obstacle to recruitment of teachers and university staff.   Private industry, on the other hand, particularly the large modern sector and resource enclave firms, pays substantially higher wages in less accessible areas or areas with few facilities or amenities.   These regional wage differences exacerbate the lack of highly educated, especially technical, staff in the more remote regions in government service.

Wage norms have been suggested as a more appropriate approach in a developing country where they can be used as "indicators to point to cases where the position of wage earners is unsatisfactory and requires remedial action". Such norms could be fixed in terms of the country's own current per capita national income; where "some employees are paid several times the per capita national income the norm acts as a wholesome reminder that this is at the expense of other workers".

Wages and occupations

Table 51 indicates that urban wages are over twice those in rural areas on average; and that administrative occupations offer wages which soar above all other, including professional activities. Again, there are several qualifications. Wages shown in this table are for employees only, therefore the professionals who are self-employed, doctors, engineers, architects, etc., with private practice, are excluded. The professional group as noted above is composed mainly of teachers, predominantly of primary school teachers, among whom a high proportion will be in the younger age groups because of the recent primary school expansion. These combined factors account for the relatively low salary ranges of professionals. The closeness of professional to clerical wages is thus not so surprising. Because up to now the numbers entering the labour force after the lower secondary level have been so few, most of those entering the clerical occupations have upper secondary qualifications equivalent to those of primary school teachers. Furthermore, newspaper advertisements suggest that entry salaries in the urban modern private sector for clerical staff with stenography and some language qualification from upper secondary-level schools are about three times those for primary school teachers in the public service. The range of wages for the clerical occupations is, however, much greater than it is for professionals.

The very low wages for farmers may be due partly to the characteristics of wage data as collected by Sakernas surveys. First, land-owning own-account farmers are not included, only those who were, in the reference week, labourers working for a wage. The agro-economic studies referred to above showed that among this landless group, and also among farmers with very small holdings, there is a considerable degree of multiple occupations, with one person moving at various times of the year from farming to casual labour on public works construction, petty trading, food

Table 51:   Index of average wages by occupation, 1978

	Total	Urban	Rural
Professional	231	165	287
Administrative/ Managerial	1 040	617	2 210
Clerical	206	180	278
Sales	117	118	96
Services	77	72	97
Farmers	49	46	65
Production workers	137	99	127
Average	100	100	100
	(Rp 14 604)	(Rp 23 601)	(Rp 10 812)

processing for sale, or work in agricultural processing
industries or transport.   Furthermore, the labour force
wage data refer to monthly wages based on work at the
main job during the reference week which, it will be
recalled, may refer to no more than one hour's work.
Against these data must be set the signs of possible
turn-around in rural wages signalled by the recent micro
village studies of the Agro-economic Surveys.[37]

Wages for production workers average out to near
the national average; wage levels in this sector, says
Manning, are highly firm-specific, with differentials of
1:4 not uncommon between modern sector foreign-owned
high technology firms and domestic low technology
firms.[38]

Evidence on wages in the construction sector -
employing less than 2 per cent of the workforce - is
subject to similar qualifications.   For example, the
1977 Construction Census reports that only a very small
proportion of labour in this sector is permanent and
full-time; since much of the construction work must be
carried out in the dry season, seasonality may also
affect the amounts and levels of wages paid.   Table 52,
which gives rates for casual labour in rural public
works, indicates that the ratio of skilled to unskilled
is about 2:1 and appears to be increasing slightly.
But these data are only guidelines prepared by regional
officials as "target" wages for labour contractors, and
the extent to which they reflect competitive regional
rates is not clear.

Male/female wage differentials

The public service does not have separate scales
for males and females, though very few females are found
in the higher ranks.   In general, in the private
sector, wages for females are well below those of
males.   Manning found that the modern sector employers
(particularly foreign-owned enterprises) preferred male
production workers, partly because of the laws
restricting employment of females at night, generous
menstruation and maternity leave and partly because of
the employers' expectations that there will be greater
turnover among female employees.[39]   The fact that
females command lower wages on average is not so much
due to male/female differentials within a firm as to the
concentration of women in low-wage industries, e.g.
tobacco processing.   This is not inconsistent, says
Manning, with high wages for females in several
industries in which a small proportion of all employed
women work.

Table 52: Daily wages of skilled and unskilled workers in construction 1971/72 and 1981/82 (in Rupiah)

	1971/72			1981/82		
	Unskilled	Foremen	Skilled	Unskilled	Foremen	Skilled
Java, Bali and Nusatenggara Barat	127	213	240	525	675	1 050
Jakarta and Sumatra	229	313	409	700	850	1 400
Sulawesi, Maluku and Nusatenggara Timur	147	227	320	775	875	1 550
Kalimantan, Irian	315	449	527	1 000	1 000	2 000

Sources: H.W. Arndt: "Regional wage differentials" in Bulletin of Indonesian Economic Studies (Canberra, The Australian National University, Mar. 1972); and R. Daroesman: "Survey of recent developments" in Bulletin of Indonesian Economic Studies (Canberra, The Australian National University, July 1981).

The tracer study also found lower average wages for
females in all occupations. The very wide differences
in sales and in farming reflected the age groups as much
as sex. In the sales occupations, most of the females
were primary school graduates involved in market or
door-to-door sales, while males were secondary school
graduates working as sales personnel for industrial and
commercial firms in urban areas. Similarly in the
"farming" occupations, a few girls from secondary-level
schools were employed in high productivity areas such as
flower farming or in demonstration work, while farming
for males represented primary school graduates working
as farm labour. On average, males in the professional
and technical occupations got higher wages than
females; when primary school teachers (who accounted
for almost all the professionals and were almost
entirely female) were separated out, average wages for
males were still distinctly higher.

The tracer study also indicated that average wages
for new entrants were about half those of the adult
workers reported for the same year for the same
occupations in the labour force surveys. This finding
tallies with that of Sundrum.[40]

V.   CURRENT AND FUTURE ISSUES - AND SOME APPROACHES

General Economic Issues

Measures to increase employment in developing
countries have been described, following practices in
developed countries, as changes in input or output
mixes: changing techniques of production through
changes in factor prices, controls by government over
exchange and interest rates and thus over imported
inputs, and by attempts to set "correct" wages in the
private sector through minimum wage legislation or by
changing the composition of output towards more
labour-intensive manufactures for import substitution or
for export.[41] All of these approaches have been used
in Indonesia.

The November 1979 devaluation of the rupiah was
directed towards increasing non-oil exports; the
expansion of manufactures and semi-processed goods
would, it was expected, have positive employment effects
as well. Recent surveys, however, suggest that the
initial success of the devaluation was rather quickly
dissipated, and the employment effects have not been
markedly noticeable. The subsidised credit policies
which have been expanded so greatly in the past ten
years have had a more pervasive effect on the economy
and have been an important component, along with other

measures, in the doubling of rice production. They may also be having some effect on small industry and trade where they are supported by a range of other policies as part of the unremitting effort of the Government to improve the lot of the "weak economic group". But the extent to which this basket of policies increases employment and the extent to which it simply improves incomes of the already employed is not very clear. In one sense, it is also not very material since the increase in productivity of the underemployed is fully as important as any increase in additional "jobs" at low levels of productivity and low wages.

To return to the basic problem of policies and programmes to increase employment, concentration on job creation leads to approaches to the problem acting primarily on the demand side, following the theory and practice more relevant to the developed countries. In Indonesia, as we have emphasised, the most intractable problem is really one of low productivity or underemployment for the vast bulk of the labour force. Consideration of this aspect points to "solutions acting primarily on the supply side, by measures to raise the productive capacity of all workers – the unemployed, the underemployed, the employed and the overemployed alike" not only through appropriate factor prices, infrastructure, credit policies and land redistribution, but quite as importantly, through education and training.[42] The increase of productivity of any group of workers will not only increase the total output of goods and services, including the share of it accruing to those whose productivity is increased, but will also increase their demand for others' goods and services.

In the long term, the two policies which can be expected to have important impacts from the supply side are reduction of population growth and the transformation of the productive structure of society through education and training – which also has an appreciable incidence on the population limitation itself.

Even in the short term, better retention of the young in school can have a sizable effect on increased demand for labour. A one per cent increase in enrolments has the effect of decreasing the participation rate (although not in a full 1:1 ratio), which in turn reduces unemployment.[43] While attainment of full primary schooling for all children will not in itself decrease the numbers entering the labour force, it will allow them to enter at a more mature age and with better skills. The education system is also "its own best customer". Both increased retention at primary, and quality improvement and expansion at secondary level, will involve employment not only of teachers, but also of numerous educational services, construction, printing, manufacture of equipment, etc.

With the economy growing by 7.5 per cent a year, and overall enrolments by 8.5 per cent a year over the past decade, it is not surprising to find imbalances within the education system, or between the education system and the economy as a whole. In this section, we will look at some of the issues arising from these imbalances, and conclude with a discussion of some policies which may assist in their solution.

There is much less talk today, at least in Indonesia, about the dangers of educated unemployment than there was a decade ago; it has been a fear felt more on Indonesia's behalf than by Indonesia itself. Because secondary and tertiary education have so far been the privilege of upper income groups, fears over educated unemployment have centred on the potential dangers of urban concentrations of vocal discontent from politically influential households, rather than on the waste of resources or the economic effects of such unemployment.

The problem of educated unemployment in Indonesia may thus be summarised as:
(1) vast numbers of primary dropouts with low rates of unemployment who at best can look forward to low productivity and low-income work;
(2) a smaller number of those with full primary education whose opportunities will be slightly better;
(3) a very small number of lower secondary school-leavers whose employment characteristics vary little from the primary school group;
(4) the academically educated secondary graduates where unemployment rates are highest but numbers small, where expectations are high and where income levels of the employed are higher¹ than for the vocationally educated;
(5) the vocationally educated who have lower rates of unemployment but who also look forward to lower average rates of pay than the academically educated;
(6) those with tertiary education where unemployment rates are low and numbers few.

Two further points may be made. First, to the extent that the present high rates of inactivity among young male school-leavers represent "discouraged workers" rather than a queue to return to school, unemployment rates of secondary school-leavers may be underestimated. Second, the view that a job means "success" and unemployment means a school-leaver is "unsuccessful" obscures the fact that a waiting period appears to result in eventual attainment of a better job; but the distinction between the "waiters" and hard-core long-term unemployment of school-leavers deserves closer study.

The mismatch issue

The ILO reports on Sri Lanka, Colombia and Kenya have attributed educated unemployment, whether at primary or secondary level, to a mismatch between the "job expectations generated by the traditional system and the job opportunities provided by the labour market"[44] and have put forward the suggestion that "to cut down the output of primary and secondary schools or to somehow expand jobs, while leaving the structure of wages, salaries and fringe benefits what it is, will not in fact solve anything".[45]   These reports, published in the early 1970s, were followed by Dore's now famous analysis of the "Diploma Disease", the symptoms of which he identified as follows:[46]

- the income premiums for those with higher over those with lower educational levels are perceived by parents and students;
- high social demand for education is engendered, and parents sacrifice willingly to ensure that their children are in the queue for higher incomes;
- high social demand for places gives rise to increased provision, often through private schools, at a pace which exceeds the possibility of maintaining quality of education;
- the decrease of quality leads to an emphasis on exams and credentials and to "employee-minded" output;
- graduates of these dilute courses cannot find jobs at expected rates of pay or in the favoured professions and ranks of administrative services;
- those who can afford to do so then continue to higher levels of accreditation, and those who cannot take jobs for which they are "over-qualified" (though not necessarily over-educated);
- employers reinforce this emphasis on credentials by using them as a screening process, constantly upgrading the educational requirements for jobs;
- high qualification levels for low-level jobs is an expensive and inefficient use of scarce funds.

To what degree does Indonesia follow the pattern Dore has observed both in developed and developing countries? Dore also suggests that the later a nation enters the modernisation process, the more marked this pattern is. Has this been, or is this about to become, the dominant pattern in Indonesia?

First, average salaries obtained by those with tertiary education have been shown to be far higher than those obtained by primary or secondary graduates. Also, the pressure of private demand and expansion of the system and consequent dilution of quality are in evidence. There is as well an emphasis on examinations – almost to the exclusion of other methods of assessment – in the Indonesian educational system.

After that, however, the focus becomes somewhat blurred. Many elements of the diploma disease are certainly in evidence, but there are also important tendencies in the opposite direction. First, although there are high rates of unemployment among secondary and tertiary graduates, the nature of the unemployment appears to be frictional, and there appears to be little evidence of their being forced into low-level, low-productivity or low-income jobs. They have, indeed, been replacing those with lesser qualifications, but so far this has been "catching up" with educational levels set many years ago but not met (such as teachers with a full 12-year education replacing those with less education in primary schools). Underemployment of secondary graduates has not yet attained significant proportions, either measured in hours worked or in income.

There is certainly pressure for expansion of higher education from those who have completed secondary school. But university education is not the only response to this: the academies which offer a degree, but provide training in a single discipline with strong employment orientations have proliferated, as have other employment-preparation "courses". Post-graduate education is being severely limited by Government to a few established faculties, and emphasis is being given to training abroad as well as in-country at this level.

Private modern sector employers do not appear to place great reliance on credentials and often prefer a drop-out with desirable attitudes to a graduate without them. The traditional private sector probably also gives greater emphasis to other considerations than to credentials, but we still know very little about recruitment to this sector. Because its job specifications are so much less clear, the civil service still relies largely on mechanistic testing for selection; this in turn is based on educational-level qualifications. Unlike the private sector, the public sector is open to all without preference for specific schools or faculties, or individual characteristics.

While thus exhibiting many of the symptoms, Indonesia does not yet appear to have totally succumbed to the diploma disease; the greatest danger in the future will lie in the degree to which expansion outstrips quality. In its attempts to control this problem, the Government will have to take into account not only the expectations of the educated for high income status jobs, but also the expectations of those providing and operating the schools, and those of prospective employers. The Government's own expectations that the schools must prepare not only for higher education but also for employment include an unspoken assumption that the population will divide itself quite clearly into those suited for higher education and those who can benefit only from training for direct entry into the labour force; this expectation may also need to be reassessed.

Apart from this special meaning of mismatch, there are other issues of mismatch or imbalance, such as that between levels of education, with massive drop outs at grades 3 or 4 of primary school; the desirable speed of expansion of secondary education, in particular with regard to quality; the desirable balance between general and vocational secondary education; the issue of job creation and productivity; wage policy and labour market efficiency and the economic and educational planning framework.

Primary school drop-out

The fact that nearly half of those enrolled in primary school leave after only three or four years of schooling represents a waste of resources: literacy and numeracy for these drop-outs have reached only an insecure level; the national language has not yet become a common tool; and selection for further education occurring, as it does, on an economic basis, is a waste of human and development potential.

Secondary school expansion

As retention rates at primary level are improved, the present heavy demand for places in secondary schools will be intensified. The issue of expansion involves decisions both as to the numbers to be accommodated in secondary schools and as to the rates at which numbers and proportions are to be reached. Unlike economic targets, educational targets have frequently been exceeded in Indonesia as in other developing nations. These targets have so far been set according to projected output from lower levels of education rather

than in accordance with any long-term view of national
needs or employment possibilities. Incentives to, and
control over, provision of places are important features
of this issue.

Educational quality

One of the most difficult questions facing
educational planners and policy-makers today is how to
reintroduce quality into a rapidly expanding system and
at the same time meet popular claims for equality. Beeby
sums up the problem in his assessment: "There are
frequently strong differences of opinion on what
constitutes improvement in quality, and these
differences are intensified by the difficulty of
defining many qualitative objectives and of measuring
progress towards them", and goes on to point out that
"qualitative change in education is rarely linear and
continuous".[47]

There is no lack of emphasis on quality in public
statements on education or even in the Third Plan; the
ingredients are seldom spelled out except as in the Plan
in the form of numbers of books printed, numbers of
teachers attending upgrading courses, numbers of
laboratories constructed, in all of which there are
targets reached and exceeded.

But still there are complaints: from universities
that entrants are ill-prepared; from aid agencies that
scholarships go unused because appropriate candidates
cannot be found; from parents who compare their own
education with what their children are receiving, and so
on. Some years ago, the decline of quality was blamed
on lack of finance, but this cannot be the entire
cause. High expenditure per pupil may indicate high
quality, but it may also indicate a high degree of
wastage and inefficiency. Few would quarrel with the
view that the quality of teachers is the overriding
determinant of quality, whatever its definition.
Indonesia now has well over a million school teachers
and perhaps some 20-30,000 teaching staff in tertiary
and other institutions, a high proportion of them
young. The problem is a massive one indeed.

The role of vocational schools

The need for technically trained manpower (and for
those trained in administrative and clerical
occupations) in developing countries has had, in
Indonesia, an almost automatic corollary: that these
future workers should be trained in schools operated by
the Department of Education. As we have seen, this

view is both inherited from the colonial period and
reinforced not only by long practice but more recently
by a heavy infusion of bilateral and international aid
for technical schools in particular; it is further
reinforced by the practice of planning by simple
extrapolation from the past.

The colonial government aimed to produce specific
numbers of specialist manpower to fill specific slots in
its administration.   Independent Indonesia aims   to
educate all its citizens to at least primary level and
to higher levels in increasing but unspecified
proportions.   It aims to turn them out not only for
government administration but also for private sector
employment and for self-employment.   Thus vocational
education has always been considered "A Good Thing";
but questions of for what and for whom, how many, where
and when, in what form and at what cost, are only now
beginning to be widely discussed.

Training for what?

About 80 per cent of Indonesia's industry is in the
rural small-scale and cottage sector, and only about 20
per cent in the medium and large modern sector, the
latter mostly urban.   The same characteristics are
probably true for commerce.   For which sector should
the technical (and commercial) schools train?   If for
the modern sector, questions arise as to how schools can
be kept abreast of technological change in industry;
unless they have access to almost unlimited funds,
equipment and teachers once installed and trained must
be used for many years.   Evidence is mixed as to the
extent to which large modern industries prefer those
with a good general education over those with technical
school training.   Among the small and medium
traditional sector the range of products and range of
technology is very wide and changes in technology can be
expected to be very great over the next decade or so.

Where?

A decision on what the schools should train for
would reduce problems of location.   In large cities
where there are dozens of secondary schools, costs of
installation of special equipment for technical schools
are being minimised and efficiency increased by the
establishment of technical training centres which
provide practical workshop experience for a number of
schools.   It should be possible to do much the same
thing for commercial schools if they are expected to
train for modern sector commercial activities.   But as

education is extended to medium and smaller-sized towns
which can support only one or two schools, problems
arise over school size, free choice of school type by
students and cost both to government and parents.

Form and cost?

In the past technical and commercial schools have
had very low unit costs. To some extent this was
because of reporting peculiarities which omit many
sources of income, but to a greater extent it has been
that vocational schools were "pale copies" of general
schools. The high cost of providing quality technical
education is now being demonstrated by the schools
receiving project or foreign aid; the extent to which
this quality can be replicated without continuing
project aid is still an open question.

The alternative of a comprehensive school with
training centred on the present technical training
centre pattern has been widely discussed, but little
work has yet been done on estimating the costs and
advantages of such a major administrative reform.

The even more basic question of whether the same
quality or a better quality of technical and commercial
education can be provided more efficiently and at less
cost outside the schools has had little discussion and
virtually no research.

Labour absorption and wages

By what means can the nation best absorb into
employment an increasingly educated labour force in
order to transform and modernise the economy? As
primary retention and secondary expansion proceed, the
nature of employment creation can be expected to shift
from the current emphasis on rural public works; the
direction in which it will shift, and the rate of
progress, will depend on whether the output of schools
and universities are given quality education or merely
"certificated" in the Dore sense.

In the past the public service, including state
enterprises, has been the primary destination of the
university output, and of a large proportion of
secondary output. The concentration in the civil
service has had an important influence on wage structure
and on the expectations of graduates. As numbers
produced from these levels increase, the proportion
going into public service is bound to change. Policy
statements put emphasis on self-employment as a means of
absorbing labour; this implies an outlook on work
marked by initiative, a wide range of skills, and

resiliency, qualities not in fact given an equivalent degree of priority in schools.

A related issue concerns the allocation of labour by industrial sectors, the degree to which agriculture can continue to absorb a high proportion of the labour force, both in farming and in other agricultural activities, and the degree to which workers who drift away from agriculture can be absorbed in industries or services.

The educated labour force has been, up to the last few years, an urban feature; the extent and the rate at which the educated can be absorbed in rural areas, and in urban areas outside the few main cities, is another aspect of this issue, as is the general Java/Outer Island balance.

How can the wage system be adjusted to contribute towards fuller employment, higher productivity, better allocation of labour, and appropriate manpower development (the four functions of an efficient wage policy identified by Arndt and Sundrum)? So far, the public sector has dominated the wage system. At the top levels, it competes through a series of supplements with the private sector, while at the middle and lower levels it maintains a rate well in excess of that being offered by the private sector, unrelated to job productivity and constituting an obstacle to expansion of employment and a major cause of the high income expectations of current graduates.

Thus it would seem that educated unemployment in Indonesia today is largely frictional, but exacerbated by labour market inefficiency. The tracer study has shown that inexperienced young workers know little about occupations, about occupational requirements and how to look for jobs. Labour market information is still highly informal, concentrated in a few large cities in the modern sector and in the public service.

Some approaches

The two basic approaches to the problem of educated unemployment are to reduce or hold down the production of secondary and tertiary graduates to meet current demand, or increase jobs to absorb however many graduates are being produced from schools and universities. The first alternative does not solve problems of unemployment, but simply shifts them from the educated to the uneducated, from open to disguised unemployment. The economy is tied into a slow rate of development and, because of the long gestation periods required, the education system cannot rapidly expand to speed it up. This approach also requires assumptions

regarding the exact number and nature of the slots to be
filled, and these are very difficult to assess
accurately unless the economy is stagnant. For
Indonesia, as for other developing countries, this
approach has been politically unacceptable, being seen
as both anti-egalitarian and inadequate for the desired
rate of development.

The second alternative, that of increasing jobs to
absorb the output of schools and universities, has been
preferred, especially since attention to the problems of
unemployment and to the potential dangers of educated
unemployment occurred at about the same time as
government resources were greatly multiplied. Job
creation was therefore emphasised in the Third Plan.

The emphasis on numbers of jobs to be created
tends, however, to obscure somewhat the basic need in
Indonesia, which is for more productive work. It is
precisely in those sectors where productivity is least
that the highest proportions of the educated are
absorbed. The expansion of the public service and the
increasingly wide range of undertakings in heavy
industry and trade by state enterprises are likely to
mean that the absorption of high level manpower by
government will continue to increase. The burden on
public finance of this concentration is obvious,
particularly when wage differentials by educational
level are still great. It is the expectation of
austere financial conditions in the coming decade which
has turned more recent attention to the necessity for
self-employment (although this is directed more to the
less educated). But the qualities of initiative,
resilience and adaptability, and the wide range of
skills which mark successful self-employment, are not
notable features of the present education system.

The rate at which education is to be expanded under
this second alternative has in practice in the past been
left to social demand to determine. While this
approach may accurately reflect parental and community
wishes, it also reflects their past experiences rather
than the future characteristics of the job market.

Other approaches which have been suggested to
better coordinate the expansion with employment include
the manpower requirements approach, cost/benefit
analysis and rate of return. The manpower requirements
approach is essentially one in which the educational
system is to adapt to the expected rate of growth of the
economy; it makes education a passive agent which
exists to fill gaps in manpower requirements set for a
target rate of growth rather than giving it the active
function of raising the possible rate of growth.[48]
Another weakness of this approach is its neglect of the

costs and benefits of education.   The rate-of-return approach, designed to meet this shortcoming, was found inappropriate because in practice it identifies the social benefits of education with private benefits from personal earnings which are not reflected in differences in marginal product to employers, especially in the public sector where salaries are not determined by the market.   The rate of return approach also assumes that the salary structure observed at any point of time will remain constant and apply to earnings throughout the working life.   The policy applications of these approaches are thus confined only to short-time periods.   These approaches also assume rigid relations between education and total output.   Education, on the other hand, is not a causal, but a permissive factor.

Because of the weaknesses of these approaches, Sundrum suggests that the only way to expand education, build up quality, and co-ordinate the output of the expanded system with other development aims is to make long-term decisions in advance.   The question of the rate at which Indonesia desires and is willing to pay for quality education for all its citizens is a concern not only of professional educators and administrators but also of the nation as a whole.   Many of the other questions concern whether certain activities are best carried on in or outside of the schools and whether they are beyond the jurisdiction of school officials.

On the broader front of the economy as a whole, the numerous suggestions and recommendations made by previous studies of employment and unemployment, on the absorption of educated labour, and on the crucial increase in productivity among both the educated and the less educated, appear to be still valid.   They include changes in wage policy away from the basic-needs-oriented minimum wage towards identification of high and low wage pockets, the establishment of wage norms, and a decrease in salary differentials linked to education .through adjustments in public service wages. Of these, only the last has had any significant acceptance and progress.   There are also the prospects of reducing unemployment through the tertiary sector. But the absorptive power of this sector in particular is little understood as yet.   Thus self-employment in current employment strategy could perhaps be improved by a better understanding of this sector.

Research and adaptation of technology also remains a promising area for improvement in absorption of the educated in agriculture as well as in industry, particularly where industry is unnecessarily capital-intensive.   Agriculture will still have to absorb significant amounts of labour;   there is only little opportunity to expand employment through land redistribution, so that programmes of extension, more attention to productive uses of agricultural output as well as to inputs, and continuation of public works appear to hold out promise.

The transmigration programmes might be reviewed to assess whether they could absorb more young educated manpower than they now do as the emphasis changes from movement of population to regional development. A potential means of increasing employment experience for new school-leavers might be investigated through National Service programmes patterned on, for example, the Civilian Conservation Corps of the 1930s in the United States of America.

Policies on urbanisation could include more attention to policies on location of educational facilities, to avoid some of the current imbalances in educational output. Provision of better educational facilities outside Java could help to reverse the present flow and direct it away from that overpopulated area.

The labour-intensive public works programmes have been shown to be useful in providing income opportunities for rural labour during the agricultural slack season. The rural social services, such as health and education, are absorbing many of the rural educated, as are rural credit schemes and rural transport.

The lack of labour market information has been noted by many, but the means of remedying this have not been clarified, particularly as it concerns the young school-leaver.

Many of the problems of lack of co-ordination between the education system and the absorptive capacity of the economy for its output are beyond the power of the Department of Education to solve alone. However, there are, of course, many steps which can be taken within the education system which, in the short term, might alleviate some of the problems of co-ordination.

In sum, the desire for rapid economic and social development so strongly felt in Indonesia may best be served by a continued expansion of the education and training system, provided that the quality can be reinstated and maintained, and provided further that the human resources so developed can be channelled into the productive sectors of the economy.

VI. SUMMARY

As the preceding sections have shown, open unemployment of the highly educated is not a major problem in Indonesia. Among the tertiary educated, it is of a temporary nature and after some period of queueing up, virtually all are absorbed. The same is true of the secondary educated; though unemployment rates are higher than for the tertiary level, open unemployment at this level too is heavily concentrated among the young and inexperienced, complicated by high expectations and lack of knowledge about the job market. They too are gradually absorbed by their mid-twenties. Unlike in most developed countries, open unemployment in Indonesia is not closely associated with poverty. Indeed, up to the present, completion of secondary school has been largely limited to the relatively well-to-do households. The main problem has been identified, not as open unemployment, but as low-productivity employment. One feature of this problem is the imbalance among levels, the ratio of the highly educated to the middle level, of professionals to technicans. Another is the high proportion of the educated in the civil service where productivity is difficult to measure.

The approach of holding back expansion of the educational system has never been seriously considered in Indonesia, not necessarily because of unemployment considerations, but because of the intensity of private demand and the legitimate desire of the nation to modernise itself through an educated labour force and society. Demand has also been principally the cause of the manner and rate at which the school system has expanded, and the resultant imbalance among types and levels of education, among regions, and among such factors as provision of teachers. Only recently has there been an increasing awareness of the need to re-introduce quality into the rapidly expanding system. "Quality" education, however defined, cannot of itself increase employment any more than increased quantity can. But increased quantity alone will not even improve productivity, and may have a negative effect on it. The improvement of education in the sense of a change of emphasis from passive to active learning, in provision of textbooks, laboratories and, above all, in more careful selection and more intensive training of teachers can, on the other hand, help to increase productivity across all levels of society. To do so, educational plans need to be co-ordinated with more general policies of economic, social and physical infrastructure over the long term.

Notes

[1] It is estimated that the population more than doubled between 1845 and 1880 in Java, from 9.14 to 19.5 million. Jan O.M. Broek: Economic development of the Netherlands Indies (New York, Russell and Russell, 1942), p. 17.

[2] E.D. Hawkins: "Job inflation in Indonesia", in Asian Survey (Berkeley, University of California), May 1966, Vol. VI, No. 5, pp. 264-275.

[3] R. Daroesman: "Finance of education", Part II, in Bulletin of Indonesian Economic Studies (Canberra, The Australian National University), Mar. 1972, p. 68.

[4] The main sources of data used in this paper are the 1971 and 1980 Population Censuses, the 1976 and 1978 Labour Force Surveys (Reports VK-KK 0062.8101) and the 1976 Inter-Censal Population Survey (Reports VUS 78-22, 78-23, 79-27, 79-28, and VP 78-01), all from Central Bureau of Statistics, Jakarta. In addition reference has been made to various reports listed in the bibliography.

[5] For a review of the transmigration programme, see P.A. Meyer and C. MacAndrews: Transmigration in Indonesia: An annotated bibliography (Yogyakarta, Gadjah Mada University Press, 1978).

[6] T.H. Hull: "Indonesian population growth 1971-1980", in Bulletin of Indonesian Economic Studies (Canberra, The Australian National University), Mar. 1981, pp. 114-120.

[7] Population of Indonesia: Results of the sub-sample of the 1980 population census, Series S1 (Jakarta, Biro Busat Statistik, 1982, Report SP.LY 0661.8201). The data for other countries are from ILO Statistical Yearbook, various years.

[8] Manning points out that "... in theory firms are not permitted to employ children under the age of 12 and may not employ children aged 12-18 on night work ... the press has noted that the employment of children below the age of 12 is widespread ... Despite this attention, the Government has not raised the minimum age even to 14 in accordance with the Basic Law of 1951". C.G. Manning: Wage differentials and labour market

segmentation in Indonesian manufacturing (Canberra, The Australian National University, Ph.D. thesis, 1979), p. 164.

9 H.W. Arndt and R.M. Sundrum: "Employment, unemployment and underemployment", in Bulletin of Indonesian Economic Studies (Canberra, The Australian National University) Nov. 1980, p. 64.

10 A. Abey, A. Booth and R.M. Sundrum: "Labour absorption in Indonesian agriculture", in Bulletin of Indonesian Economic Studies (Canberra, The Australian National University), Mar. 1981, pp. 36-65.

11 G.W. Jones and B. Supraptilah: "Under-utilisation of labour in Palembang and Ujung Pandang", in Bulletin of Indonesian Economic Studies (Canberra, The Australian National University), Mar. 1976, pp. 30-57. See also H. Redman, H. Moir and Daliyo: Labour force and labour utilization in selected areas in Java: Results of an experimental survey (Jakarta, National Institute of Economic and Social Research), LEKNAS/LIPI monograph series, Aug. 1977, 2 vols.

12 M. Blaug: Education and the employment problem in developing countries (Geneva, ILO, 1974), p. 10.

13 G.W. Jones: "Labour force developments since 1961", in A. Booth and P. McCawley (eds.): The Indonesian economy during the Soeharto era (Kuala Lumpur, Oxford University Press, 1981), p. 229.

14 C.M. Widodo and K. Damanik: "Pengalaman kerja lulusan sekolah" (BP3K, Departemen Pendidikan dan Kebudayaan, Jakarta) 1979.

15 R. Daroesman and A. Weidemann: "The role of newspaper advertisements in employment recruitment", in Bulletin of Indonesian Economic Studies (Canberra, The Australian National University), Nov. 1982.

16 D.H. Clark: "Labour market outcomes for new senior secondary school graduates in Indonesia" (typescript) (Orono, University of Maine).

17 But see Table 49 below.

18 Kompas 21 June 1978.

19 D.H. Clark, op. cit.

[20] In the 1971 Population Census, for example, a person was classified as employed if he was working at the time of the enumeration or if he had worked for at least two days during the week preceding the enumeration. The 1971 Census results were published in two series showing widely different unemployment percentages. The preliminary C series showed much lower rates than the subsequent D and E series because the latter two tended to classify incomplete and doubtful returns as unemployed to a much greater extent than the C series. The D series has been quoted in this paper. In the 1976 Inter-Censal Population Survey and the 1976 and 1978 Labour Force Surveys and the 1980 Census, the employed were defined as those who had worked at least one hour during the week preceding enumeration. There were differences also in the time of year of enumeration, but problems of seasonality have been shown to be of less importance than problems of definition and coverage in accounting for the discrepancies. The inclusion of far greater numbers of rural women in the Inter-Censal Survey who were excluded from the Labour Force Surveys was the main reason for the widely different estimates of labour force (53.7 million as against 48.8 million respectively), even though both surveys were undertaken by the Central Bureau of Statistics in the same year. (H.W. Arndt and R.N. Sundrum, op. cit.)

[21] For further details on the colonial and early Independence period of education see: Pendidikan di Indonesia dari Jaman ke Jaman; Pendidikan di Indonesia, 1900-1940 (2 vols.) (Jakarta Badan Penelitian dan Pengembangan Pendidikan dan Kebudayaan, Departemen Pendidikan dan Kebudayaan) 1977. See also Raden Loekmani Djajadiningrat: From illiteracy to university, Netherlands Indies Council of the Institute of Pacific Relations, 1942.

[22] For a description of initiatives in establishing schools see R. Daroesman, op. cit. and also W. Heneveld: "The distribution of development funds: New school building in East Java", in Bulletin of Indonesian Economic Studies (Canberra, The Australian National University), Mar. 1978.

[23] Such schools depend for their existence on the availability of teachers in existing schools for their staff, and on existing buildings and equipment which they borrow or rent in off-hours. They find students because of the unappeased demand for schooling per se, and offer teachers welcome opportunities for additional

income from such part-time teaching. It is not uncommon for such private schools to be established by a group of teachers from the "host" school; the private school of this type then becomes a kind of satellite on the older, more established (usually state) school. A high proportion of private institutions at tertiary level also operate on this principle.

[24] C.E. Beeby: Assessment of Indonesian education: A guide in planning (Wellington, Oxford University Press, 1979).

[25] Republik Indonesia: Rencana pembangunan lima tahun ketiga, 1978/80-1983/84.

[26] W. Tjiptosasmito and W.K. Cummings: "The status and deployment of teachers in Indonesia" (Jakarta, World Bank Education Project No. 5, Department of Education and Culture, Aug. 1981, mimeo.).

[27] See, for example, D.A. Tisna Amidjaja: Kerangka pengembangan pendidikan tinggi jangka pangang (Jakarta, Direktorat Jenderal Pendidikan Tinggi, Departemen Pendidikan dan Kebudayaan, 1980).

[28] Problems are also found with estimates of those with primary and no schooling. Hull analysed the differences between the 1971 · Census and the 1976 Inter-Censal Survey because it appeared that there had been a decline in the numbers of people with completed primary education between the two years; this seemed extremely unlikely in view of the great increase in primary education of the late 1970s. The problem seems to lie with the way in which questions were asked and in hasty enumeration in the labour force surveys. Because of these problems of definition, great care should be taken in the discussion which follows on average wages received by educational level or school type. T.H. Hull and Sunaryo: "Difficulties of measuring achieved schooling in Indonesia", in Asian and Pacific Census Forum (Honolulu, East-West Population Institute), Vol. 6, No. 3, Feb. 1980, pp. 9-13.

[29] See sources for Tables 44, 45 and 46.

[30] P. McCawley: "The Economics of Ekonomi Pancasila", in Bulletin of Indonesian Economic Studies (Canberra, The Australian National University), March 1982, pp. 102-109.

31 R.M. Sundrum: Development economics (Chichester, John Wiley and Sons, 1983), p. 85.

32 H.W. Arndt and R.M. Sundrum: "Wage problems and policies in Indonesia", in International Labour Review (Geneva, ILO), Vol. 112, No. 5, Nov. 1975, pp. 369-387.

33 C. Gray: "Civil Service compensation in Indonesia", in Bulletin of Indonesian Economic Studies (Canberra, The Australian National University), Mar. 1979.

34 Asian Regional Team for Employment Promotion: Manpower and related problems in Indonesia (Bangkok, ILO, June 1972), p. 64.

35 Arndt and Sundrum, op. cit.

36 ibid.

37 Collier, op. cit.

38 C.G. Manning, op. cit.

39 ibid.

40 R.M. Sundrum: "Employment policies for development and equality" (seminar paper) (Canberra, The Australian National University), Mar. 1975.

41 R.M. Sundrum, 1983, op. cit.

42 H.W. Arndt and R.M. Sundrum: "Transmigration: Land settlement or regional development?" in Bulletin of Indonesian Economic Studies (Canberra, The Australian National University) Nov. 1977.

43 R.M. Sundrum: "A macro-economic approach to educational planning", Canberra, Australian National University, 1971, mimeo.

44 Towards full employment, A Programme for Colombia, prepared by an Inter-Agency Team organised by the International Labour Office (Geneva, ILO, 1970), 350 pp. plus appendices; Employment incomes and equality: A strategy for increasing productive employment in Kenya (Geneva, ILO, 1972), 600 pp.; and Matching employment opportunities and expectations: A programme of action for Ceylon (Geneva, ILO, 1971), 251 pp.

[45] M. Blaug, op. cit.

[46]   R.   Dore: The   diploma   disease,   education,
qualification and development (London, George Allen and
Unwin Ltd., 1976), 214 pp.

[47] C.E. Beeby, op. cit.

[48] Sundrum, 1983, op.cit.

BIBLIOGRAPHY

Arndt, H.W.; "Regional wage differentials", in Bulletin
of Indonesian Economic Studies, Mar. 1972.

---; Sundrum, R.M. "Wages, salaries and incentives",
Paper delivered at a panel discussion of the Asian
Regional Team for Employment Promotion, International
Labour Organisation, Jakarta, May 1974.

Atma Jaya Research Centre. Hawkers in Jakarta. Jakarta,
Atma Jaya Research Centre, 1976.

Beeby, C.E. Assessment of Indonesian education: A guide
in planning. Wellington, New Zealand Council for
Educational Research and Oxford University Press, 1979.

Biro Pusat Statistik. The labour force situation in
Indonesia 1979: Average for the months of February,
May, August and November. Jakarta, BPS, 1981.

---. SAKERNAS [National Labour Force Survey] 1976: The
labour force situation in Indonesia, September-
December 1976: Main summary and tables. Jakarta,
BPS, 1978.

---. SAKERNAS [National Labour Force Survey] 1976: The
labour force situation in Indonesia, September-
December 1976. Jakarta, BPS, 1979.

---. Sensus penduduk [Population census] 1971: Penduduk
Indonesia, Seri D. Jakarta, BPS, 1975.

---. Statistik Sosial [Social Statistics]: Statistik
pendidikan diluar lingkungan departemen P & K,
September 1979. Jakarta, BPS, 1980.

---. SUPAS [Intercensal Population Survey] 1976,
Tabulation Series No. 3: The Indonesian labor force.
Jakarta, BPS, 1977.

Blaug, M. Education and the employment problem in developing countries. Geneva, ILO, 1974.

Booth, A.; McCawley, P. (eds). The Indonesian economy
during the Soeharto era. Kuala Lumpur, Oxford
University Press, 1981.

---; Sundrum, R.M. "An evaluation of labor market per-
formances in developing countries", Paper presented at
a work-in-progress seminar, Department of Economics,

Research   School   of   Pacific   Studies,   Australian
National University, Mar. 1980.

Daroesman, R.   "Finance of education, Part I",   in
Bulletin of Indonesian Economic Studies, VII(3), 1971,
pp. 61-95.

---.   "Finance of education, Part II",   in   Bulletin of
Indonesian Economic Studies, VIII(1), 1972, pp. 32-68.

---.   "Survey of recent developments",   in   Bulletin of
Indonesian Economic Studies, July 1981.

Garnaut, R.G.;   McCawley, P.   Indonesia: dualism, growth
and poverty.   Canberra,   Research School   of Pacific
Studies, Australian National University, 1980.

Hadiwaratama.   "Technical   and   vocational   education in
Indonesia",   Paper   prepared   for   UNESCO   General
Conference,   Belgrade,   1980,   Jakarta,   Ministry   of
Education and Culture, 1980.

Hawkins, E.   "Job   inflation   in   Indonesia",   in Asian
Survey, VI(5), 1966, pp. 264-275.

---.   "Labour   in   transition",   in   R.T.   McVey   (ed.):
Indonesia. New Haven, HRAF Press, 1963, pp. 248-271.

Hull, T.H.; Sunaryo "Difficulties of measuring achieved
schooling in Indonesia", in Asian and Pacific Census
Forum, 6(3), 1980.

---; ---.   "Was the education question on the 1971 census
wrong or has Indonesia been deschooling society?",
Indonesian Population Dynamics Project, Working Paper
No. 11. Yogyakarta, Population Institute, Gadjah Mada
University, 1978.

IBRD.   Education: Sector policy paper.   Washington,   DC,
1980, 3rd ed.

ILO,   Asian   Regional   Team   for   Employment   Promotion.
Manpower and related problems in Indonesia.   Bangkok,
ILO, June 1972.

Indonesia,   Badan Administrasi Kepegawaian Negara.   Data
pegawai   dalam   bentuk   grafik: Lampiran   buku   I.
Jakarta, Badan Administrasi Kepegawaian Negara, 1975.

Indonesia, Ministry of Education and Culture, Office of
Educational and Cultural Research and Development
(BP3K). The employment experience of school leavers:
A preliminary report stage I from a longitudinal study
of primary, lower and upper secondary school
graduates. Jakarta, Ministry of Education and
Culture, 1977.

---. The employment experience of school leavers: An
interim report on a longitudinal study of primary,
lower and upper secondary school graduates in
Indonesia. Jakarta, Ministry of Education and
Culture, 1978.

---. Teacher education in Indonesia. Jakarta, Ministry
of Education and Culture, 1980.

Manning, C.G. "Wage differentials and labour market seg-
mentation in Indonesian manufacturing", Ph.D. thesis.
Canberra Research School of Pacific Studies,
Australian National University, 1979.

Koentjaraningrat. The social sciences in Indonesia,
Vol. I. Jakarta, Institute of Social Sciences (LIPI),
1975.

McCawley, P. Industrialisation in Indonesia: Developments and prospects. Development Studies Centre,
Australian National University, Occasional Paper No.
13, Canberra, Australian National University, 1979.

Moegiadi, C.M.; Elley, W.B. "Evaluation of achievement
in the Indonesian education system", in Evaluation in
education, 2(4), 1979, pp. 281-351.

Moir, H. Economic activities of women in rural Java:
Are the data inadequate?. Development Studies Centre,
Australian National University, Occasional Paper No.
20. Canberra, Australian National University, 1980.

Palmier, L. "Occupations of Indonesian graduates",
article submitted to the Bulletin of Indonesian
Economic Studies.

Redmana, H.R.; Moir, H.; Daliyo. Labor force and labor
utilization in selected areas in Java, Vol. I.
Jakarta, LEKNAS-LIPI, 1977.

Seah, C.; Soeratno, P. Higher education in the changing
environment, Case studies: Singapore and Indonesia.
Singapore, Regional Institute of Higher Education and
Development, 1979.

Siahaan, L. et al. Japanese direct investment in Indonesia: Findings of an experimental survey. Tokyo, Institute of Developing Economies, 1978.

Simanjuntak, P. "The market for educated labor in Indonesia: Some Policy approaches", Ph.D. thesis. Boston, University of Boston, 1981.

Snodgrass, D.R.; Lindung, H.; Seroso, D. Inpres sekolah dasar: An analytical history, Development Program Implementation Study, Working Paper No. 2. Harvard, Harvard Institute for International Development, 1980.

Sundrum, R.M. "Education in relation to economic development and employment in the ECAFE region", typescript, n.d.

---. "Employment policies for development and equality", Paper presented at a work-in-progress seminar. Department of Economics, Research School of Pacific Studies, Australian National University, 1975.

---. Growth and development, Institute of Economic Growth, Occasional Papers, New Series No. 3. Delhi, Hindustan Publishing Corporation, 1981.

---. "A macro economic approach to educational planning". Canberra, Australian National University, 1971; typescript.

---. "Manpower aspects of educational planning in East and Southeast Asia", Paper delivered at the Conference on Manpower Problems in East and Southeast Asia, Singapore, May 1971.

---. Booth, A. "Income distribution in Indonesia: trends and determinants", in R.G. Garnaut and P.T. McCawley (eds.): Indonesia: dualism, growth and poverty. Canberra, Research School of Pacific Studies, Australian National University, 1980.

Thomas, R.M. A chronicle of Indonesian higher education: The first half century, 1920-1970. Singapore, Chopmen Enterprises, 1973.74

University of Indonesia, Faculty of Economics, Program Perencanaan Nasional. The dilemma of civil service wage fixing in Indonesia. Jakarta, University of Indonesia, 1975; mimeo.

Waskito, T.; Cummings, W.K. "The status and deployment of
teachers in Indonesia", Report of research
co-ordinated by Waskito Tjiptosasmito related to P3G
(Proyek Pengembangan Pendidikan Guru), World Bank
Education Project No. 5, 1981; mimeo.

Widodo, C.M.; Damanik, K. The employment experience of
school-leavers. Jakarta, Indonesia, Department of
Education and Culture, Office of Education and
Cultural Research and Development, 1979; mimeographed.

6 SUMMARY, LESSONS AND ISSUES

I. SUMMARY

1. Introduction

The upshot of this study would seem to be that schooling lays a curse on prospective workers predisposing them to unemployment, in contrast to an abundant literature on the theme "more schooling means more earnings". It shows that schooling – in the way it has been provided in the four countries studied – seems to throw up certain obstacles to the immediate entry of school-leavers and university graduates into employment.

Despite the diversity of contexts the four countries showed a curious similarity of approaches and remedies to the same problem. Not surprisingly the "four" also had common failures. · The characteristic approach was to make schools, or a large part of them, more "vocational" when unemployment went from bad to worse. This was not a wholesale, overnight transformation because the changes were effected gradually in slow steps. Viewed as a whole, however, it showed an unmistakable trend towards increasing the vocational content of curricula in schools.

It is interesting to enquire why the approach taken by the four countries does not seem to work. It is not that school approaches do not matter, even though school systems are rather slow to react in this regard; it is simply that the school systems reacted in what may be called the wrong direction. Instead of disengaging themselves from specific vocational training and concentrating on general education such as the refinement of skills in the 3Rs, schools became increasingly vocational. As it were, they used the vocational school solution to the unemployment of educated labour.

This is not to say that practical, handicraft instruction should not be given in schools, because it has its proper place in general education; but when it is given heavy emphasis, it causes problems. Certain inherent features of the short-lived technology embodied in specific vocational skills make schools an

ineffective means of delivering those skills. In fact,
it would seem that those skills are better taught either
on the job or off the job in short courses, not in
school curricula, thus leaving schools free to discharge
their proper function in general education.

This observation raises some questions. For
instance, how is it that school authorities have been
unaware, or seemingly unaware of this rather simple
inference? Why is it that they continue to use the
vocational school solution despite the attendant
difficulties of its _prima facie_ ineffectiveness?
Answering these questions adequately would require a
separate treatise on educational change, particularly on
the behaviour of "stakeholders" in this change. (See
also Turnham and Jaeger on this point, the dominance of
middle- to upper-class values as regards the sort of
schooling and training that the lower classes ought to
receive.) Certainly educational authorities, among
other vested-interest groups and important stakeholders,
tend to prefer status quo to change. There are also
overtones to these questions, one of which is the
historical context in which practical trade schooling
was foisted on colonies at the discretion of colonial
administrations.

2. On the unemployment of educated labour

As mentioned in the introductory chapter, the
notion of "educated unemployment" or, more exactly,
unemployment of the educated labour force, contains two
loosely understood elements. The first element is the
term "educated", the determination or definition of
which is rather problematic in the context of poor
countries where the quality of schools varies widely.
Similar-looking school certificates or formal
qualifications may not mean the same thing, so that they
are inadequate as indicators of levels of schooling or
for distinguishing those who are truly educated from
those who are not. Thus, level of schooling as a
measure of any formally acquired education can only be
used with great caution.

The second element is "unemployment", the opposite
of "employment" as understood in modern economies. The
fine nuances of this concept mean nothing when they are
improperly applied to poor countries. Even the simplest
notion of employment is turned to derision when working
for one single hour in a reference week is sufficient to
classify a person as "employed". Casting the definition
as wide as this tends to conceal underemployment,
grossly overestimate employment, and correspondingly
underestimate unemployment.

Hence unemployment of educated labour as thus measured tends to be rather low. In many cases the rates are well within the range associated with frictional unemployment, i.e. brief periods of unemployment that allow workers to move to better jobs. In reality, however, the problem is far more serious than would appear from conventional labour statistics.

Tanzania

A prime example is Tanzania, whose unemployment rates were 7.0 per cent in urban areas, 3.9 per cent in rural areas and 4.0 per cent for the country as a whole. Detailed calculations by educational level, however, showed much higher figures for those who had gone to school. For instance, the unemployment rate of those who had never been to school was only 2.2 per cent, but the rates were 5.4 per cent of those who had up to 4 years' schooling (Standard 4) and 7.3 per cent of those who had from five up to eight years. The unemployment rates were much higher still in urban areas (where the educated tended to forgather): about 19 per cent of those with up to Standard 4; 18 per cent of those with Form 2 (nine to ten years of schooling) and 16.7 per cent of those with Form 4 (11 to 12 years of schooling).

Underemployment was even greater. While there are no figures available for estimating underemployment by school level, there are data which show that adjustment for visible underemployment (based on a standard number of hours in a working week) would increase the country's unemployment rates to 11.2 per cent for the urban areas, 18.7 per cent for the rural areas and 18.4 per cent for the country as a whole. But if the urban minimum monthly wage of Tsh.150/ (roughly $18.00) were used as the income standard, adjustment for invisible underemployment would add 5.1 and 55.1 percentage points, respectively, to the 7.0 per cent rate in the urban and 3.9 per cent in the rural areas. Without a doubt underemployment of the "educated" would be less than that of the non-educated, using the Tsh.150/ income standard, but this might not be so if the standard were to vary with educational level as in the wage scale in government service.

These figures are from a labour force survey in 1965, because later data are not available in a usable form. Recent data perhaps reflect an official stance that does not recognise the existence of unemployment in the country. Even recently a Tanzanian M.P. was quoted as saying, "There is no unemployment in the real sense of the word because we have sufficient land" (Africa Now, Dec. 1982, p. 61).

However, indirect observations indicate that the
unemployment and underemployment that were recorded in
1965 may not have improved substantially since then.
Recent unemployment of Form 4 school-leavers, which was
25 per cent in 1976 and 32 per cent in 1981, seems to be
worse than the relative shares of unemployment in 1965
among urban workers with some schooling.

Egypt

Unemployment was also measured conventionally; this
produced figures that understated actual unemployment.
According to census figures, unemployment in Egypt was
only 2.2 per cent in 1960 and 7.7 per cent in 1976.

When these figures were broken down by categories,
however, unemployment of the non-educated increased from
1.85 per cent in 1960 to 2.5 per cent in 1976. But the
unemployment of those with at least primary schooling
rose from 6.53 per cent to 13.86 per cent between the
two census years. Further breakdown by level of
schooling revealed similar trends. The unemployment
rates of workers with primary schooling edged up from
4.04 to 6.91 per cent, but the corresponding rates for
workers with intermediate or secondary schooling
increased more than twofold from 8.37 to 19.90 per
cent. Likewise, the unemployment rates of workers with
university qualifications more than doubled from 4.26 to
10.80 per cent.

Readers who are familiar with the Egyptian scene
will suspect that the figures may be overestimates
caused partly by misreporting. Because by statute
government jobs were guaranteed to workers with at least
secondary technical school qualifications, some workers
who were in this category and who were working in
private firms might have reported as "unemployed" in
order not to be disqualified for government posts. The
extent of this misreporting is not precisely known.
However, it could only be a fraction of the 13.6 per
cent of workers with at least secondary school
qualifications who worked in the private sector in
1976. It cannot be of the same order of magnitude as
the reported overstaffing in government offices, which a
disputed estimate put at 40 per cent.

The Philippines

Like in Tanzania and Egypt, employment in the
Philippines was conventionally measured. The reported
figures, therefore, should be regarded as underestimates
of unemployment.

Long-term trends seem to indicate that open unemployment had been receding from 10 per cent in 1956 to 6.1 per cent in 1965 and to only 3.9 per cent in 1975. This rate bobbed up to 5.2 per cent in 1976 but then decreased again to about 4.9 per cent in 1978. As already noted above, these rates are low and in fact much lower than recent figures in Europe, but knowing that the figures are underestimates we have good cause for concern. For instance, an indirect estimate of total unemployment in 1972, including open unemployment and the full-time unemployment equivalent of invisible underemployment, was between 25 and 33 per cent, but by conventional measurement unemployment was placed only at 6.1 per cent.

Unemployment in 1968 was low among workers with no schooling (4.4 per cent) and those who had attended primary school (4.5 per cent). It was high among those with incomplete college attendance (17.4 per cent) but it tended to be on the low side (7.2 per cent) among those who had completed four or more years of college studies.

A different sort of measurement and its statistic, called the "non-utilisation rate", shows much higher figures. The utilisation rate of a category of workers is simply the ratio of the employed to its population, whereas the employment rate of the same category is the ratio of the employed to its labour force. Because population is larger than labour force, the utilisation rate is arithmetically smaller than employment rate. By way of consequence the non-utilisation rate is always higher than the unemployment rate. It is this yardstick that is used to gauge to what extent a poor country, which in principle has a scarcity of educated and skilled workers, is able to turn its stock of human resources to account.

The overall non-utilisation rate, so defined, for workers with at least one year of high school was 35 per cent in 1969. The rate of high school graduates was 22 per cent, while the corresponding figure for those with one to three years of college was 61.7 per cent, presumably because many of them were still at the university. Nevertheless, the non-utilisation rate was still a sizable 39.4 per cent for workers who had completed college.

Later figures in 1975 showed that while the unemployment rate of college graduates stood at about 8 per cent, the non-utilisation rate was 22 per cent, indicating that more than one out of every five graduates were not working.[1]

According to certain writers, these figures do not mean that the unemployed will never find work, even

after a protracted period of job-seeking. In their
view, unemployment of the educated labour force is a
question of flows or of waiting time, which for some
graduates can take several years.

The pattern of this flow, according to a tracer
study in 1969, showed that unemployment of graduates
could be plotted as a declining curve. It was steep
during the first year after graduation, less steep in
the second year and rather flat in the succeeding
years. From a starting point of 100 per cent at
graduation, unemployment (in terms of unweighted average
of non-utilisation rates) was down to about 36 per cent
within a year and was further reduced to about 18 per
cent in the second year. From then on the decline was
very slow: to 13 per cent in the third year about 10 per
cent in the fourth year and about 7 per cent in the
fifth year. These figures suggest that even after the
end of the third year, a significant number of graduates
were still unable to find a suitable post. Many of them
had to wait till the fifth year and for some, the 7 per
cent mentioned above, the waiting and job-search
continued. However, if the non-response of about a
quarter of the graduates surveyed was interpreted as
"unemployed", the unemployment uncovered by the tracer
study could have been much greater.[2]

There is no way of telling whether this pattern has
changed substantially for the better, even if the
conventional unemployment rate, which at the time was
about 8 per cent, eased in later years to about 4.9 per
cent in 1978. A later tracer survey of employed
graduates showed that their non-utilisation rate was
higher in 1978 than in previous years. Within less than
six months after graduation, the non-utilisation rates
were 28.2 per cent in 1963-64 and 31.2 in 1967-68 but
this rate was 44.8 per cent in 1978. The 1978 tracer
study indicated that a large number of the graduates
were in voluntary unemployment, that is, they refused to
take up jobs for one reason or another. Some of these
reasons were low salary offer, bad working conditions,
job too far away, and no opportunities for advancement.

Indonesia

Once again, the low unemployment rates in Indonesia
are the result of casting the definition of employment
very wide. Working two days or 14 hours during the
reference week was sufficient for a person to be
considered "employed" in the 1971 census. In this
census the overall unemployment was 8.8 per cent. It
was 12.5 per cent in the urban and 8.2 per cent in the
rural areas. When the cut-off point or criterion was

reduced to "at least one hour" in the 1976 intercensus population survey, the unemployment rate was only 3.0 per cent. But if the 1971 criterion had been used in 1976, the measured unemployment rate would have risen to 12.8 per cent, a full 4 percentage points increase (cf. Simanjuntak, pp. 8ff). To say the least, the employment situation was not improving.

These figures are very small compared to underemployment. The visibly underemployed – those who worked less than 35 hours during the reference week in 1976 were found to constitute about 37 per cent of the "employed", according to the criterion of working time mentioned above (ibid.).

Even with the low criterion, however, unemployment of workers with some schooling was large in 1971. As a reference point, unemployment stood at 7.8 per cent among those without schooling, but the comparable rate was 14.3 per cent among workers who had had some schooling. Among the latter, unemployment tended to vary, though not directly, with level of schooling: 9.8 per cent among those with elementary (or primary) school qualifications, 14.5 per cent among those with senior high school certificates, but 12.4 per cent among those with university degrees.

With the one-hour criterion in 1976, unemployment among the unschooled was only 0.8 per cent but it was about 8.7 per cent among those who had been to school. Again, even if the figures are lower than the corresponding rates in 1971, still the unemployment rates tend to vary upwards with educational level: 2.4 per cent for completed elementary school and 9.8 per cent for completed senior high school. The unemployment rate among those who had completed higher education was, however, only 3.3 per cent.

A sub-sample survey of population in 1978 and the census in 1980 followed the one-hour criterion used in 1976 and thus showed similarly low measured unemployment rates.

Yet when the data were broken down by age groups, the rates were nonetheless high. The 1978 survey showed that, while the overall unemployment rate for Indonesia was measured at 2.5 per cent, the rates were 8.0 per cent for age group 15–19 years old and 7.6 per cent for age group 20–24 years old. Among all those who had completed primary school the unemployment rate was 3.4 per cent, but this rate was 9.6 per cent among the 15–19 year-olds, though only 6.1 per cent among the 20–24 year-olds.

Unemployment rates were much higher at the secondary levels of qualification. Among the same age groups as above, for those who had junior high school certificates the rates were 16.6 per cent for the 15–19 year–olds and 16.4 per cent for the 20–24 year–olds. The corresponding rates among those with academic senior high school qualifications were a surprising 66.1 per cent and 26.9 per cent, respectively.

These variations clearly show that unemployment hit hard at the young educated age-groups, particularly the 15–19 year–olds who had secondary school qualifications. Even among the 20–24 year old university-educated group unemployment ran at about 27 per cent.

As a problem of the young and educated, unemployment was studied in detail by means of a tracer study. It was found that indeed for many school-leavers and graduates entry to jobs was quite a problem. About two-thirds of primary and secondary school-leavers who were unemployed had been looking for work for more than 8 months after graduation (Widodo and Damanik, 1979). About 40 per cent of secondary school-leavers were still looking for jobs one year after graduation and 25 per cent were still in quest of employment one year later (IBRD, 1982, p. 117). There were also many school-leavers who were waiting for admission to further studies in the schools of their choice. Hence, the transition process which was often recorded in surveys as unemployment might have been a leisurely process of awaiting re-entry to further schooling or of unhurried job seeking, especially for public sector jobs.

However, all these remarks about how serious or otherwise educated unemployment has been in quantitative terms in Indonesia should not obscure the fact that the main problem is a variety of underemployment. It is not of the conventional sort reported in population censuses or in labour force surveys, but rather that of work with very low productivity. Most of the country's talented and educated youth aspire to work in the public sector or in the government bureaucracy. They are thus fatally attracted towards this blind alley rather than to other possibilities of more innovative and productive work in certain parts of private industry.

Whether in Indonesia, Egypt, Tanzania or the Philippines, unemployment (as measured) was always higher among the younger age groups than the older ones. The rates varied from one country to another and from one socio-economic context to another, but the pattern remained the same, something like an incomplete inverted U: unemployment was usually lowest among the least schooled, highest among those with middle-school qualifications, then somewhat less among those with the university degree, presumably because the last mentioned had a better _entrée_ to public-sector employment than those with lesser qualifications.

There are several plausible explanations to this observed pattern. First, schools may have overproduced school-leavers and university graduates in excess of what the economy can absorb. In general this "overproduction" is manifest, and its supposed causes have been thoroughly surveyed elsewhere (Blaug, 1973, 1977). However, the hypothesis that except at the very top the overproduction is a function of the number of years spent in school is difficult to defend, because the output of schools is usually much larger at the low than at the high levels of academic achievements. For this hypothesis to hold water, it requires a further assumption that, towards the far end of educational attainment, the demand for "educated" workers shrinks even smaller than the output of the institutions of higher learning, an assumption that remains to be investigated.

Second, it may be that the celebrated "pattern" mentioned above is only an illusion. It is possible that there exists an inverse relation between unemployment and the time spent in job-seeking, because workers who have never been to school have more time to look for work, and because the longer the time one spends in school the less time one will have for situation-hunting. This contention implies that if the data were "controlled" for time spent in labour markets, the observed differences in unemployment rates between school levels would become attenuated and the pattern would cease to exist.[3] If so, the problem would be reduced to one of overproduction, pure and simple, for which the remedy is obvious, i.e. curtailing production. But this oversimplifies the problem by negating all other causes, e.g. certain features of schools and labour markets.

It is perhaps conceivable that the relationship between unemployment rates and schooling may be totally different from the pattern just observed. However, this is implausible, as the following two cases suggest. The first case is that of a zero relationship, i.e. after "controls" for time spent in the labour market. This case has already been mentioned as quite unlikely. The second case is that of a negative relationship, the reverse, of what was observed, i.e. the more the schooling the lower the unemployment rate; this is plausible if the unschooled and the schooled prospective workers were to compete for the same jobs in the same labour market. But this condition is speedily ruled out by labour market segmentation which hinders different categories of workers from competing for the same jobs. Without

job competition little remains of the supposed advantage
of the schooled workers over the less schooled and
unschooled, as regards the time needed to find jobs. If
this is so unemployment is no longer inversely dependent
on schooling but depends directly on the conditions of
the labour market within each segment; hence, the
implausibility of a possible negative correlation as
mentioned above. This inference leaves us only with the
third or last case, i.e. the positive correlation that
was observed earlier.

Third, the speed of labour absorption in the labour
market varies with educational level. In the third
case, above, the speed is slower among the "educated"
than among the non-educated workers and is dependent on
certain features of labour markets. On the one hand
employers are rather rigid as regards hiring standards
and on the other the prospective employees are no less
inflexible than the employers. This is in part a
mis-education explanation, a subject to which we shall
turn later.

Between countries, the observed pattern was so
general that it must have had causes that rendered the
different contexts irrelevant. We considered a number
of labour market policies that the countries used for
directly containing unemployment and then drew
inferences from the effects of those policies. Our
general impression was that the pattern occurred despite
the policies. There was even good reason to believe
that the policies worsened the situation without
altering the observed pattern.

Attention was also directed at systems of schooling
and training as an explanatory variable. The systems
varied from one country to another so that this might
easily be dismissed as inconsequential. Surprisingly,
however, the content and general logic or "ideology" of
what appeared to be different systems were fairly
similar among the four countries.

II. LESSONS

It was not the object of the study to propose any
policy specific for each country, because recommendatory
roles pertain to specialised missions that are
undertaken at the request of a member State. Nor was it
the intention to supplant the recommendations of
missions to any of the countries being studied, but
simply to expand a knowledge base or shed light on a
grey area, namely, the use of schools and training as a
means of alleviating unemployment.

The expansion of the knowledge base is a matter of
drawing lessons from diverse political economies. The

diversity, however, was not without common features, not only in their problems and policy measures but also in their failures. Thus at the outset, learning how to avoid those failures is a good lesson in itself.

To simplify our task of presentation, we have treated the supposed economic causes as given. That is, we consider economic conditions as a context or background to highlight the general effect of poor economic performance on unemployment. There is, of course, a further reason, that is, by treating the economic conditions as given, we are able to sharpen our focus on certain diagnoses and measures that governments usually take when joblessness appears.

A.   Direct intervention in the labour market

Direct intervention has many forms, ranging from guaranteed jobs, rapid expansion of schools, and school-like measures such as national volunteer service and military services, to permissiveness in migration.

1.   Guaranteed jobs in the public sector

This was a natural consequence in Tanzania because the output of the university was much less than the requirements of public sector employment. But it was an extraordinary measure used in Egypt for conscripts, secondary technical school-leavers and university graduates. The result was heavy overstaffing in public sector employment. A further result was to induce an increased demand for schooling, especially at the secondary and tertiary levels, and for schooling of the academic sort. Hence, the next rounds of demand for guaranteed jobs increased in scale and constituted a problem far greater than before.

2.   Reducing the labour force

The measures under this heading are like statistical exercises. The object is to label a large part of the unemployed in such a way that they are excluded from the labour force.

Expansion of the school system

Keeping working-age children and young adults in school directly reduces the number who will be looking for work. This is useful until a point is reached when any further increase in enrolment will be neutralised by drop-out rates and later by increased numbers of school-leavers and graduates. In countries whose population is mostly young, say, less than 21 years old, extended schooling may have kept the labour force participation rates and unemployment rates statistically low. This may have been true in the Philippines and to a limited extent in Indonesia and Egypt, but not in Tanzania where enrolment rates have not as yet been high.

Military service

Military service reduces the civilian labour force. Retaining people longer in the military service may keep them from demanding civilian jobs. Used in Egypt, this measure may have had the unforeseen result of impelling secondary workers (defined as children, women and the elderly) to look for work. Hence, it may have had the exact reverse effect of increasing the size of the labour force and of swelling unemployment as well.

National service

In Tanzania this was a para-military service, engaged mostly in civic work in village development and in some instances in police duties. This national service was intended to instil and develop socialistic attitudes through direct service to the people. It was also used as a stepping-stone to jobs in government service. As a para-military activity the national service reduced the size of the civilian labour force, an effect similar to that of military service.

In Indonesia national service has been in the form of a youth volunteer programme, not as a para-military organisation but as a student-action programme. Student volunteers go out to villages to work with full-fledged government officials in food production campaigns, sanitation drives and literacy projects, all of which constitute a quasi-apprenticeship or induction programme to government jobs in the villages. Whether this significantly increased employment of educated labour is not definitely known, but the programme has been considered successful; at least it has defused campus restiveness. Again, the overall statistical effect is like that of prolonged military service which smooths out the entry and re-entry of large numbers of school-leavers to the labour market. But unlike the military conscription in Egypt, the student volunteer programme in Indonesia could not have induced secondary workers to join the labour force, because the volunteers were primarily those who could afford to forgo looking for work as a matter of urgency.

3. Control of the size of
    the educated labour force

Growth of secondary and higher education has been
strictly controlled in Tanzania and this seems to have
nipped in the bud the problems of educated unemployment
known in many poor countries. However, the strict
control has not only bred a certain form of élitism but
has also pushed unemployment and underemployment to the
less educated, and perhaps further down to the
non-educated group.

In countries where higher education has been
allowed to expand as fast as it could – and even faster
with foreign aid and loans – the application of controls
to check or slow down further expansion has been
extremely difficult. Indonesia and Egypt were in no
mood to step on the brakes, while the Philippines found
that for every brake that might be applied there would
be stiff opposition. Proposals for structural reforms
of the Philippine educational system to adjust it to the
manpower needs of the country were internally defeated
by a claim that education has goals that are much higher
than mere manpower needs (Castillo, 1973). Even the use
of a national examination for entrance to post-high
school studies has been effectively opposed and
neutralised.

4. Control of wages

Even though wide wage differences between workers
at different levels of schooling were thought to be the
driving force that accounted for educated unemployment,
the countries studied never suggested the use of wage
control as a remedy. It would seem that the wage
differences between educational qualifications
(hereafter called the wage differentials) tended to
widen if they were not held constant, as was observed in
countries where employment in the public sector was very
large. So, if wages in this sector were amenable to
manipulation, their impact on reducing demand for
schooling and on the supply of educated labour ought to
be very great. But this possibility is illusive
because, as is widely known, government bureaucracies as
institutions appear to have the ability to protect their
interests very well.

It has been argued, however, that wide wage
differentials could be reduced by increasing the supply
of the educated labour force – provided quality could be
maintained. How this would happen was not described,
but it would seem that the argument revolved around the
reduced average wages of the new cohorts of secondary

school-leavers and university graduates who would be
toppled into the traditional unprotected sector. Hence,
the apparent reduction of wage differentials would be a
statistical artifact rather than any real change in the
structure of wages, especially in the modern sub-sectors
of the economy. Besides, according to the credentialism
theory of labour markets, "educational expansion is
unlikely to have much impact on earnings differentials
because an increased flow of graduates will simply
promote upgrading of hiring standards..." (Blaug, 1976,
p. 847), a phenomenon that was observed in Indonesia
(Hallak, 1980, pp. 160ff).

Part of the difficulty in the use of wage control
lies in the general unpopularity of preventing wage
rises for productive workers and in the financial burden
of increasing the wages of the huge number of workers
who are at the bottom of the wage scale. This
difficulty is made worse by the presence of modern
sector private firms whose financial "clout" can draw
scarce skills away from government service or allure
them directly from schools. Hence, the use of wage
control as a device for minimising excessive imbalances
in the labour market tends to have little operational
value.

5. Permissive emigration

Allowing nationals to emigrate for employment is
not an active policy but rather a reactive one, in the
sense that no government openly exports workers while
professing acute shortages of skills. To say the least,
if it were an active policy of any government, it would
be played very "low key". In countries with severe
unemployment, extensive unpoliced borders and
unrestricted travel, people emigrate in search of
gainful employment. In Egypt this migration has brought
in substantial remittances that went to pay for food
imports. Similarly, this type of migration has helped
to augment the Philippines' foreign currency reserves
and has spurred effort on the part of the Ministry of
Labour and Employment to devise schemes for protecting
the country from short-term fluctuations in skill supply.

In a more general sense, emigration could lead to
some form of human capital formation through work
experience and other means of skill acquisition.
Further, it could alter the outlook of governments (and
their economic advisers) regarding the powerful driving
forces of labour markets, how these markets interplay
and how skill scarcities appear or vanish.

A new outlook about the way in which the labour
market fuctions in the real world might have some

positive effects. It could lead to better co-ordination between schooling and vocational training in industry, and perhaps it might improve employment planning as well. A new outlook might also develop an awareness of the limits of certain policies. For instance, when labour-importing economies are in the doldrums they become protective of their own unemployed workers and restrictive, if not openly discriminatory, against foreign labour; emigration for employment may thus not be feasible all the time. Moreover, the altered outlook could be responsive to new possibilities that occur only intermittently, such as supplying the skill requirements of growth industries when labour-importing economies undergo structural change. However, this observation assumes that the skills are not quickly developed or acquired, that the labour-exporting countries have them in plentiful supply, and that the skills are better exported than utilised at home. Most of all, it suggests a free flow of skilled workers, perhaps through international agreements, among countries.

B.   Indirect intervention through schools
       as training systems

While most of the direct interventions in the labour market discussed earlier did not seem to bring about clear-cut positive results, the indirect ones described below tend to have long-term effects that are disadvantageous to pupils and students and to the economy as a whole. The indirect ones were in small step-by-step changes which taken together reflected the belief that certain instructional reforms could bring about increased employability of school-leavers and university graduates.

1.   Increased vocational instruction
      in schools

This intervention has many forms. It ranges from emphasis on practical work in primary schools to specialised occupational training in technical schools. In Tanzania a great deal of teaching and learning time was allocated to what were called "self-reliant" activities in school garden plots and farms. There were also post-primary school craft centres for some pupils who did not manage to enter the lower secondary schools, vocational schools for a few students who were unable to get into the upper secondary schools, and technical schools for some of those who could not be admitted to the university because of the very limited number of places available. This suggests that side by side with

general education in schools, there was a parallel
vocational school training system that emphasised
increasingly specialised instruction in specific
vocational skills.

In Egypt a pattern similar to that of Tanzania
seems to exist, except that because of less restrictive
control the vocational schools tend to become
assimilated to the general education schools.
Vocational schools proliferate, retain their names but
later get transformed into schools for higher studies.
Hence, the vocational schools seem to be a roundabout
way of gaining access to university studies, with
students squandering valuable time to learn practical
skills that will only be hoarded. That time should have
been used for university preparatory studies to begin
with.

The situation in Egypt was not entirely different
from that of Indonesia, where vocational schools were
described as "pale copies" of general academic schools.
Because well-qualified teachers and funds are very
scarce or because vocational schools are much more
expensive to establish and maintain than academic
schools, the former were unable to be what they ought to
be, namely, truly good vocational schools.

But the emphasis on vocational instruction did not
stop at the secondary vocational schools, where students
were approaching maturity and were about ready to assume
responsibility in the world of work. The vocational
emphasis was also present in general academic schools
where it would seem that practical instruction was
stressed most at the primary level, less so in lower
secondary and least of all at the upper levels. The
emphasis seems to correspond to drop-out rates which are
greatest during the first few years of schooling. This
gives the impression that the target of practical
instruction was the potential drop-out rather than those
who would stay on.

The same thing seems to have happened in the
Philippines. Vocational secondary school graduates had
difficulty, not to say great difficulty in finding
gainful employment in keeping with their training. So
most of them went on to post-high school studies,
especially when many vocational secondary schools were
upgraded to degree-granting technical colleges in
agricultural science, fishery, electricity,
auto-mechanics or in construction and building trades.

However, unlike in Indonesia, Egypt and Tanzania,
the graduates of vocational secondary schools in the
Philippines were not in principle debarred from entering
university studies. This was true provided certain
entrance requirements were met. For most colleges,

passing the national college entrance examination (NCEE), was sufficient. However, a further and more rigorous examination was required by prestigious schools, in which a vocational school background was a serious handicap.

This handicap had been experienced by village high school graduates whose instruction was reported to be the most practical. Later effects of this handicap may be observed in the differences in wages and absorption rates between secondary graduates of vocational and general academic schools. Although these differences might be correlates of socio-economic background, they would be difficult to rule out as the influence of school background too or as the joint effects of these two factors. If so, the vocational schools put their graduates from humble family origins at an even greater disadvantage.

2.   Redirection of attitutes towards work
     and village life

This sort of intervention was not a simple redirection of attitudes towards work because civics or political education was also involved. In Tanzania "education for self-reliance" was intended to prepare not only the hands but also the minds of school children for socialism and work in the villages. Likewise, National Service as a civic and para-military service was designed to expose the volunteers - as they were called - to the realities of socio-economic conditions in the villages. It was also intended to provide the school-leavers and university graduates with opportunities to serve the people, in the hope that the opportunity and exposure would transform colonial attitudes into something refreshingly positive.

That this expectation was fulfilled at a desirable level could not be said categorically. But there is evidence that the school-leavers were also village leavers. The school-leavers migrated to towns and cities, keeping the density of literate and educated workers constantly low in the villages, despite the massive reforms and expansion of the primary school system.[4]   More ominously, certain innovations in education for self-reliance were feared to have adverse effects on the educational achievements of pupils. Hence, there was an urgent need for qualitative improvements to reverse the deterioration.

In Egypt attitude transformation was not reported as an explicit objective of educational programmes, nor was this so in Indonesia despite mounting concern over the lack of interest on the part of students of

agriculture in work in rural areas. However, volunteer
programmes for secondary and university students in
Indonesia were calculated to inculcate and further
develop in the students a liking for government posts in
the villages. How successful these programmes were in
terms of attitude transformation was not known.

In the Philippines the development of attitudes
towards work has not been a formal part of any subject,
except in pre-vocational studies in primary (elementary)
schools and in vocational subjects in secondary and
technical schools. In recent years, however, food
production campaigns in schools (to counter food
shortages and increasing unemployment) have placed
increasing emphasis on the development of work
attitudes, not only in practical studies but also in all
subjects. As a campaign slogan had it, "WORK IS THE
CORE OF OUR CURRICULUM".

However, a study among elementary school pupils in
the Philippines has shown that the way to develop
favourable work attitudes seems to be less through the
hands (by increasing the use of learning time for manual
work) than through the mind, that is, through subjects
that have a high mental content (Leonor, 1981). The
study showed that achievement scores in science,
mathematics and reading had a much higher coefficient of
correlation with work attitude scores than the latter
with practical subjects.

Thus the redirection of attitudes towards work
through the teaching of practical subjects appears to
have little value, either as an end in itself or as a
means - if at all it is a means - of alleviating
unemployment among school-leavers. While it may not be
disputed that favourable attitudes are indeed necessary
for job satisfaction and work commitment, experience in
Tanzania and in the Philippines shows that the means
used for inculcating those attitudes were not
unequivocally successful. This suggests that if those
attitudes have to be developed, recourse should be had
to better measures than the use of schools.

3. Diversification of specific skills and their labels

In principle diversification of skills should
follow economic development (rather than the other way
round) as work processes become increasingly complex and
specialised. Accordingly, training for those skills
should be diversified and specialised. This trend was
noted in Tanzania from post-primary school craft
centres, secondary vocational schools to specialised
technical schools. It would not be a surprise to

encounter this developmental trend also in university studies, that is, in the increasing separation of areas of concentration or major subjects. This trend, however, was less marked in Tanzania (following the British model) and Indonesia (following the Dutch model) than in Egypt (British, with much American influence) and in the Philippines (American model).

In Tanzania and Egypt, where secondary schooling is composed of lower and upper cycles, diversification starts in the lower cycle by branching out to several study tracks or occupational streams. The occupational streams increase and occupational labels tend to become more and more specific. This increasing specificity seems to be a hindrance to occupational mobility, not only in shifting tracks in the course of training in school but also in responding to changing job opportunities. It also accounts for the observed persistent shortages of certain skills side by side with surpluses of others.

In the Philippines, secondary schooling consists of only one cycle lasting four years, but diversification also exists. There are a number of vocational secondary schools, consisting of schools of agriculture, trade and fishery, in addition to general academic and special science high schools. Diversification does not end at the high school level, because further studies in Philippine universities have become even more occupationally specialised. There is a rich variety of occupationally specific courses leading to college degrees.

This diversification has both positive and negative aspects. It is useful in rapidly growing economies which require increasingly specialised knowledge and skills, and in fact the innovations in this field have been responses to perceived new manpower requirements of growing industries or, in many cases, of public services. Training programmes for these requirements have new courses and labels to match. Hence, the impression that these programmes have been going hand in hand with personnel and manpower requirements, a fact which in principle ought to reduce structural unemployment and promote economic growth.

But training programmes in schools do not immediately "self-destroy" as soon as they have filled the new manpower requirements. In training that lasts four years, the time-lags are very long, with the result that these training programmes persist when the need for them has withered away. The luckless trainees suffer from a long waiting time for jobs, until almost any job with lower pay and inferior working conditions will be an acceptable alternative to prolonged idleness.

This situation can be long and hard, because job opportunities can change rather quickly, whereas skill-specific labels do not. Like leeches, old skill-labels stick and are difficult to shake off, while new ones are equally difficult to acquire, especially from training that lasts four years or longer. The result is that the trainees tend to be "boxed in" by opportunity sets that are defined by skill labels. The more vocationally specific those skills are, the more restricted are the opportunity sets.

It would seem that even if new skill-specific training programmes are responsive to new opportunities, the trainees are not. The reason for this contradiction is that the training is specific to opportunity sets whose technological life cycles may be rather short. Soon after their life cycles the opportunity sets become irrelevant; the graduates trained for them are rendered obsolete or exist in varying degrees of obsolescence.

Moreover, the newness and responsiveness of training programmes cast their own shadow. Old programmes ossify and seldom react to obsolescence. They continue to survive, even if they are weakened to the point of inutility.

Thus it is that vocational school graduates tend to have longer job waiting time than general secondary school graduates. Besides, the vocational school graduates tend to have lower earnings on average, perhaps not only because of occupational inflexibility but also for socio-economic reasons, the chief one being the disproportionately large number of financially poor students in vocational schools whose social connections and information network to good jobs may not be well developed.

This rather general observation extends also to college graduates in the Philippines, where post-high school education tends to be very diversified and occupation-specific, even to the point of being almost skill-specific. As noted in the country study, the employed college graduates were working in many fields other than their specialised subjects, giving the impression of flexibility despite their specific training. But the reality behind this was the lower average earnings of the graduates when they worked in fields other than their own. This refers only to those who were fortunate enough to be employed, of course, and certainly not to those who were unemployed and unable to shed their specific skill labels.

4. Upgrading quality

"Quality of education and training" has a familiar ring. It has been extolled as the remedy to the many employment problems of school-leavers and university graduates in poor countries. Conversely, deterioration of quality, especially at the 3R level, has been supposed to be the source of those problems.

Qualitative deterioration may be ascribed to many causes. In Tanzania it was blamed on what were described as the "unprecedented curricular reforms" that put too much emphasis on activities that were remotely related to scholastic achievement. In Indonesia it was attributed to the rapid expansion of the school system. This was also the case of Egypt where rapid expansion led to a falling off in teaching standards on account of overcrowded classrooms and poorly trained teachers. In the Philippines, quality may have suffered marginally from "democratisation" or widening of access to schools.

Given these supposed causes, the corresponding measures to improve quality appear simple. Rapid expansion of school systems ought to be slowed down; school reforms should concentrate on the fundamental skills such as the 3Rs; and perhaps the democratisation of access to schools should be reversed.

But these measures, simple as they may seem, are not easy to apply. Moreover, any qualitative improvement would follow certain nuances of quality that might vary from one social class to another or from one country to another. Tanzania, for instance, may insist upon the development of socialistic attitudes as the primary concern of her school system. Indonesia and Egypt may wish to improve the staffing and provision for their vocational and technical schools, and the Philippines could continue working on selection and admission procedures. All this suggests that measures to improve quality might well espouse the existing design features of school and training systems and would deepen the roots of these features, including those that engender occupational immobility.

III. ISSUES

At the core of the preceding lessons and observations are issues, on which decisions about remedies are based and on which much of success or failure of the remedies depends. The first of these issues is that of wage differentials, namely, whether wage differences between workers at different levels of schooling ought to be narrowed down as a cure for educated unemployment. The second issue is that of

appropriate designs of school and training systems to
cope with dynamic labour markets and minimise the
emergence of educated unemployment. The third issue
touches on certain provisions of the ILO Convention No.
142 on human resources development: how flexible should
school and training systems be and how may this
flexibility be achieved, as called for by Article 2 of
the Convention? In the following discussion we lay bare
the elements of the issues.

1. Wage differentials

The issue regarding wage differences between
workers at different levels of schooling is seen in two
opposite perspectives. On the one hand the wage
differentials are regarded as the evil cause of educated
unemployment; as such, they ought to be narrowed down to
a point at which they would attract only a sufficient
supply for an existing demand. On the other hand, they
are seen as a powerful device for recruiting scarce
talent. In this view the wage differentials should be
left unaltered to serve that purpose.

In theory, wages as prices of labour profoundly
influence the upswings and downswings of the supply of
and demand for labour. Wage differentials spur and
steer a demand for schooling which, after a sufficient
time-lag, may define a supply of educated workers.
Because these differentials attract supply, the wider
they are the greater is the force that attracts that
supply, usually in the direction of a surplus. The
surplus - again according to theory - should drive the
wages downwards, thereby attenuating the wage
differences.

In practice, however, wages tend to be somewhat
"sticky": they can rise or increase at times but seldom
move the other way round. Partly because of this
property, wide wage differentials persist. Indeed, wage
differentials have been cited as the primary cause of
educated unemployment and they have been the object of
policy measures. But measures such as direct wage
controls, for instance, are difficult to devise and even
more difficult to enforce, even in centrally planned
economies. Recourse to indirect controls is just as
difficult and complicated. In many cases, indirect
controls may slow down the widening of the
differentials, but in the end they at best only maintain
the status quo.

Increasing the supply of school-leavers and
university graduates has been suggested as a means of
breaking down the wage differentials. But this does not
seem to work, because when supply increases employers

simply upgrade their hiring standards rather than alter their wage scales.

However, the opposite suggestion, namely, tight control of the growth of upper secondary schools and the university, has had some measure of success in Tanzania. This has effectively counteracted the force of wage differences and has prevented the emergence of educated unemployment of personnel with high levels of schooling.

But all these observations derive only from one view of wage differentials, i.e. from equilibrium models of labour markets.

The opposite view stems from disequilibrium models. It also considers wage differentials as a powerful force, a force of attraction that employers use as a recruiting device to cream off talent from a labour supply of heterogeneous quality (Drazen, 1982). The wage differentials, then, are particularly useful in contexts where the quality of output of school and training systems varies widely, even at the same level of formal qualification.

This view seems to be in keeping with the contemporary scene in poor countries, at least in the countries in this study. Rapid expansion of schools systems spreads men, money and machines somewhat thinly, and it in turn erodes quality. Quality suffers not only from these factors but also from the increasing supply of pupils and students of inferior preparedness for further study.

In this context the wide wage differentials are not dysfunctional phenomena that cause educated unemployment; instead they are social institutions that serve to distribute scarce talent to the highest bidders. In the latter sense, much of what is regarded as educated unemployment is simply a transition process of job-search, whose remedies are entirely different from those that would be required in equilibrium models of labour markets. Well-functioning labour markets through good occupational information and guidance systems, for instance, could shorten job-search and reduce structural employment.

2. Appropriate designs of school and training systems

It is observed that the usual response of governments to rising educated unemployment is to "vocationalise" the school system, not only by introducing more vocational content into existing curricula but also by establishing more and more vocational schools. The effects of this response are

detrimental to the quality of basic schooling at the 3Rs
level (Beeby, 1966, Ch. 1) and are questionable even at
the economic level when low absorption rates and low
earnings are taken into account. This then raises
serious doubts as to the usefulness of that response and
as to the wisdom of its continued use, especially in
countries which already spend vast sums on vocational
instruction. If one includes the value of technical
assistance in this field from bilateral donors and
international organisations, the financial implications
of these doubts are very considerable.

Akin to these doubts is the question why the
vocational school solution produces the detrimental
effects mentioned above. The answer seems to lie in the
characteristics of vocational schools and the
technological life cycles of skills in labour markets.
We will describe these features in turn.

During colonial times the vocational schools were
plausible enough answers to the specific manpower needs
of governments, usually for personnel in the civil
service. Requirements for military officers were
fulfilled by training in military schools; requirements
for medical officers were satisfied by training in
medical schools; and those for officials in agriculture,
forestry, fishery and in urban industries were met by
training in schools in these fields.

The training requirements were not solely in
specific occupational skills but also in general
education, so much so that the short cut was through
integrated formal education which consisted of an
amalgam of academic and practical subjects. The
integrated curricula required four years in the
Philippines and five to six years (two cycles) in
Indonesia, Egypt and Tanzania. This length of time was
of little consequence in the context of a fixed demand
for personnel for the civil service. But when demand is
not fixed as in open labour markets, spending so much
time on a training cycle leads to serious problems.

The long duration of the training cycle is the
critical factor because it is long enough for technology
and employment opportunities to change. This change can
be rather swift in very specific skills, so that
obsolescence may set in even before the pupils or
students trained in them leave school. This happens not
just in theory but also in practice, because vocational
schools can hardly keep abreast with industry in terms
of up-to-date equipment and teachers.

Besides technological change there is also another
form of obsolescence due to changes in opportunities.
Existing opportunity sets for which training is
undertaken may not be there four years hence. The

result is the commonly observed mismatch between job
requirements and qualifications, a situation that
induces long waiting and searching for good jobs rather
than a ready acceptance of inferior ones.
  We can generalise this observation into the
following. Curricula are designed for a range of
employment opportunities which are called the
opportunity sets. The sets are represented as columns
in Diagram A, Figure 5. At the time a curriculum is
designed (and implemented) the opportunity set is known
to be at its location at Time 0. A year later the
opportunities change or move to a new location under
Time 1. A small part of the new opportunity set will be
different from the original one. After another year
this difference increases, and so on until the fourth
year or later when the new opportunity set will be
almost completely different from the original for which
the curriculum was designed in the first place.
  An extreme form of Diagram A is Diagram B in which
the skills taught are so very specific that they will be
completely obsolete in relation to the skills required
by available jobs a year or two later. An extension of
this notion is shown in Diagram C. Curricula are
redesigned, say, at four years' interval, to suit the
opportunity sets known at the time. But because of long
time-lags, technological change and change of
opportunity sets, the opportunities envisaged by the
redesigned curricula are never met. Under this
condition the vocational schools become degenerate
solutions for reducing educated unemployment.

  3. Convention No. 142: Human resources
     development

  We now turn to the ILO Convention No. 142
concerning vocational guidance and vocational training
in the development of human resources, which stipulates,
inter alia, that

    "Article 2...each Member shall establish and
    develop open, flexible and complementary systems of
    general, technical and vocational education, ...
    and vocational training, whether these activities
    take place within the system of formal education or
    outside it" (emphasis supplied).

  The accompanying Recommendation No. 150 on the same
topic repeats the above provision and lays down, in
Paragraph 5(2), that ILO Members should aim in
particular at "establishing patterns of systematic
vocational training in all branches of economic activity

Figure 5: Dynamics of vocational school curricula and
          employment opportunity sets

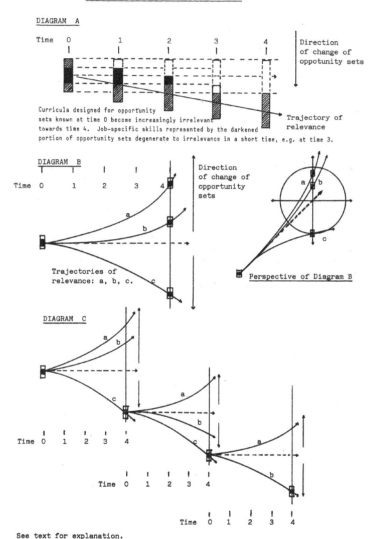

DIAGRAM A

Curricula designed for opportunity sets known at time 0 become increasingly irrelevant towards time 4. Job-specific skills represented by the darkened portion of opportunity sets degenerate to irrelevance in a short time, e.g. at time 3.

DIAGRAM B

Trajectories of relevance: a, b, c.

Perspective of Diagram B

DIAGRAM C

See text for explanation.

and for all types of work and levels of skill and responsibility" and "facilitating <u>mobility</u> between different lines of training, within and between the various occupations..." (emphasis supplied).

The key notion in these provisions is flexibility of which two forms are obvious: flexibility of the system itself and flexibility of its product, i.e. the trainees. What the foregoing country studies showed is that schools and training systems may well be responsive - even though usually they are not - yet they leave the trainees occupationally inflexible. In responding to rising educated unemployment, the countries showed some flexibility by increasing the vocational content of curricula and by establishing many vocational schools. But this may have impaired the quality of learning in the 3Rs, which in turn may have been to the detriment of trainability and adaptability to new work opportunities.

Further, many institutional features of the systems develop rigidity rather than flexibility. First, as mentioned earlier, long training cycles make practical instruction in schools an ill-timed preparation for new work opportunities that change. Second, occupation-specific or skill-specific labels and certificates do not readily match new job requirements, thereby engendering mismatches and disqualification, especially in a labour market that is in surplus. Third, vocational schools are - without a doubt - very expensive to establish, equip fully and maintain. These factors tend to limit the number not only of schools but also of students, unless quality is sacrificed, which is often the case. This in turn implies that the students are not only inadequately trained but are also difficult to retrain. The latter is due to an insufficient level of general education as well as to a low standard of vocational instruction. Moreover, retraining becomes impossible because access to training opportunities is extremely limited, partly because of overspending in expensive vocational schools rather than in less costly non-formal training courses. All this makes the vocational school-leaver inflexible in terms of poor trainability and occupational mobility.

If indeed flexibility of trainees were the objective, then school and training systems ought to be redesigned for it. Work in this area and related areas could make the Convention and Recommendation more useful and could encourage ratification by many more member States.

Notes

[1] It should be noted that these data were from a survey with low response rates.

[2] It is assumed here that every graduate joins the labour force immediately after graduation. But for the 22 per cent non-utilisation rate to carry an unemployment rate of only 8 per cent implies that out of a population of 100, 85 were in the labour force of which only 78 were working. Obviously, 15 were not in the labour force for one reason or another. Further, 7 out of the 85 were unemployed.

[3] This supposition is derived from fragmentary evidence from tracer studies of university graduates, showing that "unemployment concentrates in the first months of entry into the labour force" (Psacharopoulos and Sanyal, 1981, pp. 41f). This evidence also reveals decreasing unemployment towards later months but never indicates when unemployment will eventually disappear. Some of these studies cover waiting periods lasting two years and a few up to five years, yet unemployment of the cohort being traced has not sunk near zero. Besides, much of the data presented did not take into account the non-response rates, which in some cases were substantial. One of these studies has more than a quarter of the graduates "not responding", which when accounted for could increase the reported unemployment rate and the waiting time.

[4] This observation supports the proposition that villages have a capacity to absorb educated people. The limit of this capacity is defined by social and economic conditions which when exceeded will give way to urban migration as brain or skill overflow.

BIBLIOGRAPHY

Beeby, C.B.   The quality of education in developing
countries.   Harvard University Press, 1966.

Blaug, M.   "The empirical status of human capital theory:
A slightly jaundiced survey", in Journal of economic
Literature, Vol. XIV, Sep. 1976, pp. 827-855.

---.   Education and the employment problem in developing
countries.   Geneva, ILO, 1973.

---.   "Educated unemployment in Asia with special reference to Bangladesh, India and Sri Lanka", in Economic
Bulletin for Asia and the Pacific, Vol. XXVIII, No.
1/2, June-Dec. 1977, ST/ESCAP/47, pp. 120-137.

Castillo, G.T.   "Education for agriculture", in Philip
Foster and James R. Sheffield (eds.): Education for
rural development.   London, Evans Brothers Ltd., 1973.

Drazen, A.   "Unemployment in LDCs: Worker heterogeneity,
screening, and quantity constraints", in World
Development, Vol. 10, No. 12, 1982, pp. 1039-1047.

Hallak, J.; Busa, I.; Jalil, A.; Sayuti, A.   "Education
and work in Indonesia", in J. Hallak and Francoise
Caillods (eds.): Education, work and employment - I.
Paris, UNESCO/IIEP, 1980, pp. 149-191.

IBRD.   Indonesia: Financial resources and human development in the eighties.   Report No. 3795-IND, 3 May 1982.

ILO.   Human resources development: Vocational guidance
and vocational training.   Geneva, 1974.

Leonor, M.D.   Unemployment and the education system in
Tanzania.   Geneva, ILO, 1983; mimeographed World
Employment Programme research working paper;
restricted.

---.   "How attitudes towards work develop: Evidence from
Project Soutele, Philippines, 1975".   Geneva, ILO, 1981
typescript.

---.   Education and productivity: Some evidences and
implications, Geneva, ILO, 1976; mimeographed World
Employment Programme research working paper;
restricted.

Leonor, M.D.   Duration of unemployment and first job
earnings: Upper secondary vocational school graduates,
Ayuthya, Thailand, 1970-1974.   Geneva, ILO, 1976b;
mimeographed.

---.   "Non-formal education and rural development in
Seameo countries", Journal of Agricultural Economics
and Development, Vol. V, No. 1 (1975), pp. 36-50.

Morio, S.; Zoctizoum, Y.   Two studies on unemployment
among young people.   UNESCO, 1980.

Psacharopoulos, G.; Sanyal, B.C.   Higher education and
employment: The IIEP experience in five countries.
UNESCO/IIEP, 1981.

Rado, E.R.   "Unemployment among the educated in Pakistan".
Geneva, ILO, 1976, doc. PAK/73/014.

Sanyal, B.; Perfecto, W.S.; Arcelo, A.A.   Higher education and the labour market in the Philippines.   UNESCO,
1981.

Simanjuntak, P.J.   "Educated unemployment in Indonesia:
A preliminary report", in Technical papers of the
Employment and Income Distribution Strategy Proposals
for Repelita III.   Jakarta, ILO Office, 1978;
typescript, restricted.

Tanzanian survey. "Presription for a critical situation", in Africa Now (London), No. 20, Dec. 1982,
pp. 49-70.

Turnham, D.; Jaeger, I.   The employment problem in less
developed countries.   Paris, OECD, 1971.

Turnham, D.J.; Hawkins, E.K.   The employment problem and
World Bank activities.   Washington, DC, IBRD, 1973;
mimeographed staff working paper No. 148; restricted.

Versluis, J.   Education and employment: A synthesis.
Geneva, ILO, 1978; mimeographed World Employment
Programme research working paper; restricted.

Widodo, C.M.; Damanik, K.   The employment experience of
school-leavers.   Jakarta, Indonesia Department of
Education and Culture, Office of Education and
Cultural Research and Development, 1979; mimeographed.

INDEX

Underlined page numbers refer to tables.

Abbreviations: (E) Egypt
                    (I) Indonesia
                    (P) Philippines
                    (T) Tanzania

academic qualifications (E) 60
administration, salaries in (T) 48n
  see also bureaucracy
agriculture
  labour absorption by (I) 235-6;
  teaching of (E) 94-5, (I) 210, (T) 39-40;
    opposition to 42
  wages in (I) 220, <u>221</u>, 222, 224
aid, foreign (I) 212, (T) 3, 46
Arndt, H.W. (I) <u>223</u>
Arndt, H.W. and Sundrum, R.M. 219, 233
Arusha Declaration (T) 37, 41, 47-8n
Asians (T) 31

Beeby, C.E. 197, 272
Blaug, M. 178, 257, 262
bureaucracy, growth of (E) 72, 75, 91; (T) 30-1, 33

capital goods imports (T) 32
Castillo, G.T. 120, 261
central planning (E) 60, 73-7, (I) 211-12
child labour (E) 68, 80, (I) 197
civil service (P) 109
  educational levels in (I) 210
  see also public employees
Clark, D.H. 184, 188
class distinctions in education (E) 57, 88, (T) 41
college enrolment (P) 149, <u>153</u>
  by specialisations (P) <u>154-5</u>
colonial era 5, 272, (E) <u>80</u>, 81, (I) 191, 214, 231,
  (T) 28, 41-2, 46, 47n5
community service (I) 199-200
compulsory education (E) 56, I 195, 197
co-operatives (I) 213
Corpuz, O. 110
cost of living and wage level (I) 219
credit policies (I) 224-5

curricula
  changes in (I) 198-9, (P) 131
  employment opportunity sets and 273-4
  overcrowded (E) 90
  reform (E) 92-3 (P) 119-21, (T) 37

decentralisation (I) 212
devaluation (I) 224
development
  employment-creating 5-6, (I) 170
  planning (I) 212
  regional (I) 212, 236
  rural (I) 212, 222, 223, (P) 111
Diaz, R. 121-2
diploma "disease" (I) 227-9
Dore, R. 33, 39, 227-8
Drazen, A. 271
drop-outs 264, (I) 197-8, 226, 228-9

East African Economic Community 29-30
economic growth (E) 75, (I) 234, (T) 17, 18-19, 31-3
economic policy (I) 213
economic trends (I) 169-70, (P) 109-12
educated unemployment 250, 256, 271, (E) 58-60, 72,
  252, (I) 169, 178, 188, 189-90, 191, 226, 233, 236-7,
  254-8, (P) 5, 114, 157-8, 252-4, (T) 3, 11, 23, 44,
  251-2
  causes of (E) 97
  concealed in low-skilled jobs (P) 130
  employment creation to absorb (I) 234-6
  forms of (P) 133-4
  meaning of 8
  vocational schools solution to 249, 263-5, 271-5
  see also unemployment
education
  academic (E) 88, 93-4
  as investment (P) 126-8, 133
  basic (E) 93, (P) 124
  class distinctions in (E) 57, 88, (T) 41
  compulsory (E) 56, (I) 195, 197
  constrained optimum model (P) 160-3
  cost (I) 195, 196, 235, (P) 127-8, 134-5, 136, 157-8
  cycles (E) 56
  demand for (P) 124
  drop-out problem 264, (I) 197-8, 226, 228-9
  employment creation by (I) 225-6 232
  for self-reliance (ESR) (T) 3-4, 11, 33-4, 37-40, 45,
    265
  formal and non-formal 8, (I) 198

education (continued)
  free (E) 56, 59, 68, 70, (I) 192
  general 3, (P) 127; and vocational 268, (I) 214
  higher (I) 218, (P) 149, 153-5
  history of (E) 80-9, (I) 169-70
  market-determined (P) 124-7, 133, 158-9
  non-formal (P) 121-2; and formal 8, (I) 198
  opportunity for, inequality in (P) 132-3
  planning (P) 159
  policy changes in 4
  private (E) 88, (I) 169-70, (P) 5, 109, 124
  quality of 265, 269, (I) 230, 232, 237, 271, (P) 131
  returns on, and supply of graduates (P) 161-2
  rural (E) 57, 92, 96, (T) 26, 34, 38
  short instruction time (I) 199, 211
  specialist 266-8, 273-4, (I) 182, 184, 218, (P) 115,
    117, 118, 126-8, 134, 154-5
  state participation in (I) 213, (P) 125, 131-3, 159
  unemployment relief by, see unemployment; see also
    curricula reforms; graduates; labour force,
    educated; political education; primary
    education; schools, school-leavers; secondary
    schools; students; teachers; technical schools;
    universities; vocational education.
educational levels
  labour absorption by (I) 258, (P) 147, 149, 152
  labour force (E) 80, 82-7, 90-1, (I) 172, 174, 175,
    178, 202, 203, 210-11, (P) 147, 151-2;
    public/private (E) 86-7
  occupations and, labour force by (I) 181, 202, 208-9,
    210-11
  population by (E) 90-1, (I) 200, 201, 202, 203, (T) 22
  rural-urban migration by (T) 25
  unemployment by (E) 67, 77, 252, (I) 178, 179-80, 183,
    188, 190, 191, 255, (P) 112, 113, 143, 146, 147,
    251, (T) 14, 44
  wages by (I) 214, 215, 216
elitism (T) 41
emigration 262-3, (E) 55, 60, 262, (P) 122, 123, 124,
  262
employment (T) 11, 17, 21
  creation (I) 170, 224-5, (P) 133, (T) 5-6, 30
    education and (I) 225-6, 232, 234-6; rural (I) 169
  definition (I) 171-2, 250-1, 254
  graduates (E) 66, (P) 115, 143, 156, 157
  guaranteed 4, 259, (E) 55, 58-9, 70, 72, 74-6, 98,
    252, (T) 259
  hiring standards 262, 271
  male/female (I) 184
  multiple job holding (I) 169
  opportunity sets 273-4

employment (continued)
  overseas, training for (P) 122-4
  primary and secondary workers (E) 80
  private sector (E) 66
  public sector (E) 60, 74-5, (T) 30-2
  recruitment, public/private (I) 217
  registers (I) 184
  rural (I) 233, 235-6, (P) 119
  rural/urban (E) 77, 78-9, (I) 169
  sectoral (E) 77, 78-9, 80, 82-5, (T) 20
  waiting periods 257-8, 268, 273, (I) 177, 227,
    (P) 143, 147, 148, 150; reasons for delay
    (P) 150-1, 254
  see also educational levels, labour absorption, labour
  force, school-leavers, vocational education
entrepreneurship (T) 31-2
evening classes (E) 96
expatriates
  control by (T) 28-9
  displacement of (T) 30-1
exports (I) 211, 224, (P) 111, (T) 30-2

fees, school (P) 134-5, 136-7
food self-sufficiency (T) 211, (P) 111

GNP per capita (E) 4, 55, (I) 5, (P) 5
graduates
  employment (E) 66, 70, (P) 115, 143, 156, 157
  meaning of 6, 99n
  numbers of (E) 71
  reducing supply of (P) 118-19
  unemployment (E) 67, 68, 252, (P) 114, 254
  vocational training (E) 60
  voluntary services (I) 199-200
  see also educational levels; employment, guaranteed;
    universities
Guruli, K. 29

Hallak, J. et al. 262
hours of work 178, (E) 59, 70

illiteracy (E) 66, 67, 68, 90-1
  see also literacy rate
import substitution (I) 211
independence, aftermath of (I) 169, 191-2, (T) 3, 28,
  41, 46
indigenisation (E) 74, (T) 30-1, 46

inflation (E) 59, (I) 211
International Labour Office (ILO) 43, 75, 273, 275
International Monetary Fund (IMF) (T) 31
interest rates, low (P) 110, 133

labour absorption (P) <u>156</u>
  by educational levels (I) 258, (P) 147, 149, <u>152</u>
  by school type (P) 147, <u>152</u>
  rural (I) 233, 235-6
labour, educated
  absorption (P) 114-15, <u>116-17</u>, 188
  emigration (P) 122, <u>123, 124</u>
labour force (I) 171-2, (T) <u>13</u>
  by age groups (I) 172, <u>173</u>, 178
  children in (E) 68, 80, <u>(I)</u> 197
  educated, size of 261
  male/female (I) 172, 175
  rural/urban (I) <u>173</u>
  see also educational levels
labour, forced (T) 42
labour, illiterate (E) 90-1
labour-intensive public works (I) 170
labour market 258
  Arab 56
  equilibrium and disequilibrium models 271
  inefficiency (I) 233
  intervention in, direct 259-63, indirect 263-9
  policies 258, (E) 68, 70-80
  skill supply to (P) 128-30, 149, 161-2
labour migration 262-3, (E) 55, 60, (I) 170, 184, 211,
  214, 236, (T) 17, 23
  see also emigration, rural-urban migration
labour non-utilisation rate (P) 253-4
Leonor, M.D. 39, 43, 120, 266
literacy rates (T) 23

Manning, C.G. 222
manpower planning (P) 132, (T) 31, 42
marketing costs (T) 32
memorising in schools (E) 89-90
mental agility 2, 4, (T) 45
migration, see emigration, labour migration, rural-urban
  migration
military service 260, (E) 55, 59, 72-3, 80
mis-education 1, 2, 89-91, (E) 80, (I) 258
missionaries and education (T) 41-2
Mohamed Ali 80-1
Morrison, D.R. 35, 39-40, 42
multiple job holding (I) 169

National Service 265, (I) 236, 260, (T) 36, 45, 260
  see also military service
nationalism (T) 30
nationalisation (E) 58, 74, (T) 29-30
Ndunguru, S. 40
newspaper job advertising (I) 184
North-South dialogue 32
Nyerere, J.K. 30, 36, 48
Nyerere, President M.J.K. 30, 36-7

oil crisis, impact (P) 111-12
oil income (I) 5, 212
overseas contract workers' emigration (P) 123
overseas employment, training for (P) 122-4
overstaffing (E) 91
  guaranteed jobs and 4, (E) 58, 70, 72, 75
  see also employment, guaranteed

Pancasila (I) 213
payments in kind (I) 216
planning, see central planning, development, manpower
  planning
population
  by educational levels (E) 90-1, (I) 200, 201, 202,
    203, (T) 22
  growth (I) 170-1, 225
  statistics (T) 47n2
political
  change (E) 55, 58
  economy (T) 28-9
  education (T) 33, 37-40, 42
polytechnics (E) 93
preparatory schools (E) 93
primary education (E) 93, (I) 192-3, (T) 23
  drop-outs 264, (I) 197-8, 226, 228-9
  enrolment rates (E) 57, 71, (I) 192
  school-leaver crisis (T) 34
  universal (I) 192, 195
  see also educational levels
private education (E) 88, (I) 192, 194, 214, (P) 109,
    124-5, 132, 143
  enrolment (P) 138-9
  fees (P) 134-5, 136-7
  results (P) 140
  unemployment after 5
private property, sequestration of (E) 74-5
private sector (I) 216-17
  employment (E) 66
  open-door policy (E) 73-5

private sector (continued)
  recruitment (I) 218, 228
  wages (I) 217, 219, 224
productivity (I) 225, 234, 237, 256, (T) 31
protectionism (T) 32, (P) 110,
public employees (I) 210, (P) 109
  illiterate (E) 91
  incomes (E) 76-7, (I) 214, 216-17, 219-20, 222,
      232-3, 235, (T) 48n7
  recruitment (I) 217-18, 228, 234
  see also bureaucracy
public sector employment (E) 60, 74-5, (T) 30-2
  guaranteed 4, 259, (E) 55, 58-9, 70, 72, 74-6, 98,
      252, (T) 259
  short working week (E) 70
  wages (E) 76-7, (I) 216-17, 219-20, 222, 232-3
public works (I) 170

regional
  development (I) 212, 236
  wage variation (I) 219-20, 223
rural areas
  development (I) 212, 222, 223, (P) 111
  education (E) 57, 92, 96, (T) 26, 34, 38
  employment (I) 233, 235-6, (P) 119
  industry (I) 231
  neglect (P) 110
  teachers (E) 57
  underemployment (T) 12, 16, (I) 174
  unemployment 3, (I) 174, 178
  wages (I) 221, 222, 223
rural-urban migration (E) 77, (I) 233, (P) 110-11,
      (T) 23-4, 38, 265
  by age and education (T) 25
rural/urban
  labour force (I) 173
  unemployment (E) 61, 62, (I) 174, 176, 177, 179
  vocational education (I) 231-2
  wages (I) 220
Rweyamamu, J.E.   29

salaries of officials (T) 48n7
Sanyal, B. et al. 114, 126, 133
Schädler, K. 41-2
school-leavers
  attitudes to employment 256-6, (I) 184-6, (P) 266
  employment 5, (E) 4-5, (I) 5-6, 181, 186, 187, 188,
      (P) 133, 114-15, 116-17, 118, 147, (T) 3-4, 44-5;
      guaranteed (E) 55, 58-9, 70, 74; search for
      (E) 182, 184-5, 188

school-leavers (continued)
  meaning 7, 99n7
  overloading employment absorption capacity (I) 6,
    257, (T) 23, 33
  unemployment (E) 67, 68, 72-3, (I) 181-2, 184-6, 187,
    188, 255-7, (P) 119, 157-8, 253, (T) 34, 44, 252
  see also educational levels
schools
  as production centres (T) 34
  certificates (T) 46n1
  class distinctions in (E) 57, 88, (T) 41
  enrolment in (T) 21-22, (E) 71, (P) 149, 153, (I) 192,
    193, 194
  examinations 261, (I) 199, (P) 265
  expansion 259-62, 271, (E) 4, 57, 71, (I) 170, 191-4,
    228-30, 235, 237, (P) 124-5, 132, 134, (T) 21-4,
    34, 44, 261
  location (I) 238, (P) 128
  praxis (T) 39
  strikes (T) 34-7, (T) 40-3
  see also education, primary education, secondary
    schools, vocational education
secondary school-leavers' unemployment (E) 67, 68, (I)
  256-7, (P) 119, 157-8, (T) 44
secondary schools (E) 93-4, (I) 191
  examinations (E) 56, (P) 118-19, 132
  general/vocational balance (I) 197-8, 218
  growth (I) 192-4, 229-30, (T) 21, 23
  shortage of places at (T) 34-5
  streaming 267
  see also educational levels, technical schools,
    vocational education
self-employed (I) 202, 232-5
short working-week policy (E) 59, 70
skills
  acquisition of 2, (T) 43
  diversification 206-8
  market (P) 128-30, 149, 161-2
Smith, W.E. 29
socialism (E) 58, 68
  education for (T) 30, 33, 44
  see also education for self-reliance
socio-economic policy (I) 213-14, 216, 224-5
students' revolt (T) 34-7, 40-3

Tan, E. and Uy, B. 133
teachers
  employment of (P) 115
  quality of (I) 199, 230, (T) 35
  rural areas (E) 57

teachers (continued)
  training (P) 125, 135; colleges (E) 89, 92, (I) 185,
    194, 199, (P) 134; graduates of (I) 204, 207
  technical schools (E) 56, 60, 89, (I) 198, 231-2,
    (P) 264, (T) 42-3
  curricula (P) 119-20
  upgrading of (E) 94-5
technological change 231, 272
Thomas, R.L. 31, 42, 45
Tobias, G. 31
tracer studies 6, (T) 27, (P) 114-18, 120, 143, 147,
  (I) 181-88, 256
training, meaning of 7-8
transmigration (I) 236
Turnham, D. and Jaeger, I. 250

underemployment (E) 58, (I) 6, 174, 178, 225, 228, 237,
    251-2, 255-6, (P) 112, 141, 143, 157-8, 253,
    (T) 12, 15-16
  rural (I) 174, (T) 12, 15-16
  visible and invisible (T) 15-16, 47n3
unemployment (E) 4, 58-9, 60-1, 252, (I) 2, 169, 171,
    178, 181, 237, 254-8, (P) 112-14, 135-6, 147, 252-3,
    (T) 11-12, 13-15, 17, 23, 27, 251-2
  after vocational education 3, (T) 42-3, 45
  between schools (I) 6, 182, 188, 256, (T) 44
  by age group 256, (E) 61, 62-5, 66, (I) 174, 176,
    178, 180, 188, 189, 255, (T) 14
  by labour categories (P) 141, 142, 143
  causes of fall in (P) 141
  duration (E) 72, (P) 114-15, 148, 150-52, (I) 174,
    177, 183,

  experience and (I) 184; by sector and occupation (P)
    143, 144-5
  graduates (E) 67, 68, 252, (P) 114, 254
  illiterates (E) 66, 67, 68
  in labour surplus conditions (P) 157
  macro-economic diagnosis of 1
  male/female (E) 61, 62-5, 66, (I) 174, 176, 177, 178,
    179, 183, 189-90, (T) 14
  measuring (I) 171
  origins of (T) 28-33
  primary and secondary workers (E) 61, 65, 66, 72-3
  relief measures 259-62, 269, (E) 59-61, 70, 72-3, 91,
    96-7, (P) 118-24, (I) 170; conscription 260,
    (E) 55, 59, 72-3, 80; economic (T) 45;
    educational 249, 258-61, 263-5, 271-5;
    disadvantages of (I) 227-9, 233, (T) 44-6;
    national service 260, (I) 236, (T) 36, 45;
    levelling of wage differentials 261-2, 269-71

unemployment (continued)
  rural 3, (I) 174, 178; and urban (T) 12, _13_, _15-16_,
    (E) 61, _62_, (I) 174, _176_, _177_, _179_
  visible and invisible (T) _15-16_, (I) 174, 178
  see also educated unemployment, educational levels,
    school-leavers, secondary school-leavers
universities (I) 192
  enrolment in (E) 71, 95; by faculties (I) 202, _204-6_
    faculties (I) 203, 267; technical (E) 88-9
  expansion of (I) 193, (P) 132, (T) 44
  graduates by faculties (I) 203, _207_
  reform (I) 199-200
  Supreme Council and employers (E) 95-6
urban growth (P) 110-11
urbanisation policy and school location (I) 236

Valentine, T. 31
vocational education and training (E) 4, 56, 89, 92-8,
    264, (I) 181, _187_, 197-8, 200, _201_, 218, 230-1,
    264, (P) 119-2I, 132, 134, 264, 268, (T) 34, 39,
    41-2, 263, 266-7
  as solution to unemployment 249, 263-5, 271-5
  curricula and opportunity sets 273-4
  earnings following 3, 268, (P) 120
  employment after (I) 211, 264, 266-8; by
    occupations (I) 202, _208_, 210
  flexible 273, 275
  graduates' (E) 60
  ILO Convention on 273, 275
  non-formal (P) 121-2
  policy change during 4
  rural/urban (I) 231-2
  specialised 266-8
  strikes in (T) 40-3
  unemployment after 3, (T) 42-3, 45
voluntary services (I) 199-200

wages (I) 232
  after vocational education 3, 268, (P) 120
  by educational levels (I) 214, _215_, 216
  by occupations (I) 220, _221_, 222, _223_, 224
  central planning impact on (E) 76-7
  control of 261, 270
  cost of living and (I) 219
  differentials, reduction of 261-2, 269-71
  government policy's impact on (E) 76-7
  male/female (I) 222, 224
  minimum (I) 219, 235
  norms (I) 220, 235

wages (continued)
  private sector (I) 217, 219, 224
  public services (E) 76-7, (I) 216-17, 219-20, 222,
    232-3, 235, (T) 48n
  regional (I) 219-20, <u>223</u>
  rural (I) 221, 222, <u>223</u>
  urban/rural <u>(I)</u> 220
War Department schools (E) 81
Widodo, C.M., and Damanik, K. 256
Williamson, J., and DeVoretz, D.J. 120
World Bank 43-4, 49n10, 256

Printed in the United States
by Baker & Taylor Publisher Services